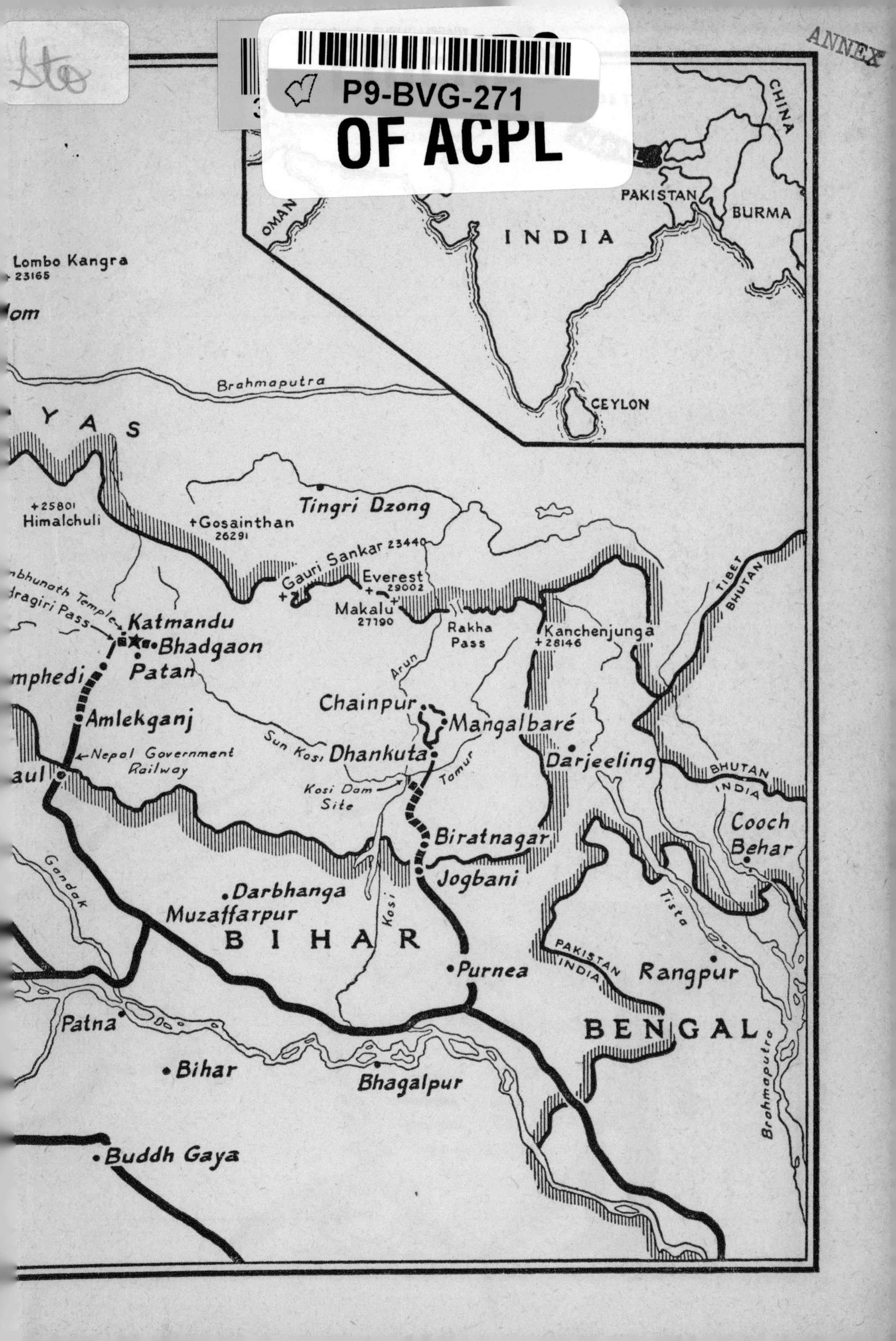

Sto
P9-BVG-271
OF ACPL
ANNEX
CHINA
OMAN
PAKISTAN
BURMA
INDIA
CEYLON
Lombo Kangra
23165
Brahmaputra
YAS
+25801
Himalchuli
+Gosainthan
26291
Tingri Dzong
Gauri Sankar 23440
Everest
29002
Makalu
27790
Rakha
Pass
Kanchenjunga
+28146
TIBET
BHUTAN
Katmandu
Bhadgaon
Patan
Amlekganj
Nepal Government
Railway
Arun
Chainpur
Mangalbaré
Sun Kosi
Dhankuta
Tamur
Kosi Dam
Site
Darjeeling
BHUTAN
INDIA
Cooch
Behar
Biratnagar
Jogbani
Gandak
Darbhanga
Muzaffarpur
Kosi
BIHAR
Tista
PAKISTAN
INDIA
Purnea
Rangpur
Patna
BENGAL
Bihar
Bhagalpur
Brahmaputra
Buddh Gaya

SEARCH
for the
SPINY BABBLER

AN ADVENTURE IN NEPAL

BOOKS BY DILLON RIPLEY

Trail of the Money Bird

Search for the Spiny Babbler

SEARCH
for the
SPINY BABBLER

AN ADVENTURE IN NEPAL

BY DILLON RIPLEY

ILLUSTRATED

HOUGHTON MIFFLIN COMPANY BOSTON
The Riverside Press Cambridge
1952

The author wishes to thank the National Geographic Society for permission to include in this book the illustrations copyrighted by them in 1950

The Riverside Press
CAMBRIDGE · MASSACHUSETTS
PRINTED IN THE U.S.A.

To Mary

Acknowledgments

THERE ARE MANY to whom I owe a great deal for what has gone into this account of my visits to Nepal, and perhaps most important are those institutions which have sponsored my two collecting trips there, Yale University, the Smithsonian Institution, and, in the case of the second trip, the National Geographic Society. To these institutions and to their officers who have encouraged, helped, and sponsored me I am everlastingly grateful. I must especially thank the National Geographic Society for generously allowing me to use photographs and other original material in their possession. To my friends on the trips, and particularly to Edward Migdalski of Yale's Peabody Museum staff, I cannot begin to express fully enough my thanks for their assistance and generous help, as well as their unfailing companionship.

The rulers of Nepal at the time of our visits, particularly His Highness the Maharajah Mohun Shamsher and his son, the Minister of Foreign Affairs, Major General Bijaya Shamsher, went out of their way to treat us with confidence and consideration. I can only hope that they will understand that we are very grateful, and that in my writing of this book I have been prompted by my great interest and indeed affection for their country and its inhabitants both avian and human. Certainly I have felt it a signal honor that the Nepal Government allowed us such complete freedom of movement in their hitherto forbidden hinterland.

My friends in India, the then American representative, George R. Merrell, the present representative, Loy Henderson, my distinguished colleague, Mr. Salim Ali, the late and incomparable Mrs. Sarojini Naidu, and many others, have been of the greatest help and assistance throughout my trips. To me they have all represented kindness and co-operation itself. The future of Nepal, indeed the future of India and its vital relations with the United States, are complex and vexing problems in these dark days. I am convinced of the good will and integrity of those leaders I have known in Nepal and India and I believe they will work to their utmost for good in the future.

And finally to my wife who has untiringly assisted me with the preparation of this book, I dedicate it with much gratitude and a full heart for her constant help.

DILLON RIPLEY

YALE UNIVERSITY
NEW HAVEN, CONNECTICUT
April 1951

Contents

List of Illustrations

facing pp.

SEARCH
for the
SPINY BABBLER

AN ADVENTURE IN NEPAL

I

Introduction to Nepal

NEPAL is one of the most remote and inaccessible, and at the same time one of the most beautiful, places in the world. A kingdom five hundred by one hundred miles, its fifty-four thousand square miles of territory are spread at a perilous angle along the ridgepole of the Himalaya Mountains. Mount Everest is in Nepal, and a whole lesser galaxy of the highest mountains in existence. From the uninhabitable waste of peaks which Nepal and Tibet share as a common border, the mountains slope down through rugged forest and farm-clad slopes to the foothills and beyond to a belt of lowland plain known as the Terai. Across the Terai, thirty-odd miles beyond the foothills, lies the southern boundary, the border between Nepal and India. On the west, climbing through the hills, Nepal meets the Indian District of Kumaon; on the east, her neighbor is the semi-autonomous State of Sikkim, now under Indian control. Within this great spread of territory from near sea level to the tops of the mountains lies a whole array of climates. Perpetual summer bakes the sun-drenched fields of the lower Terai, part of the vast alluvial plain of Central India. This is the plain of the Ganges and its multitude of tributary rivers, not long ago geologically, in early Pleistocene times, a great bay of the sea.

The northern part of the Terai bordering the foothills is still covered with magnificent subtropical forest. North of this again lie the hills, first the Siwalik Range, four-thousand-foot ridges of sandstone and clay, then a series of narrow inner valleys, the "duns," and beyond, the first ridges of the main Himalayas. Through these serrated hills sweep the tributary rivers, rolling down from the heights unbridled and awesome in the summer rains, sweeping all before them and devastating huge areas of the plains. Hidden among the ridges, in a gem-like valley of its own, lies Katmandu, the capital of Nepal, a secluded storied city, out of the world, beyond time, the "Jewel in the Lotus."

If Nepal's geography has served to make it remote, its people have conspired to keep it inaccessible. From the welter of half a hundred tribes, each in its mountain fastness, has arisen a government of the unconquered Gurkhas, the most warlike of all the people of the hills. Today Nepal consists of perhaps a dozen tribes under the firm hegemony of the Gurkhas, who rule from Katmandu, where still cling the receding vestiges of a more ancient culture of the former rulers, the Newars. The dominant tribes are united also in a state of Hindu orthodoxy which surpasses that of most of the rest of Hinduism and which now dominates the Tibetan form of Buddhism lingering among the highest hills.

Since the earliest times Nepal has been closed to foreigners, particularly to non-Hindus or non-Buddhists. Although the rulers are laymen, there has always been a strong theocratic tinge to the Government. In all history perhaps only two hundred Europeans and two dozen Americans have journeyed into Nepal, and virtually all of these have traveled only up and down the prescribed route from the plains to Katmandu and a radius of fifteen miles around its small valley. In former days the ruler, the Maharajah-Prime Minister of Nepal, invited Viceroys of India and their guests to winter shooting parties in the Terai Forest, in one or two special areas where tiger, rhino, and miscellaneous smaller game were produced in abundance. Viceroys were never invited to Katmandu, as it was thought that this might imply a domination of Nepal by the Government of India, an implication which the Nepal rulers were zealous to avoid.

To me and to my fellow ornithologists, students of birds around the world, Nepal has always had a particular fascination because of the researches of a single man. Brian Hodgson was a consumptive clerk in the British East India Company at the beginning of the last century, who was given the choice of going home to die in England or in a post in the hills. He chose the latter, and was sent to assist the then Resident appointed by the Company to the Court of Nepal. Hodgson lived and thrived, becoming in the process an outstanding student of the natural history, ethnology, and linguistics of the Nepal Himalayas. He succeeded the Resident, and lived in Nepal from 1821 to 1843 as a diplomat and negotiator during some of the most tumultuous times in the country's history.

Meanwhile Hodgson's studies on birds were monumental. He recorded some five hundred and sixty-three species from Nepal, all from specimens brought in to him by Nepali hunters, for like every other foreigner he could not travel beyond the confines of the Katmandu Valley. One hundred and fifty of these species he described for the first time to science as new species, giving in most cases as type locality simply "Nepal." In the subtropical regions of the world, birds are not particularly migratory in their habit, as they are in Europe and North America. In these regions, with a tolerable food supply the year round, birds are characteristically sedentary rather than migratory. The great variety of habitats in Nepal from the plains to the higher mountains allows an equal variety of species to inhabit the area as a whole. Of this multitude of species many tend to be confined to specific zones of altitude or vegetation.

As the knowledge of the birds of the Indian Peninsula and related areas became more complete, it was realized that Hodgson's work was really the cornerstone for research in the whole area — far more than simply Nepal territory. He was the first to have written about many bird species which ranged the whole length of the Himalayas, fourteen hundred miles, from Kashmir to Assam. His collection of over nine thousand specimens, with drawings and manuscripts, which eventually was presented to the British Museum, was the greatest single collection from the whole region.

A century later, however, much of Hodgson's work needed to be verified and extended. Many of his specimens had disappeared. Others were now so worn and discolored, "foxed," as the technical term is, that they were useless. Still others resembled a cross between a rag and a hank of hair. The last forty years had seen a tremendous growth in evolutionary studies with the developments in genetics. Parallel with this had come a great interest in studies of the evolution of species in nature. The initial steps in evolution, the isolation of contiguous populations, the creation of geographical subspecies, recognizable subgroups within a species, had become a most fertile field of evolutionary research. The long continuous chain of the Himalayas with its profusion of species would be a veritable gold mine for such research, but for this new specimens were desperately needed. Hodgson's original material had given the species their names, but his material was now too old and too fragmentary to serve the needs of the present-day research workers in speciation and other evolutionary studies. Nowadays, too, the range of a species must be pinpointed. Thus, Nepal had become a sort of question mark, a focal point to ornithologists.

My work in bird studies before and during the Second World War, when by good luck I was stationed in the East, had gradually directed me to research in the fauna of the general region known as the Indian Region. In this region the keystone, Nepal, had assumed more and more importance in my mind. It beckoned and challenged. I wanted to get fresh material from Nepal and to study the whereabouts of the break which occurred in the fauna within its boundaries. A great number of Himalayan bird species have two or more distinct subspecies, varying in size and color primarily, from west to east along the mountain chain. Whatever the extrinsic outward barrier which helped to determine this "break" in the species, it must be somewhere in Nepal. I wanted to range into the back country, in western and eastern Nepal where no collectors had ever been, and to try to make a thorough sampling of the avifauna.

As it happened, it seemed to be a bit of sheer luck. I spent the winter of 1946–47 collecting in India for Yale University and the Smithsonian Institution. I had gone back to India to start the first of a series of trips to collect specimens in out-of-the-way localities which had been missed or passed up by the earlier workers on Indian birds. My Indian colleague,

Mr. Salim Ali, and I had hopes of preparing an up-to-date work on birds of the Indian Region, a task which was sorely needed. In addition, I wanted to get raw material for speciation studies. The American Chargé d'Affaires in New Delhi that winter was George R. Merrell, a friend from war days, who put me up when I visited the capital to outline my plans to various Government officials. As I talked to him about my projects, he suddenly asked me why I had never thought of going to Nepal.

"What are the chances?" I shot back.

The chances turned out to be very good. George had recently been to Katmandu to conduct the first negotiations on the exchange of diplomatic relations between the United States and Nepal. He was on excellent terms with Nepal officialdom, as indeed he was everywhere in the East. There has seldom been a more popular representative of America in southern and eastern Asia than George Merrell.

George solved the problem by arranging one of his characteristic luncheons. There was a varied company, a minor Maharajah, a Sikh Congress leader, a Persian Princess, a delightful Czech couple who earned their keep by playing tennis for Indian rulers (this was before the days of the Indian Union), the new Counselor of the American Embassy and his wife, and my first Nepali acquaintance, Colonel Rana, Consul-General for Nepal in India. George introduced us, politely extolling each to the other.

Colonel Rana was a short, plump man with a clever face and a smooth, diffused manner. I explained my interest in Nepal birds, a subject of which the Colonel had apparently hitherto been unaware, and he eventually promised to write to the Maharajah enclosing a letter of introduction which

George would write. I faced the future with small hopes. It seemed to me that in the eyes of the Colonel I must be a very unimportant person. After all, there was no money and certainly no prestige in birds. And an ornithologist belonged to an undefinable category in the social scale. George, however, was more hopeful. He felt the Maharajah would be interested. After all, I was harmless, neither an economic royalist nor a missionary. Later, Merrell had to redraft his letter of introduction, as in it he mentioned that the Colonel had had lunch with us. The Colonel thought that the then Maharajah-Prime Minister might take exception to his representative having a meal with casteless persons. A Martini, yes, but a meal, no. So I began my introduction to Nepal.

I had learned meanwhile from George something about the Government of Nepal which has no recent parallel except that of Japan under the Shoguns. Like Japan, Nepal had a King, an hereditary Head of the State revered as an incarnation of the god Vishnu, but a King of his own palace only; and a ruler, the Maharajah-Prime Minister. Both posts were hereditary, the King's descending from father to son in the normal way, the Prime Minister's descending by age within a single family in a complicated roll of succession. To be eligible for this roll of succession, a member of this family, the Ranas, must have been born of a mother legitimately wedded to her husband, and in addition of a caste high enough to eat rice in her husband's presence. Once these important weeding-out stipulations had been satisfied, the actual date of birth provided the order of succession. Thus, a Maharajah tends to be succeeded by his next oldest legitimate brother or first or second cousin, a device which insures that the new ruler shall be a man old enough to be able to catch up the reins of power. In autocratic Asian circles a succession involving a minor is usually a good excuse for a revolution.

Merrell further explained that at present to all intents and purposes power is concentrated within two families of the Ranas, the sons of the late Maharajah Chandra, of whom the eldest is now Maharajah, and the sons of Chandra's younger brother, the recently retired Maharajah Juddha. Both these men were nephews of the celebrated Jang Bahadur, the formulator of modern Nepal history, who consolidated his power as Prime Minister by a timely and sweeping elimination of his rivals and thus entrenched the Ranas as rulers from the eighteen-sixties on. So much of Nepal's recent history should be in the mind of anyone who goes there.

Some two months later, my assistant, Edward Migdalski, and I were busily collecting birds in the Biligirirangan Hills in South India when a telegram came from Merrell informing us that permission had been received for me to visit Katmandu and a radius of fifteen miles around it for a four-month period. We took stock of our supplies and equipment and considered our time schedule. We were due back in the United States in the spring. Furthermore, the season would not be too propitious for collecting. As the spring advanced, the plumage of birds becomes worn and abraded. Specimens taken at this time would be less useful than later in the autumn or winter, when the annual moult has been completed, and the feathers are pristine. Still, even some collecting around Katmandu would be worth while; and so we evolved a plan. We would spend our last collecting month in Nepal, secure as much as we could, and use the opportunity to make friends with the Government officials and see if we could propose a return trip at a later date into the western and eastern unknown parts of the country. After all, if we only spent one month we should still have three months of our original permission to go on; and certainly no one would ever get a permit to visit the excluded areas without first journeying to the capital and making contact directly with the Maharajah and his Court.

For some reason luck continued to be with us. We made the trip, spending from mid-April until mid-May in and around Katmandu. With our two assistants, two young taxidermists from Portuguese Goa and Ceylon, we managed to accumulate six hundred bird specimens and a number of mammals as an extra dividend. In addition, I prepared a memorandum for the Maharajah outlining the vital need for an ornithological exploration of outer Nepal, trying if possible to infuse some of my sense of excitement in the cause, an excitement which had been sharpened by the work that we were already doing.

Our final audience with the then Maharajah, Sir Padma Shamsher, who has since retired and gone to live in India, was full of tension. I had submitted my memorandum through one of the officials and we were on tenterhooks. At last, during a pause in the conversation, I "popped the question." Had His Highness read my memorandum?

The Maharajah smiled in a benign but vague way and turned to the Commander-in-Chief, his Number Two, the man who would some day succeed him. General Mohun smiled benignly, too, and uttered the single fateful word, "yes." And so it was agreed.

Ed and I returned to the States in the spring, and for over a year I was busy in research on my Indian specimens,

Meanwhile I hoped and planned for a return to the Mountain Kingdom, a real return that would include marching up along the two main tributary rivers which drain the western and the eastern parts of the country. Such a trip would demonstrate where a lot of the rather mysterious bird species described by Hodgson and merely labeled "Nepal" really came from. It would solve a number of evolutionary problems, and incidentally such a trip would also involve exploration of territory unknown to any outsiders. With these points in mind, I approached the National Geographic Society and found a ready willingness to help support a real expedition to Nepal. Again Yale and the Smithsonian Institution favored the project, and this time, too, officers of the Department of State gave generously of their time and assistance. Official letters from the three sponsoring institutions were dispatched through the Department in order to confirm the verbal agreement of 1947, and I settled down to wait, meanwhile drawing up our plans.

Months later I was thrown into a state of consternation by the receipt of an official reply from the new Maharajah, Mohun Shamsher, addressed to the newly accredited American Minister to Nepal. The main part was as follows:

"Much as I would have liked to give Mr. Ripley the required permission I am all the more sorry to have to tell Your Excellency that taking into consideration the great difficulty of transport and lack of amenities of life in the interior of the hill [*sic*] as well as the temperament of the local people it has not been thought advisable to permit Mr. Ripley to visit the Kosi and the Karnali Valleys. If he desires to visit the Terai only necessary permission will be granted to him it being of course understood that we shall not be held responsible for the safety of his life in the course of his tour in the Terai."

This was a terrible blow. The Terai lowlands would yield little of the ornithological interest that a trip into the mountainous valleys might produce. I would hardly be justified in mounting an expedition to return again to Katmandu and then to travel in the Terai. In my quandary I called up Joseph Satterthwaite in the State Department, a friend from our short trip to Katmandu. He and his party had come to Katmandu to sign a treaty opening diplomatic relations between the United States and Nepal while Ed and I were collecting there. His advice was practical and to the point.

"By all means go yourself and talk to the Maharajah," he said. "You know him and he knows and likes you. It is far better to talk directly than to write letters to people twelve thousand miles away."

Backed up loyally by the three supporting institutions, I decided to do just that. The spring and summer were spent in procuring equipment and arranging for the personnel of the trip. Edward Migdalski would come with me again, and I was in constant correspondence with Salim Ali on the recruitment of two additional bird taxidermists from Bombay. Brian Hodgson had performed nearly as great a work on the mammals of Nepal as he had on the birds, and I was anxious to make a real collection of small mammals on this trip. On our previous stay in Katmandu, we had made only a meager beginning on the mammal side, for the collecting of natural history material is such a specialized form of work that it becomes impossible without a considerable staff to bring back a successful mixed bag. Two graduates the preceding spring from Yale, Howard Weaver and Richard Mack, volunteered to train themselves as mammal collectors. They would pay their way out to India, and after that the expedition would finance their trip and their collecting. They studied skinning and trapping during the summer, and I was in high hopes that they could learn the subtle trapping techniques necessary for catching small mammals in the jungle.

In India a National Geographic staff photographer, Volkmar Wentzel, and his young English assistant, Francis Leeson, would join us. I had not met them, but had been told on all sides that they were both capable in their field and delightful companions, and so they proved to be. Francis especially, with his fluent Hindustani, was often invaluable. Two friends, Sidney and Gertrude Legendre, had been with us for a month on the previous trip in India. They had been a great help to us and grand company. Now, although, to our great grief, Sidney had died very suddenly, I urged Gertrude to come anyway, even for a brief visit, to see some of the strange country that we hoped would be revealed to us. She might come out later in the winter.

For the whole group I must buy tents, tables, chairs, cots, cutlery, cooking equipment, and food. Weight would be a major problem where porters must carry all our gear on their backs. We had already found that above the plains of the Terai, man is the only beast of burden in Nepal. I was at great pains to get tents of the lightest weight and whatever variety of dehydrated foodstuffs could be purchased in the United States. Then there was the question of the collecting equipment. In order to shoot birds to be made into museum skins, it is necessary to have some sort of dust-shot ammunition. We standardized our equipment, by getting five sixteen-gauge shotguns with a variety of different-sized load shells for larger birds and small game. In addition, we took along small auxiliary barrels which fitted the sixteen-gauge chamber, and from which we could fire a thirty-two caliber brass cartridge about the length of a long rifle revolver cartridge, loaded with dust shot. Fired from the sixteen-gauge, this small load would spread so rapidly that a tiny bird the size of a wren could be killed, without damaging its feathers, at a distance of no more than ten or twelve feet. And kill them we unfortunately must. We could never know properly the birds of the Himalayas unless we had fresh specimens. Fortunately the same situation does not apply in Europe and North America, where our species are now in the second main stage of bird study, the specimens being so well known in museums that the binocular and the notebook have taken the place of the shotgun and the museum tray.

For mammals we would need a variety of small traps and some special lures and baits. In addition, for all our specimens we must take along museum labels to be affixed to each one, catalogues, pins, cotton wool, arsenic powder, sawdust, or other drying agents, salt for large mammal skins, and a variety of skinning tools, scalpels, shears, snips, and forceps. Then there were special trunks for the specimens which contained drying trays. All of these and all the varied gear, including our khaki clothes, boots, and long woolly underwear, had to be packed and crated and shipped months before we planned to arrive ourselves. It was a busy summer complicated by ill health on my part, shipping strikes which made the arrival of our equipment uncertain, and the added insecurity of our future plans inside Nepal.

As much time as could be spared from planning and purchasing our supplies was put in on making a list of the mammals of Nepal, with many of which I was unfamiliar, and also with lists of the bird species of Hodgson's time so far unaccounted for. What had happened to the Mountain Quail, *Ophrysia superciliosa*, last met with in the Indian Himalayas near the western Nepal border in the eighties of the last century? Was it extinct, and if so why? It had been a grassland species found apparently at five to seven thousand feet altitude. Perhaps it still existed in western Nepal, where presumably conditions at that altitude were more stable and untouched than in the highly populous neighboring province of India. Could we get any news of the Pygmy Hog in the Terai? A strange miniature species of wild pig, it was known from only a handful of specimens. There were other birds, as well, the Spiny Babbler, *Acanthoptila nipalensis*, collected by Hodgson's men and simply labeled "Nepal." Was it a highland bird, a lowland species, did it live in grassland or forest? There were supposed to be seven specimens in the British Museum, but only five could be located, all faded and worn. I had never seen the species. And what of the Pinkheaded Duck, that strange creature with a soft milk-chocolate-colored body and an angular head of brightest Schiaparelli "shocking" hue? Was it a relict from some vanished age when brighter, stranger creatures roamed the shores of Pleistocene seas, still to be found in jungle pools in the Terai? There were endless questions to be answered.

Ed, Howie, Dick, and I left finally in October, planning to meet Wentzel and Leeson in Calcutta. We sailed via France and then flew by air from Brussels direct to India. En route we had fun and a modicum of work at the Paris Natural History Museum. Our gayest time was the night of our arrival in Paris, a never-to-be-forgotten event when plans went completely awry. The hotel had given up our rooms, there was a taxi strike, the boat train was delayed, Paris was packed with United Nations delegates, and the serious-minded members of an expedition representing Yale University, the National Geographic Society, and the Smithsonian Institution found themselves parked all over the city in the sole remaining bedrooms to be found — in what are now genteelly known as "Maisons de bon accueil." Ill-reputed though these houses might be, they were comfortable enough, but for me the night was made more complicated by a date with a girl at Maxim's at the end of which I found I had run out of francs and she had to pay our rather staggering bill. It was a memorable night and the source of many a reminiscence later on on chilly evenings round the fire in the mountains. I had no idea, too, how useful our experiences in Paris would be to us later on in Katmandu.

A few days later we were winging our way out to India. The vagaries of international air travel today are reminiscent of an old-fashioned milk train which makes all the stops and keeps a schedule of its own. Apparently the air-line people often feel that the mere privilege of being on a plane is enough. There should be no reason for the passenger to carp if he is sixty hours late or if the plane suddenly goes to Rome instead of Zurich. We finally made Calcutta in the middle of the night. It was my first glimpse of the country since independence had been achieved. A zealous, partially literate policeman was on duty checking passports. When he came to mine, I was fascinated to see him taking down my name as "Mr. Litchfield Connecticut" (my home address). It made me feel like a male bathing beauty. He was an aggressive man and seemed to know his business better than I, so after an attempted explanation I let the whole matter ride.

In Calcutta we embarked on a busy program. Wentzel and Leeson were here waiting for us with their quota of the camera supplies that we would need. The customs and police officials were cordial and friendly, but there were mountains of red tape to be waded through before we could land our vital equipment. Some of it had been landed in Bombay instead of Calcutta and had disappeared in the overcrowded port which had become a sort of quagmire. The two new Goanese taxidermists, Toni and John, appeared and Ed started training them in. All in all it took us three weeks before we could see daylight ahead. Finally there came a day when we posed for some rather insipid pictures of ourselves shaking hands with each other in front of the Victoria Memorial on the Calcutta Maidan or green. This was what I called the "off into the Blue department," an aspect of expeditions which all proper explorers are supposed to undergo. Eventually we got the train tickets and arranged for hiring a truck to take our mountain of boxes, bags, and bales to the station. Then I wired to Katmandu to the Durbar, as the Maharajah's office is called, that we would be reaching Raxaul, the town on the Nepal border which marks the beginning of the route up to Katmandu, on November 16, 1948. The die was cast. We were off to see the Maharajah, to see if after all our trip halfway across the world was going to be worth while; to find out if we could climb up into the river valleys, into the unknown mountains.

We made Howrah Station in good time on the morning of our departure. The truck was unloaded and our baggage weighed in. After piling the luggage into all available crannies of our train compartments, there were still nearly two tons of stuff to be put into the baggage car. Coolies, station-masters, bystanders, and ourselves — everyone shouted and fussed and rushed about aimlessly through the seething, tangled mass of humanity that lined the platform. Dante's Inferno could be no worse than the hot, sweaty, jumbled multitude packing that squalid barn of a place. We fought our way into the train. We found our places amid the piles of gear. We made sure that the baggage car was attached to the same train and that our boxes were in. Some instinct had warned me to get to the station a good long time ahead of train time. My instinct is far from infallible, but it worked this time. We had just made sure that everything was all right when, by some fantasy of timing known only to itself, our train proceeded to depart half an hour early. We were hot and dirty and tired, but anyway we were off to Nepal.

II

Return to Nepal

JUST TO GET TO THE BORDER of Nepal is a special experience. In the future it may well be that air travel right into the valley of Katmandu will be the rule. The older way is one for hardier souls. The first fifteen hours or so out of Calcutta are easy enough. The railways are broad-gauge affairs, comfortable to ride in, moderately clean, and there are a few station restaurants that will prepare a meal and serve it in the compartment. But then there is the Ganges to be crossed. Except at Banaras there are no bridges. The railway line simply comes down to the river bank and stops. Hundreds of yelling porters descend upon the train, the luggage is unloaded and carried piece by piece on their heads down the bank to a fat glowering steamer ferry, panting with the constant effort of engulfing and disgorging vast hordes of insect-like passengers. We always seemed to make our crossings at night in a bedlam of shrieks and cries, with weird Daumier-like shadows and flickering streamers of light cast upon the struggling masses surging in and out.

Long hours would be passed waiting for the inscrutable movements of these ferries. On the opposite bank, a mile or two away, a new world of strangeness and squalor would emerge. This was the domain of the Oudh Tirhut Railway, the longest meter-gauge line in the world, which spreads its spider web of track a thousand miles across the baked and barren plains of India's States of Bihar and Uttar Pradesh, as the old United Provinces are now called. The movements of the Oudh Tirhut were shrouded in mystery. Timetables existed and were often consulted by confident clerks, who advised airily about our program from the security of an office in Calcutta, but in reality the trains had been making their own separate plans for years.

By a series of letters to the Oudh Tirhut Railway, launched into space and always unacknowledged, I had ordered that a "Double First Tourist Car" should meet us at the ferry. By some alchemy unexplained to me the "Double First" car turned up, and on future occasions appeared also, sitting cozily on a siding waiting for us. The fare for six first-class railway tickets covered the hire of this carriage which had two compartments fitted to sleep three, each with a bath compartment, and an additional cubbyhole at the end for three servants. By crowding a bit, the six of us could fit in with most of our luggage. In the cubbyhole we could squeeze Toni and John, Rao, our new bearer, and Abdul the cook, as well as a small Gurkha boy, Bagam, who had been hired in Calcutta to do errands. The heavy crates and boxes still had to be shipped by baggage car, and usually one or other of the taxidermists or the three servants would also ride in that car, just to see that everything was all right.

The advantage of the Double First was that it was switched from train to train when, as usually happened, we had to change from the "Number Three Down" at Gorakhpur or some other junction, to the "Number Forty-Seven

Up." The Oudh Tirhut was full of these changes, most of which had to be made in the middle of the night. At least we could stay in the same car even if the noise and confusion prevented sleep.

Added to all of this was the dirt. The Oudh Tirhut Railway has apparently not had the funds or the inclination to spruce up its rolling stock for a very long time. Our car would invariably be missing such appurtenances as electric light sockets (wrenched out by persons unknown), switches for the much-needed fans, or leather covers for the bunks, which were usually upholstered only with non-bedbug-proof jute sacking. Superimposed on this was always a heavy layer of grime. Usually the water in the toilets ran out early on the journey. Sometimes odd accidents happened, such as the time we had a toilet that collapsed because it had not been properly bolted to the floor. It was always hot in the daytime, so that all possible windows had to be kept open, which added to the dust and cinders already within. As a final straw, food was usually very hard to come by. We wisely had taken K-rations along, but even they can pall in the forty-eight or more hours that it always takes to go anywhere on the Oudh Tirhut Railway.

Thus, the approach to Nepal is a highly distinctive one, guaranteed to induce a very special mood of dejection and doubt. Only as the train wheezes and rattles along for the last three hours of the trip, the last thirty miles or so from Sagauli to Raxaul, is there any change. Then comes a new lifting of the heart. The train trip is nearly over. The unknown lies ahead. But anything is better than the old Oudh Tirhut. Then, too, we were lucky in November. The last hour it was brilliant and sunny. There ahead, above the heavy grayish ground haze, lifting clear and translucent to the north, were the wreathed shoulders and the shining snow peak of Dhaulagiri, sixth highest mountain in the world. The effect was magical. It was possible to imagine a certain effervescence in the air suddenly, a breath of coolness, of cleanness. So always the Himalayas have affected people in India, weary of the plains, but here especially the mountains exercise a particular influence. The mountains of Nepal are still unknown, unclimbed, breathing forth an atmosphere of mystery.

For Edward Migdalski and myself coming to Nepal was a familiar ordeal, with its changes of trains, shifting of mountains of luggage, and general atmosphere of dirt and gloom. For the others it was a revelation. Besides, this time we were approaching the capital with considerable trepidation, not knowing for certain whether the Maharajah would agree to our plans after his disheartening answer to my letter. We did not know whether luck would still be with us.

At last there came a sign, "Raxaul," and we were at the edge of Nepal. The station was a gloomy brick shed piled high with boxes wrapped in jute sacking, destined for Katmandu. Across the tracks was a white-painted steel fence with a wide gate. Beyond, in Nepal territory could be discerned a few huts and a brick wall enclosing a house and garden. There were also sidings and sheds for some railway cars which made the Oudh Tirhut Railway look huge by comparison. This was the Nepal Government Railway, a narrow-gauge affair which runs from Raxaul twenty-nine miles across the Terai north toward the base of the hills.

In the look of the place there was nothing to distinguish India and Nepal. It was the same flat Terai land, stretching away into the distance, covered with the same whitish dusty soil with a checkerboard of small fields, each planted with grain so thinly that the stalks stood apart and could be counted. In places there were clusters of mud walls, the thatched roofs covered with melon and gourd vines. The only color relief to this dusty monotony was the occasional feathery tufted patch of yellow-green bamboos or the mango trees, sometimes in thick clumps, sometimes spaced wide apart and open.

In all this the people seemed much the same, only the Nepali national dress began to be noticed. This was more apparent in the men, a tight-fitting pair of trousers usually made of white cotton, rather like baggy jodhpurs. Above the trousers came a wide shirt worn with the tails out and tied, rather than buttoned, in an ornamental way across the chest. The shirt was also of cotton, and over this was worn a coat when the wearer could afford it, usually of cotton drill in the warm weather or of tweed in the winter. Most distinctive of all was the cap worn by the Nepalis, a cotton skull cap with a peak, which is sewn in such a fashion that it is a bit lopsided, the peak being off center, slightly over the right side. This cap might be white or black or of some hand-blocked pattern in rich bright colors. Only officials and high dignitaries wore the black beaver rounded pillbox-style cap, which in a hard black felt form is often worn by Gurkha troops or orderlies in the British or Indian armies.

Women's clothes consisted for the most part of Indian-style saris, the wrap-around drapery which may be made of anything from cotton to elaborately brocaded silks or damask. Under this the women wore a skirt or slip and a short waist, which left the midriff bare if the lower garment was a skirt. The women from the hills wore a distinctive dress — a very wide skirt of colored cloth with an enormous sash winding round and round the waist to produce a mediaeval "enceinte" effect. Over this was worn a rather tight jacket with the same sort of strings to tie it over the breast as the men used; a scarf or shawl over all. These hill women were fond of silver coin and glass or china bead jewelry, and their husbands loaded them down with ropes and ropes of coin or bead necklaces and bracelets, showing off in this way a good part of the family wealth.

A few of these hill people were always moving in or out of Raxaul, giving the place color and strangeness. On the platform when we arrived there was a tall Nepali in the jodhpur trousers, shirt, coat, and peaked cap. He saluted us smartly, and then stroked the dangling mustache which most Nepali men would not dream of being without, and smiled a bit shyly. I recognized him as the man who had greeted Ed and myself the previous year, and smiled back. My Hindustani was good enough for me to catch the gist of his speech. It was a word of welcome, with the notice that we would stay at the Nepali Guest House, the brick affair across the tracks, surrounded by its own wall. Hordes of coolies materialized as they always do at these moments, and the stationmaster, a dignified old gentleman in a blue tweed coat and a filmy cotton "dhoti," strode over to see what the fuss was about. There was very little fuss. We gathered up our cameras and light gear and strode through the gate in the white fence into Nepal.

The Nepal State Guest House in Raxaul was a squarish brick building with a bow in front making a two-story porch. In front there was a small garden within the wall, with neat half-moon flower beds full of color. In the yard were several "gul mohur" and other ornamental trees, and in these perched a few somnolent crested starlings, brown with yellow bills and feet, calling at monotonous intervals a querulous "cheep." The few small open holes in the brick of the eaves of the guest house were inhabited by owls about the size of a scops or screech owl. They made themselves known by a shrill disconcerting series of shrieks, "kee-ek, kee-ek, kee-ek," mostly just after dark. In addition, at least two small species of bats lived in cracks in the plaster and board of the inside of the guest house and fluttered about in the gloaming.

On our first visit Ed and I had been herded into one very small room on the ground floor, an introductory experience of Nepal hospitality calculated to add to the railroad mood. This time our treatment fell into much the same pattern. Although we were at first ushered upstairs with considerable grace and given the run of the slightly more elegant top floor, it was made known to us that this was only temporary. One of the mighty ones, a top-flight member of the Rana family, was about to arrive on his august way to Delhi, and before he took the train, he would rest for a few hours in the upper rooms. A President or a King could not require more preparations or more awe in advance of his coming, and the visiting foreigners who might happen to be official guests of the State were made to feel like real interlopers, which of course they were in the eyes of the Nepalis. We could have our tea upstairs, but after that we would have to go down again to await the departure of the Rana.

Upstairs there were two bedrooms connected with a hall and a sort of sitting room. As is so characteristic of Indian architecture, there were doors in every wall of every room, sometimes two doors to a wall, so that when all were open, everything could be seen in every direction. Tea was brought to us at the table in the central room. From there we could look into the principal bedroom which had been readied for the Rana, with a brass bedstead in the center beside which stood a two-foot-high brass spittoon. In our room there was a table in a corner covered with a large white cloth.

We sat about rather dully, the weight of our luggage and the cares of planning weighing on our minds. It was always this way at intervals. We had come so far. Now we must plan for going on. Meanwhile there was a sort of hiatus of the mind. Suddenly there was a scuffling of feet and a shrill outburst of angry-sounding Nepali. It was a monologue delivered in a crescendo, and came nearer as several people hurried up the stairs. Into the room burst a smartly dressed fat man, obviously a Personage of some sort. His trousers and shirt were of good material, dyed a bright pink. His coat was of fine tweed, and he wore a round black pillbox hat of beaver. With only an angry, disgruntled glance at us, he continued to fire off a string of epithets at the cowering janitor and his assistants. The white cloth was whisked away, revealing silver trays of sweetmeats, large red apples, oranges, and bottles of soda water. For us, having left the fresh fruit of Calcutta behind and already inured to eating out of tin cans, this seemed like opulent fare. The trays were hurried away to some recess, and we were urged again a few moments later by the tremulous janitor to move below to the lesser bedrooms on the ground floor.

If anything could be designed to make one behave with ill grace, it was this sort of folderol. It was almost irresistible to react pettishly to such trifling incidents. I know that I for one stalked downstairs feeling rather small and silly. Whenever this sort of thing happened in Nepal, I used to reason with myself if I felt put upon. I would try to rationalize my feelings. I would think, "Oh, well, you're only angry because you're used to being just a little better than everyone else in a place like India, where a white man has an advantage. Now you're upset because a Nepali, albeit a member of the ruling family, is being treated better than you are." This talking to oneself usually helped, but not always.

The fat personage belonged to a class of people in Nepal who spend their whole lives as secretaries, assistants, or aides of various sorts to the two ruling families, that of the King, and, more particularly, the Prime Minister's family, the Ranas. They traditionally surrounded their master with a screen of adulation, and everything they did was calculated to feed his and their sense of self-importance. I always found the members of the ruling families themselves most polite and gracious. Normally the more important the man, the more courteous he would prove to be. This could not be said, however, of their minions, and it was the attitude of these small fry that has served in the past to create such a feeling of resentment among visiting foreigners.

I was reminded of this feeling not long ago when reading the account of Dr. Hoffmeister, who journeyed to Nepal in 1845 as physician for Prince Waldemar of Prussia. When they were met near the border by Dil Bikram Thapa, nephew of the then Prime Minister, Mathabar Singh, Hoffmeister remarks how "most ludicrous scenes were caused by the officious zeal of his twenty or thirty vassals, all of whom watched his every movement." These same kinds of vassals were just as officious over a hundred years after.

A few minutes later the tiny Nepal train arrived at Raxaul Station from upcountry. Having deposited the ordinary citizens at the station platform, the train then came on another hundred yards to the back door of the guest house to debark the Rana. Bagam, my Gurkha boy, having been born and brought up in Calcutta, was having his first experience of life in the land of his fathers. He was all ears and eyes, and would scuttle back and forth to us huddled in our small room downstairs with news of the great events. The Rana was apparently a young man, a General in rank, therefore a "First-Class" member of the family in the Roll of Succession, who was accompanying his sister to Delhi where she was to be married to an Indian Prince. With her were twelve women attendants or "bridesmaids," as Bagam whispered to us, "very pretty too," all of whom scuttled upstairs in the dark to the upper rooms so as not to be seen by us.

Fortunately these recitations were interrupted by the announcement that dinner was ready across the tracks in the Indian station restaurant at Raxaul. We trooped over to a small fly-specked room in the dingy brick building where a soup-stained white cloth had been spread over half of a dirty table. The other half was left bare for the casual traveler who might come in from the "Number Seven Down" train which was due any moment. A stunted man with a pot belly put on a white coat to act as waiter. On his head was a turban of the made-up, sewn-together sort which waiters wear. Across the front was a red band with a brass "K" for Kellner's, the restaurant concessionaires of the railway. The lower half of the turban was black with sweat and grime.

We were given a sort of mulligatawny soup, a mutton

curry and rice, and a custard for dessert which was somewhat of the consistency of soft apricot-colored cement. To alleviate this disappointment I called for something to drink. A perfectly good-looking bottle of Canadian Club whiskey was produced, but on closer investigation the second disappointment of the evening came when the bottle proved to contain what appeared to be Cyprus brandy.

Meanwhile the train had pulled in, and several portly gentlemen came in and sat at the bare half of the table and ordered tea, cigarettes, and drinks. We then were stared at, minutely and carefully, in that concentrated way which is characteristically Indian, but which seems so impolite to the foreigner. When I first experienced it, I used to try staring back, but that never did any good, and might in fact be worse, as it could lead to a long conversation.

We stayed long enough for the Rana to be ready to leave by the time we walked back across the tracks through the gate. Three special cars had been drawn up to be attached to "Number Seven Down." The first was a first-class carriage of double the length of an ordinary one, which we dubbed the "How-do-you-do, My Public, How-do-you-do, My People," carriage, for the Rana and his sister. Then came a second-class carriage for the twelve bridesmaids, and a third-class one for a detachment of Gurkha troops as a guard and official escort. The first-class carriage fascinated us, because it had evidently been made especially for Princes of Ruling Houses of India. In the center was an open porch between the two compartments which had a gilded brass balustrade and an especially wide flight of steps leading toward the ground, with gilded brass bannisters. Apparently this car was made for impressing the populace. At wayside stations the Great One could make a properly regal appearance and receive adulation from the humble public. It was far more impressive in design than anything I had seen for Presidents on stump-speaking tours at home.

The guards in their carriage interested us. They had heavy canvas cases over their rifles, well designed to make them completely ineffective for use in a hurry, but perhaps the threat was enough. There had been lots of violence on the Indian railways in the last few months, with passengers being robbed, stabbed, and thrown out of the carriages, and on our trip from Calcutta we had kept a loaded shotgun handy in the compartment.

By the time we reached the guest house again, the débris from the visiting Rana's party had been largely swept up and we were allowed to take over the top floor. The spittoon reserved by the janitor for Ranas had been removed, the empty soda bottles stood like little soldiers against the wall, and only a few stray petals from the flower garlands carried by the ladies had escaped the sweeper's notice, and lay about the edges of the rugs. Finally our beds were ready, our bedding rolls arranged on them and the mosquito nets set up on frames of poles, and we were able to sleep for the first time in three days in the comparative comfort of a bed on solid ground.

The morning brought our first experience of Abdul as a cook. I had hired him in Calcutta, a saturnine man in his late forties, a Mohammedan from Lucknow who had an excellent string of recommendations from Army wives who had liked him as a bearer, children's nurse, and cook. His lack of volubility somehow made me feel confidence in him. This was to be our first experience of his prowess. I had ordered breakfast at seven to give us a chance to get out for a walk through the surrounding countryside. We would have orange juice made from powder, porridge, powdered coffee, tinned bacon, and fresh eggs and toast. At six we were up watching the dawn light gilding the mountain tops in the distance with a golden-pink glow. Smoke was rising from the cook house and there was definitely a bustle going on below. By seven the table was set. By seven-ten we were all waiting and beginning to be restless. The mists were lifting on the fields and the flocks of cattle and goats were being led out for the day's grazing. I went below to accost Abdul. The cook house was so full of smoke that I reeled back stifled. Finally copying Abdul and Rao I groped in squatting, and knelt down by the fire rubbing smoke from my eyes. There were two fires going. Over one the eggs, which had apparently been fried an hour before, were being kept warm. Over the other, water was boiling.

"What about porridge?" I asked.

"Yes, sir, porridge making now," was the smothered answer.

"Well, hurry up, Abdul, for Heaven's sake."

Another hour went by while we tinkered with cameras, got out our shotguns and ammunition, and fiddled about upstairs. Now it was broad day. The mist had burned off long ago. The last villager had returned from the early morning trip to the fields with his little brass water pot, his "lotah," which in India is always used instead of toilet paper. It was long past time to be up and off.

"Abdul!" I shouted for the tenth time. Francis Leeson, who had been in the Indian Army and spoke Urdu and Hindustani, went down to try his luck. He came back as mystified as I had been.

"He's made the milk now" (our milk was also powdered), "but I can't find the porridge," he reported.

"Abdul!" we all chorused.

The poor man had no sense of timing. He couldn't seem to get everything ready at the same time. The other servants seemed to be sunk into a kind of apathy. There was nothing to do but wait and finish up all possible chores and arrangements beforehand. We unpacked our collecting guns, auxiliary barrels, and ammunition. I wrote letters, telegrams, gave a long list of instructions to Bagam, who was to wait for some of our heavy luggage and stay with it in the Nepali town a mile up the tracks while we went on the following day up to Katmandu. Breakfast finally arrived as we were about ready to start in on the tin plates themselves. We wolfed it down, and as Ed, Howard, and I started out of the back gate across the fields to look for birds, I glanced at my watch. It was just ten-thirty, a bad augury for bird collecting.

But the country round Raxaul is not ideal for bird collecting anyway. Fifty years ago this was the beginning of the continuous array of forest which stretched across the plains of the Nepal Terai to the foothills. In those days the Terai was a fearsome place, a heavy belt of jungle interspersed with swamps and the rocky bed of streams. In the rainy season it was a vast morass and celebrated as the world's worst malaria spot. Today the jungle is confined to the narrow six-mile belt on the northern fringe of the Terai next to the beginning of the foothills. South the twenty or more miles to the Indian border, the country is exactly the same as the adjacent parts of Bihar and Uttar Pradesh, dry dusty flat land, all cultivated except for the occasional swampy patch or stream bed.

We walked north from the guest house along the bank of a small stream. The path to the stream passed through two small villages, collections of wattle and daub huts with thatched roofs covered with melon and gourd vines. Some of the houses had rude designs about the doorways, white-painted figures of birds or prancing animals. Over the doors were tacked small hand-blocked cuts on crude paper of gods and goddesses, reminders that the Hindu autumn festival of Dasshera was recently celebrated. The designs around the doorways made me think of those I had seen in Orissa, south of Calcutta; reminded me, too, that these people were Indians, not Nepalis, probably descendants of laborers imported from the provinces to the south into Bihar a generation or two ago to work in the fields of indigo, a great crop in India at the turn of the century. Land hunger being what it is in India, these people had probably settled here across the border rather than return home when their contracts were up. Here they could work for some absentee landlord as sharecroppers, but probably at a better rate of return than in India where taxes were heavier. Perhaps they would some day own their own land, the universal dream. In front of each hut was a large round bowl-shaped cattle trough made of cement in which the family pair of bullocks were fed a mixture of water and chopped-up grain stalks or rice hulls. Beyond lay the bullocks or buffaloes themselves, tethered to stakes and lying dreamily in a soft bed of manure, most of which would be saved and dried later for fuel.

We walked on, through a grove of bamboos, feathery and yellow-green. It was empty of birds. Four little boys armed with slingshots sat in the path in the center of the grove. They were idly plucking the feathers from a green Willow

Warbler, certainly small game but still edible. In the heavily cultivated areas of India and here in adjacent Nepal it was a matter of wonder to me that any birds at all survived, so intense and so efficient were the children with their catapults.

Fortunately the boys didn't follow us, another habit of little boys which was usually a great nuisance, and Ed, Howie, and I parted company. My course lay along the stream itself. It ran deep down in a bare canyon with overgrazed brown slopes. Nothing stirred, and it began to seem hot. The sun's glare was intense. Suddenly two birds went up along the stream, a pair of Red-wattled Lapwings, a large decorative plover with nicely patterned black-and-white wings and a loud, insistent cry, "Did-he-do-it, Did-he-do-it?" We could eat these, and I fired, bringing one bird down in the stream. A scramble below to the bank and I could just reach him in the shallows. As I clambered up again, I almost regretted shooting the lapwing, for in my haste to get down I had stepped into a mass of human dung, a fate likely to befall anyone who strays off the beaten path near a village.

By the end of an hour and a half, when further search had revealed one Willow Warbler and a White-eye, a small yellow-greenish warbler-like bird, in bushes near the stream, I was thoroughly depressed. If this was going to be what bird collecting in Nepal was like, I for one would be happy to go somewhere else. But certainly it was partly Abdul's fault.

On returning, I found little to cheer me. Ed had gotten a little green barbet, a bird about the size of a bluebird with a massive stubby bill which sits in the top of a tree all day and says "tock, tock." English people in India have dubbed it the Coppersmith, so insistent is its little "tock-tock" call. Ed had also gotten a brown tree pie, a long-tailed species of Indian magpie usually found in any patch of scrub near a village, and a small brown migratory flycatcher. Howie had shot a tree-pipit. Summing up, I was glad that we were to leave Raxaul next day.

It had been good, though, to get our equipment out. The shotguns seemed to be in perfect order. The auxiliary barrels fitted properly, and the small thirty-two cartridges fired well. Then, too, these few rather uninteresting birds would serve to give Toni and John a little more practice in skinning. We started in on our catalogue, writing down these first specimens from Nepal, and filling in the details on their labels — the color of the eyes, the fleeting colors of the soft parts, so-called, the bill and feet, which would fade and darken after a time. Some birds, like the lapwing, had small lappets or wattles of naked skin about the face, and the color of these had to be catalogued as well. Then the date and the altitude of the collecting place must be recorded, and any notes on the song, habits, or occurrence of the bird which might be of future interest. All of this work meticulously carried out, and the bird skins properly made, would form the difference between a good and a poor collection.

Meanwhile Howie and Dick had been sorting out mammal traps and getting their equipment ready. Kurt and Francis were equally busy with their cameras and films. Our plan was to go up to Katmandu for approximately a ten-day stay at the capital. We would take with us just what we needed for that time in the way of clothes, food, and film. For the social life of the place we would need dinner jackets and business suits. For the bird and mammal collecting we would need a supply of ammunition and taxidermist's gear. The

On the trail near Chisapani we came on several parties of Tibetans, one led by this lama from Shimbuling Gompa near Mount Kailas. Here he demonstrates his trumpet made from a human thighbone, and one of his ceremonial drums.

The old lady of Rekcha.

Don Pal, the mighty hunter.

rest of our heavy luggage, including the tents and most of our supplies, would stay here at the Nepali town of Birganj, about a mile from Raxaul. The local governor, or "Burra Hakim," as he was called, of this District of Nepal, Colonel Rana, another offshoot of the family, came to call on us and told me that he would be responsible for our equipment if I would leave Bagam with it as a watchman.

This would save a lot of effort. Whatever happened as a result of our coming interview in Katmandu, if our permit was only for the Terai, we should have to come back to Raxaul again. If we had luck, and the Maharajah consented to our original plan to visit the western and eastern parts of the country, we should still have to come back. The interior of Nepal is so inaccessible, with such a dearth of roads, that if you want to travel from one part of it to another, the best plan is simply to go south until you hit the Indian border, find one of the many branches of the Oudh Tirhut Railway and take a ticket going east or west to the nearest point of the border, and then start walking. Most Nepalis seem to do it in preference to going over the mountains if they have a long journey ahead. Even a lot of the internal Nepal mail is transported that way.

Finally we had finished our repacking and sorting out. Bagam was dispatched by flatcar with the cases in his charge to Birganj. We were packed and ready for the single train a day which leaves Raxaul for Amlekhganj, twenty-nine miles to the north at the base of the foothills. I had sent a further telegram to the Durbar in Katmandu announcing our schedule. The train was supposed to leave at eight-thirty in the morning. By getting up at dawn we were able to coax Abdul to produce a breakfast at seven-thirty, a remarkably speedy accomplishment. Everything was packed, loaded, and carried onto the platform by eight-fifteen. But then it appeared that the stationmaster had forgotten our reservations and had made no provision for us. There was only one first-class compartment on the toy-like train, and that was reserved for one of the lesser Ranas who happened to be going up to Katmandu that day. No such problem as this could be solved without the appropriate shouting all round. When it appeared as if we should have to stay another day in dreary Raxaul, a final paroxysm of shouting on all our parts brought action. A battered second-class compartment car was attached to the end of the train, and we with all our goods and chattels piled in. Toni, John, Abdul, and Rao joined the eighteen other people who were already crowded onto various projecting parts of the anatomy of the engine, there being no room whatever in any of the remaining compartments, and as we climbed in over our baggage, there came a pant and a wheeze, and we jolted off.

This morning there were no mountains to lift our hearts as we pulled away across the baked plains of the Terai. The hills lay behind a haze of dust and mist. Only a big blue roller flew away from the telephone wire, showing us in a flash of sheer beauty his azure and turquoise wing pattern. And then I saw a black drongo on the wire, and then a kestrel. Along the stream there were some egrets and cattle herons, and in the middle of a swampy place we spied four Black-necked Storks. Even here in the flat, baked plains there were some birds left, to be looked at and enjoyed, to take away frustrations and to gladden the eye.

III

The Road to Katmandu

THE ROAD to Katmandu is as old as history, but Nepal is still perhaps the least known country in Asia. Since the earliest days of communication between civilized centers, between India and China, Nepal has been known and spoken of, but the route across the icy passes, the highest in the world, which connect the country with the east across the backbone of the continent, has rarely been traversed.

Nepal, however, has always been a magnet to visitors in spite of its inaccessibility. Buddha was born here, in the Terai at a spot called Rummindei, the Lumbini Garden of legend, in the year 563 B.C. In 250 B.C. the great Indian Emperor Asoka, the memorable convert to Buddhism, helped to start the tradition of pilgrimages which has continued ever since. He visited Rummindei and caused a memorial to be erected to Buddha's memory, after which he also traveled to the central valley of Katmandu and erected four large "stupas" around the town of Patan, monuments to record Buddha's undoubted visit to the valley itself.

The road up from the plains winds over hill and dale in a deliberately difficult and tortuous route which has been easy for the inhabitants to defend, and which has tended to discourage all travelers except the devout pilgrims. Our trip was in its own way a pilgrimage. The number of zoologists who have visited Nepal could be counted on the fingers of one hand. After the redoubtable Hodgson, there have been no real successors. Surgeon John Scully served the Residency from 1876 to 1878 and collected a few birds which were presented to the Indian Museum in Calcutta. Lieutenant Colonel R. L. Kennion, British Envoy at the Court of Nepal in 1920 and 1921, sponsored some bird collections along with an extensive collection of mammals made by a Goanese-Indian collector of the Bombay Natural History Society called Baptista.

More recently collections have been made by Lieutenant Colonel F. M. Bailey, British Envoy in 1934–38, and by several of his guests during his stay in Katmandu. The only foreign ornithologist to visit any part of Nepal outside of the valley was Mr. Herbert Stevens, who collected along the East Nepal border during the course of his extensive visit in 1922 to the neighboring semi-autonomous State of Sikkim. In 1947 Dr. Walter Koelz, an American, made a bird collection in the central Katmandu Valley and along the route up to it. This collection and the one of some six hundred birds made by Ed and myself during our first month in and around Katmandu in 1947 had been the only two recent collections by ornithologists in Nepal, prior to our return in 1948.

Our train journey lasted for a good four hours. Considering that the distance is less than thirty miles, this must be unique. Of course we stopped. We stopped wherever possible, the first place being Birganj, the Nepal town a mile or two up the tracks from Raxaul. Colonel Rana, the local Governor, appeared, very natty in riding togs and complaining of his gout, which he felt should not be attacking him at fifty-five. He apologized for the mix-up about our railway tickets and ushered us into still another second-class carriage, this time moving out the traveling Rana's womenfolk who were occupying it and who scuttled back into their master's compartment. I was fascinated by the Governor's style and his completely overbearing manner. When some hundreds of the local folk crowded about us too closely on the platform as we stood talking, he suddenly shouted out at the top of his lungs the Nepali version of "scram," a word which sounded rather like "hirndo," and everyone melted away as if he had turned a high-pressure hose on them. I admired his technique, but knew in my heart that I for one would never be able to achieve anything approaching it. One has to be backed up by the power of "the high, the middle, and the low" to accomplish such a miraculous effect.

Eventually the train started again when Colonel Rana had formally said farewell to us. He waved his hand in a signal to his aides who then told the engineer that he was allowed to proceed. We wound off, jolting and rattling across the plains of the Terai, stopping at several small villages to take on water for the overburdened little engine. The train was so packed with people that besides those attached to various parts of the engine there were scores sitting on the tops of the carriages or holding on to the doors and windows. At one stop a small elephant with his mahout or driver-keeper diverted us and the crowd. The elephant was a young one and almost as big as the engine. We took pictures of the two together, each in its own way rather primitive means of transport.

At last the cultivated fields heavy in rice stopped, and we

came to dry scrubby grazing land, spotted with thorny bushes on the top of which sat shrikes looking for insects to catch and impale on the thorns. Occasional huge flat-topped trees, silk-cotton trees as they are called, stood out above the landscape. On them perched gaunt-headed vultures or sometimes a single marabou stork. We saw a jackal threading his way in among the bushes. Although the rains had only ended two months before, the dust and the dry river beds, the lank leaves and the waiting vultures, gave the impression of a semi-desert country, but at least it was country and not the squalid surroundings that pass for country in the overpopulated vicinity of Raxaul.

Then came the beginning of the forest, the continuous belt that parallels the foothills for a stretch of about six miles. We were in it now and going up a slight grade, the engine panting for dear life. The trees here were mostly "sal," the famous timber tree of the Himalayan foothills; but these were small ones, for the area had been cut over. Nothing moved among the trees except wandering bands of buffaloes and cattle being grazed as they headed up with their herders toward the hills. A few white spider lilies shining in the underbrush attracted our attention. We hung out of the windows looking for signs of life among the trees and enjoying the comparative coolness and greenness of the forest after the heat of the open country.

At long last we wound around a bend and puffed into Amlekhganj, the railway terminus. Here the train would rest awhile and regain its strength for the journey back to Raxaul in the afternoon. The town was a mere collection of huts, tea stalls, and sheds for the numerous rattletrap busses which go on into the hills. We got out and went up to a room in the station over the ticket office where in comparative privacy we could sit and eat our K-ration lunch.

Meanwhile Toni, the more active of the bird skinners, would oversee the horde of coolies who descended on our luggage. In the midst of opening tins of sardines and meat paste, we all took turns rushing up and down to supervise this operation and to make sure that our gear was loaded onto the roof of the mail bus, a slightly less dilapidated-looking Chevrolet of ancient vintage. There was a tremendous amount of palaver about where we should sit, and in fact if there would be any seats for us at all. Nothing could ever be achieved restfully in Nepal any more than in India. There always seemed to be a tumult of shouting about every arrangement or stage in our progress. Finally it was decided that we could have two seats next to the driver and four in the sort of cage which occupied the space behind the driver's seat. In this cage were two narrow benches made for midgets with a space between designed for passage, not for knees. The six of us squeezed into the front seat and the cage along with John and Toni and our cameras and knapsacks. Behind in a great tangle of arms and legs and sacks and boxes, the rest of the available space was occupied by twenty-eight people, bodies if you will, piled helter-skelter. Different bits of clothes or a face distinguished Abdul and Rao in the forlorn welter. More stuff was piled outside on the top and three or four men managed to perch there also. When we finally lurched away from the back of the station, I doubted very much that we would be able to travel the twenty-eight miles up to Bhimpedi, the terminus of the motor road.

The trip was certainly exciting. The road was well laid out and covered with good firm gravel. At intervals there were bridges over the rivers, excellent bridges for the most part of steel girders painted red. However, the approach to each bridge was a curve where the road left the embankment along the river and swerved toward the stream. Around these curves we went lickety-split and onto the narrow bridge swooping and plunging so that it seemed a miracle that half the truck's body was not left hanging on the girders. Then, too, the road surface of the bridge was made of wooden planks, many of them rotten or missing and all of them loose. We plunged forward and over the planks with a rattle and a roar as if the driver thought that momentum alone would carry us across. All the while the planks cracked and snapped and we bumped over the gaps so that it seemed as if our trip was going to be a one-way affair. Sheer mental paralysis prevented me from stopping the bus then and there and walking the rest of the way.

The scenery, however, was beautiful and that made up for the queasy feeling. As soon as Amlekhganj was left behind, the hills began. These first hills were the Siwaliks, a range of low sandstone and clayey hills. They have been described as older geologically than the main Himalayas behind. Between these hills and the true Himalayan foothills to the north lay the "duns," a two- or three-mile-wide series of valleys separating the two ranges. The Siwalik Hills and the duns, like the Terai, were clothed with thick sal forest in early times, much of which has been lumbered nowadays. Along the road we saw mostly Himalayan pine, a delicate long-leafed type reminiscent of the turpentine pines of the southern United States. The effect was dry but not dusty; the hills seemed a faint green, lightly covered as they were with pine, occasional sal trees, and bracken fern. The rivers had worn deep channels through the hills, making precipitous cliffs in places, sheer and naked dull gray sandstone, the color of a factory wall. They seemed too sheer to stand by themselves without the aid of man-made cement.

We went up and on through a long curved tunnel, the bus just scraping the sides. There were watchers stationed here, who called through the tunnel ahead of us to each other in drawn-out alpine tones, warning that a vehicle was coming. This tunnel was an important step in making the road, for formerly there was only a narrow pass over the ridge above, the Churia Ridge, which has played such an important historical part in the defense of Nepal from outsiders. Not until 1816 was Nepal ever successfully invaded from the plains when General Ochterlony, the East India Company Commander, stormed the Churia Pass and shortly afterward signed a treaty between Great Britain and Nepal which has continued in force down to the present day.

Beyond the ridge the road ran down into a lovely broad valley full of mustard in flower, a sheet of yellow lying across the land, solid and bright. With the greener inner ridges rising behind, it was superb, a sight to lift the heart, holding promise of excitement and splendors beyond. Here we began to see dripping springs and miniature streams coming down the hillsides in a blanket of ferns and moss, a real thrill after the barrenness below. I saw my first forktail, an elegant slim black-and-white thrush with a long divided tail which flew out from a mossy cleft beside the road.

We whirled down the valley raising a great dust cloud which eddied in through the back, dispelling the illusion of greenness and moisture. After a mile or two the valley closed in again and a long winding narrow ascent began. Here we conveniently had a flat tire and so could stretch our cramped legs. It seemed a miracle that all the tires had not given way long ago. The driver and his assistants, who filled the steaming radiator with water at all possible opportunities, somehow seemed to know their business. The tire was whipped off and changed in jig time.

Then we started again, panting up the incline. In this valley the first ridges of the outer Himalayas proper pressed about us. The character of the rocks and soil had changed. Great boulders spattered the hillsides and lay in jumbled heaps in the stream bed. This was no soft, eroded sandstone. The ridges swept up steeply on each side clothed with scanty grass and trees, with broad scars where the soil had washed off and gravel and rocks had been revealed. The gravel formed long screes down the hillsides, the route of avalanches swept down by the rains. The effect was mournful. The whole topsoil of the valley seemed to be doomed. Once the trees had been removed and the grass grazed off by the goats and cattle, nothing could withstand the violent rains. Year by year less would be left until the rocks of the hills would stand out quite naked, desert and skeletal in place of the former solid rich jungle. We did not know it yet, but this would be the sight that would confront us everywhere in the foothills of Nepal.

At last we came to Bhimpedi, a long winding street beside the largely dry river bed of the headwaters of the Rapti River. Bhimpedi is a caravan town, about four thousand feet above sea level, full of hostelries for the peasants and coolies who traverse the road. There were a few wayside temples and lots of hole-in-the-wall shops from which peered blasé shopkeepers and their even more blasé small dogs. This was the first town where we saw a sort of mongrel breed of Nepali dog, halfway between a small woolly terrier and a Pekingese. The breed was better the higher we went up into the hills. The dogs got shaggier, merrier, and more vivacious, but down in the lower villages they were less shaggy, silkier, and apathetic.

Beyond the main part of the town the road simply petered out into the river bed. There was a house here, a sort of headquarters for the Government Office which controlled the hire of coolies for the road. The arms and legs in the bus resolved themselves once more into people and a great dismantling went on. Meanwhile we asked ourselves, "Where do we go from here?" and looking almost straight up could just spy out a ribbon of trail winding directly up a hill on the opposite bank of the stream. Once the baggage was unloaded and I had finished wrangling with the mail-bus driver about our fare, we turned our attention to the question of getting coolies. From Bhimpedi on the sixteen or so miles where the motor road began again in the inner Katmandu Valley, virtually everything going into this capital valley went on the backs of men, and women, too, for that matter. There was an electrically driven ropeway, a fearsome-looking device of high steel towers and a continuous cable carrying small wooden platforms at intervals of a hundred yards, which paralleled the trail. On this we could have put some of our trunks or sacks of food weighing between one and four hundred pounds and have them carried over the hills at a nominal fee. This time, however, we were traveling comparatively light. We turned to the question of coolies.

Two years before, in 1947, Ed and I had been surrounded by hordes of eager coolies when we had arrived at Bhimpedi.

Now there were very few. The manager of the business proved to be a young man of about twenty with a soft voice and a shy manner who had no control whatever over his boisterous charges. Yet notice had been sent ahead of our coming. There were the proper number of ponies waiting for us, each with a blue-uniformed pony man sent by His Highness's order. What was wrong with the coolies? The young "mukia," as he was called, seemed distracted by something else. He wouldn't put his mind on our case as I talked with him. I began to wonder if we were going to get up the hill after all. We would need about twenty-eight full-grown men for our loads and so far there were only twenty men and a few spindly boys. I refused the boys.

"I will not take boys," I said firmly. "I will have to pay them the same as the men and they can only carry half as much."

"But they are sent here to learn the trade," the young man mewed at me sideways, looking into the distance where his own thoughts apparently rested. "There are no others," he added.

We were evidently trapped. I resorted to the device which always made me feel like one of the nastier characters in *Penrod and Sam.*

"You must find me coolies," I said loudly. "Otherwise, I shall complain to His Highness" (the Nepali version of saying, "Look out, I'll tell teacher!"). At least it made the mukia look at me for a moment.

"Take some men now, sir," he said. "And we will send the rest after you later when we get more coolies in."

This would never do. I had visions of our bags still being in Bhimpedi when we returned.

"I must have twenty-eight men now and immediately," I said again, and in a rather menacing tone repeated the threat about "telling teacher." These attempts to generate fear were always unpleasant and exhausting. I longed for the little rest house ahead high up on the hill. It was four-thirty already and we had had a hard day.

The mukia strolled away deep in thought, his aides clustering about him with pencils and sheets of paper totting up lists of coolies and pony men. The available men and spindly boys meanwhile began placing our effects in their wide-mouthed carrying baskets. I got Francis Leeson to tell the small boys in so many words that we were not having them. They looked woe-begone and tried to heft the loads encouragingly to show how strong they were.

"No, no, no," I said angrily, but with a sinking feeling. After all there were no others around.

Then I saw what was distracting the mukia. A great procession of ponies, people on foot, and "dandies" — large hooded palanquin-like affairs carried by six or eight men — suddenly appeared at the bottom of the trail from the hill above. Then I noticed, too, that down on the dry river bed there was a station wagon waiting and a truck. The mukia and his assistants scuttled away down to the cars. The procession arrived. Swiftly and efficiently everything was shifted into the car and the truck, several heavily wrapped-up passengers alighted from the dandies and we could see, even at that distance, the mukia bowing and scraping. It was evidently an important Rana and his ladies on the way down to India, perhaps to Calcutta with "gallstone" trouble, a favorite excuse of lesser members of the ruling family when they wanted to get away for a shopping spree and a bit of dalliance in the fleshpots. The cars started up and whizzed by us full of complacent plump faces. We returned to our wrangling.

It was no use. After three quarters of an hour, we started off on the ponies while some twenty men and an assortment of the boys trudged after us, each with a huge carrying basket on his back full of our stuff, Toni and John, Abdul, and Rao bringing up the rear. The track was not easy, in places the ascent over thirty degrees, but it has been much improved in the last few years. We wound on and on, up through light groves of pine and straggly grass until at the end on a spur we saw the fort of Sisagarhi over six thousand feet above sea level. The fort was like a toy fort, stone-walled but tiny, a sort of musical-comedy fort complete with soldiers and a bugler who blew Nepali variations of taps most of the evening. Above was a small traveler's town with a two-story stone rest house complete with fires, electric lights, and hot tea waiting.

We arrived about six. The view over Bhimpedi and on to the Siwalik Hills and the farther plains was obscured by a sort of pink mist, a wonderful diffused sunset that was almost solid to the touch. It was cold by nightfall, and we fell onto our cots after dinner completely exhausted. The change to the hills, the brisk cold, the firelight, and the good dinner which Abdul with his usual agonizing slowness finally produced, all acted like a tonic. Again we realized that we were glad we had persevered and come after all.

The next day was a mingled trial and pleasure, a sixteen-mile jaunt partly on foot, partly by pony, up and down, up and down over two mountain passes. The first was about a thousand feet above the Sisagarhi Rest House. By telling

Abdul and the coolies that we planned to be off by six, we finally managed to get away by seven-thirty. It was a wonderful clear day, and when we reached the first pass, I felt that we were turning our backs on the twentieth century and walking somehow into the sixteenth. The view was superb, a deep valley three thousand feet below, full of purple shadows with a ribbon of a stream glancing in the light where the sun could catch it. Above were lined up ranges of hills reaching back ever higher until at the last among the clouds was a solider substance, the snow peaks, lost in a world of tempest and violence of their own.

We plunged downwards, slipping and sliding on the loose gravel and pebbles of the path. There were remnants of trees here and there, especially away from the path. Some of the bushes were sporting small pink berries and had attracted flocks of bulbuls, the yellow-vented and red-vented kinds, merry crested birds with a pleasant warble. Crowds of struggling coolies surged up from below, panting under their loads. Among them were a few Tibetans, for now was the beginning of the annual winter migration of Tibetans down from the higher country beyond the passes.

These Tibetans consisted of several types. Mostly they were coolies, carrying down bales of wool and felt and "ghee" (clarified butter) for some Tibetan businessman. Occasionally we passed lamas, the priests who come down on pilgrimage to Buddhgaya or some other holy spot in the Buddhist legends. Then there were always a few beggars, the gypsies among the Tibetans, strolling players of various sorts who dance and sing and offer their womenfolk to the casual passer-by. Some of them seemed almost demented as they capered and grimaced and leapt about us, fawning and whining, "baba, baba," with outstretched hands. I saw one half-crazed-looking woman, naked to the waist, running to an old campfire and thrusting her enormous wild tangle of hair into the ashes, dusting it all through, screaming the while at the top of her lungs. Maybe she had decided she just couldn't stand her infestation of small friends one minute longer. As the Tibetans never bathe except ritually twice a year, they are usually well populated with fleas, nits, and other little ones.

The spectacular sight, however, was reserved for us when we reached the Markhu Valley below. We came upon an automobile being transported *out* of the central valley. It seemed hard enough to get a car *into* the valley, but to take it out again seemed really unnecessary. It was an old Mercedes limousine and was being taken down to India to be sold. To transport a car in Nepal was relatively easy. A framework of poles was made, the car driven on, and then the wheels and the bumpers were removed — nothing else — and a dust cloth placed over all. Then, if it was an ordinary car, sixty men simply bent down, picked up the framework, and walked off, chanting and stepping in time, a measured careful pace. For the largest vehicles one hundred and twenty men were used. It seemed simple but unbelievable, especially over the passes. As all big things like cars were much too heavy for the ropeway, they have had to be brought in on men's backs. The biggest single items were big cars and trucks, some of the generating equipment for the hydroelectric plant, and the four-thousand-pound bronze equestrian statues which every reigning Maharajah since Jang Bahadur has had made for himself for erection in the central squares of Katmandu.

The valley along which we now trotted our ponies was beautiful. The track was rather flat after the almost vertical descent, and was dotted with small villages near the river. The river itself wound through a fantastic mass of boulders, some as large as houses, washed down in the summer rains. Dippers, those strange little brown wren-like birds, perched on the edge of the torrent or flew upstream with their loud whistle. I shot one near a village and the echoing boom of the gun brought a great host of boys and men running down to the bank to see the fun. One, bolder than the rest, volunteered to wade for me, retrieved the bird, and was rewarded with the empty cartridges and a copper coin. The dipper has wonderful thick felty feathers, like a sea bird, for its excursions on the bottoms of stream beds, and even has the musky smell of a sea bird, too, rather like the smell of a petrel or shearwater.

Beyond the houses were fields aglow with mustard or young winter rice or barley. Here and there were cherry trees in flower, delicate bursts of pink. The breeze came up and started blowing the stalks of the green crops hither and yon, rippling and playing over the surface of the fields so that they seemed like lengths of pastel-colored moiré silk. The breeze crossed the trail, too, whipping up dust devils, and making the dried shocks of corn on their racks rattle and rustle. House sparrows were trying to nest in the stored corn. The houses were bright with new coats of beige, puce, and terra-cotta-colored paint over the stucco. Everything was still shining and neat from the annual autumn Dasshera festival. The corn had been stacked in the yard, gourds and melons hung from the eaves, and there were small woodcut pictures on paper of Kali or Lakshmi pasted over the doors with daubs of writing in scarlet paint, apparently good-luck phrases and charms. Some of the houses had hanging effigies under the eaves. One was the carcass of a dog, another a stuffed otter, a third a civet skin. Withered flowers and tufts of colored stuff were intertwined in long strings which hung across the roadway at intervals from house to house or tree to tree. In places they had been strung right across the river like a spider's bridge.

We plodded on, on through more cultivation, along a dusty track, then across the stream on rude earth and fagot bridges, made newly after every washout. For the wet summer weather there were a few steel suspension bridges on a slightly higher track. In the villages small tables had been set up along the road with tea or water and sweet cakes for travelers. In places these roadside stands were doing a land-office business. We began to feel very hungry. One of the pony coolies had unwillingly consented to carry our small lunch bag. He had dropped it once or twice so that one of the thermos bottles was broken, but we still had one with water in it. That with bread and meat paste, sardines, cheese, and chocolate made a welcome lunch. It was two o'clock and we still had one more pass to climb.

This last pass, Chandragiri, was a trial. The climb was straight and steep, the path, which had at some time been paved in the form of crude steps, was largely washed out, so that each step was irregular. Masses of coolies were on their way up, carrying charcoal, and others on their way down with new pottery. Some of the litter-like dandies went by, each carried by four coolies. In them were three teen-age Nepali boys on the way back for the holidays from a school near Darjeeling. They wore colorful striped school caps, and one with the wispy beginnings of a mustache saluted us solemnly in English much to the admiration and delight of his chair coolies.

At last we reached the crest. There was a huge "chaitya" here, a stucco mound used by the Buddhists as a memorial. There was a small Nepali rest house, too, and hundreds of coolies were sitting by the side of the path, smoking and chatting as they leaned back against their great wicker packs which were supported by wide stone seats placed for the purpose. The upper slopes here were still heavily wooded with rhododendron trees and thick bushes. Flocks of small birds on the hunt passed in a stream across the trail where it was narrow between the trees. We strode on eagerly to the other side of the chaitya.

Here was a revelation. Looking over the crest of the pass, framed in the thin, moss-draped, twisted branches of silver-leaved oaks and rhododendrons, Katmandu appeared. The central valley spread out and away to the east in a myriad of terraced fields and dotted, toy-like towns. In the center lay the capital, the white blocks of palaces and public buildings standing out clear and unbelievable. A single white needle of a tower stood up in the center, the famous "Folly" of Bhim Sen, built by the Prime Minister of the eighteen-thirties. Beyond we could see the sacred rivers winding through the valley, shining, ribbon-like. All round were grouped the darker hills, and high above, rising over the clouds, massive, corrugated, were the snow peaks, Anapurna, Himalchuli, Gosainthan. The names rang out in imagination, as strange, as far off as mystic Xanadu.

We clattered on down the other side, now gaining, now losing the view through the trees. The woods were full of a gay four-note whistle, the call of the Black-capped Sibia, a soft chestnut-colored babbler, probably first found on this spot by Brian Hodgson over a hundred years before. At the end of a long last decline we came out of the woods to open fields and a small village called Thankote. In the village square under a huge banyan tree was a small Ford and a dilapidated truck waiting for us. The hunchbacked chauffeur clambered out of the Ford and saluted us, smiling. He recognized Ed and me. We climbed wearily into the car, squeezing in as best we could. I told the truck to wait for our luggage and gave each of the blue-clad pony men a two-rupee tip. The car grunted and came to life and we jolted away, down the valley road to Katmandu. For a moment it was as if we were back in the twentieth century, but only for a moment.

IV

The Valley

THE DRIVE into Katmandu in the gloaming was intriguing. In the half light we could catch glimpses of people walking along the road — coolies carrying burdens, travelers of various sorts, a throng of people all on foot. Now we seemed to hurtle past them in our little car giving us a new sense of isolation from our fellow wayfarers. We passed terraced fields, little towns with shops and people staring out, and in the distance views of other towns farther away across the fields. Finally we rattled across a long bridge over the Vishnumati, one of the two sacred rivers of the valley. It joined the Bagmati, the larger of the two, at the city of Katmandu itself. Wreaths of mist floated over the shrunken stream, dyed a glazed pink in the last shreds of the sunset. Through the mist twinkled the electric lights of Katmandu. On we went along a narrow dusty street and finally stopped at a corner where a door in the wall proclaimed our guest house. The door faced on a small square in the center of which, illuminated by the street lights, was a white marble statue under a marble canopy of the present King standing resplendent in robes, orders, crown, and sweeping plumes, the whole a mixture of European and Oriental styles.

The guest house itself was placed well back in a roomy garden full of "gul mohur" and casuarina trees. The house was prettily designed of brick with stucco trim, and consisted of a central room with bedrooms leading off on two sides, each with a bath, a closet-like room equipped with wooden wash-hand stand, tin tub, and chamber pot. Behind in the back of the yard was a range of cook houses and servants' sleeping quarters. For our visit a number of Victorian chairs and a settee elegantly upholstered in mauve brocade had been provided for the living room, as well as rugs, a table or two, and cots in the bedrooms. There was a chest with crockery in it, a fire in the fireplace, and tea was waiting for us. I recalled most of the servants, a sort of janitor and his son with droopy mustaches who had been there before, and a young, rather elegantly dressed sweeper who looked unexpectedly superior for his job of emptying the chamber pots. Later on, dinner was produced by the guest-house staff, an excellent dinner of soup, mutton, vegetables, and custard, all of which was on our bill when we came to leave.

The Nepali system of having guests was a distinctive one. Fundamentally, of course, guests were not wanted. It has only been in recent years that there have been any at all. The British Residents — as they were called formerly, now Ambassadors — have been able to have a quota of guests of their own each year, and the vast majority of the few hundreds of Europeans who have visited the valley since the first two Jesuit priests passed through in 1661 have come this way. The first British Resident representing the East India Company was installed in Katmandu in 1802. The new Indian Ambassador may also have guests. The Nepalis themselves have had almost no guests. There have been only the occasional visiting diplomats or foreign missions, or, more recently, a few experts of one sort or another — engineers, geologists, sometimes a doctor or a dentist. All these have always had their expenses paid by the Durbar, although the visits of the accredited Minister from the United States to Nepal have now been put on a business basis, with a bill being presented to the State Department after each trip. Such guests were supposed, however, to tip heavily.

Guests of our sort — that is, people like ornithologists — whose visit seemed to hold no direct commercial gain for the country, or amelioration of any aches or pains for the Ruler, naturally were given only free lodging and light. Food, transportation, and other incidentals were all to be paid for, and of course tips were expected also. Being a guest in Nepal has always been expensive no matter what your category.

We were exhausted after our day over the passes, and it was not long before we were sound asleep in our sleeping bags on the cots in the bedrooms. The November air was on the crisp side. Next morning an old friend came to call on us early, Mir Subha Maniram Bhandary, a Durbar functionary whose responsibility was the welfare of guests. We remembered him well from our previous trip when he had been somewhat less fulsome in his greeting. Then Ed and I had been strangers belonging to a curious profession whose social status was obscure. This time the Indian newspapers had been full of our coming. We were famous apparently, and the Maharajah liked us. Maniram was effusive. He reminded me of a courtier, well versed in the writings of Machiavelli.

After a considerable amount of circumlocution Maniram came to the point and prepared a tentative schedule for us to meet His Highness as well as to visit points of interest about the valley. For a guide on our peregrinations Maniram produced his son, Laviram, a younger and slightly less elegantly turned-out version of himself. Maniram was invariably plumply resplendent in his smart pale pink or blue jodhpurs, his tweed coats sporting an array of Parker 51 pens in the breast pocket and the luxurious-looking soft black beaver pillbox hat with a large gold insigne on the front. An incongruous note was that he always went everywhere on a small British motorcycle.

"Petrol is very expensive in Nepal," he would explain with a grimace.

"You have a large family?" I asked.

"Yes."

It was Maniram's most characteristic word, spoken with a distinctive sideways bob of the head which Laviram minutely duplicated. I always felt that it was impossible for Maniram to say the word "no."

"It is very expensive to educate sons," and Maniram sighed.

For a moment I thought that we were going to be able to communicate with one another as humans in the twentieth century, and I prepared to sympathize with him about his sons, but the mask descended and we turned to general topics. It was arranged that we would if possible visit the library where Wentzel and Leeson could perhaps photograph some of the rare illuminated manuscripts.

Maniram stood up and prepared to leave.

"Please arrange that we have some time for shooting," I added. "We should like to go to His Highness's preserves at Naggarjung, and to Gokarna and Godaveri if His Highness will permit us."

If we were to be refused permission to go into the hills, it would be doubly important to get in some collecting around the valley. Katmandu itself is about forty-seven hundred feet above sea level. The surrounding slopes go up to eight thousand feet, and in places were still clothed with scrub forest. All the birds and mammals at this altitude would be mountain species, not found below five thousand feet. I did not say anything in advance to Maniram about our hopes.

"I must leave now if you will permit me," said our visitor with exquisite tact. "I am going to the American Legation. It is possible that your new Minister will come to Nepal in the next few days." Maniram bowed out.

A hundred yards or so up the road toward the parade ground was a much grander guest house which Maniram always called the American Legation, a bit of wishful thinking on his part, although it was in truth the house where the visiting American Minister and his suite stayed on the annual visit from New Delhi. This house boasted the only flush toilet and Frigidaire outside the confines of the British Embassy.

That day we confined ourselves to Katmandu. We were too stiff from our jaunt to want to do very much. From the guest house and the square with the King's statue there was a road which went straight up a slight rise to the edge of the Tundi Khel, the famous parade ground, a half-mile by a quarter-mile of wonderfully flat turf running north and south, broken only by a reviewing stand in the center, a raised circular platform built around the roots of a giant banyan tree. The road formed the western edge of the parade ground. It had circles at intervals around the elaborate equestrian statues of former Maharajahs. The first of these and the most animated was a statue of Jang Bahadur, the greatest of the Maharajahs, great-uncle of the present ruler, who sat reining in his spirited charger and gazing behind him with drawn sword resting on the animal's rump in a manner reminiscent of the well-known statue of General Outram in Calcutta. Jang Bahadur stared back toward a small square which opened off the Tundi Khel and contained the "Folly" of Bhim Sen, the slender tower nearly two hundred feet high that we had noticed from the pass, built, so it is said, by an earlier Prime Minister, great-uncle of Jang, to "amaze the populace." It has become a landmark visible from all over the valley.

We walked along the road stiffly, past the squads of recruits always drilling, past the barracks and the small temple which bordered the parade ground. This temple, the Mahankal, an insignificant-looking structure surrounded with a high stucco wall and overhung with heavy trees, always interested me because it was used alike by Hindus and Buddhists in the best non-sectarian style, each believing that the image within represented a god in their own pantheon. Would that we could do the same!

Farther on, a broad new road headed off to the west away from the Tundi Khel. We turned left on this new road, Juddha Road, as it was called in honor of a former ruler, uncle of the present Maharajah. This was the modern shopping center of Katmandu. On each side were small stores, selling radios, groceries, curios, and a garage or two complete with gasoline pumps. We went into one of the grocery stores to buy some tinned food. The interior was fascinating. There were so many glass counters that it was necessary to edge sideways to get between them. In them was every sort of article — bars of soap, toothpaste and powder, the

Indian sort guaranteed to wear down the teeth in short order, jars of honey, chutney, tins of spaghetti, United States Army K-ration tins from surplus stores in Calcutta, celluloid dolls and Christmas favors and oatmeal cereal. In the center of the shop was an enormous brass bedstead that must have come from the Crystal Palace Exhibition, so covered was it with rococo designs. The mattress and springs had been removed to give more floor space for cabinets. From the ceiling hung a great array of electric fans, chandeliers, and miscellaneous wares including several dozen umbrellas and canes. The effect was like a cave with stalactites pressing down just overhead and stalagmites reaching up from the floor in all directions. Unfortunately, the tins were all several years old and priced at their weight in gold. Furthermore, there was no tinned meat as Nepal has always been a very orthodox Hindu country.

Still farther on, we came to Katmandu's leading curio store, another welter of exhibition cases. Apparently glass-fronted showcases have become a "must" to create sales. I hated to think of all the coolies required to transport the plate-glass sliding doors alone. Nepal never having been afflicted with tourists has always been deficient in curios. The valley has been famous for centuries for the woodcarving done by the Newars, the tribe who formed its earliest inhabitants. The temple windows were always intricately carved wooden screens with interior board shutters. The old temples and the larger houses and palaces had magnificently executed carvings. The modern version, however, carved into picture frames, lampstands, and other bric-à-brac, somehow seemed to lack the quality of the old. The Newars also did wonderful work in brass and fine jewelry, but the present-day gewgaws, made of thin brass inset with colored glass instead of gems, seemed a far cry from the originals. Even in inaccessible Nepal the leveling process has occurred in taste and creative art which the machine age has brought to the rest of the world. It seemed curious that the effect should be felt in remote places in which the cause itself was not apparent.

We tried to look for antique pieces, but as always these were hard to come by. Occasional bits of brass or wooden carving could be found if the curio-shop men were given advance notice, and sometimes carved relics in crystal or lapis-lazuli. A few jewels even appeared, but for the most part these were modern, the stones and settings cut and made in India.

The end of Juddha Road came at a great square after passing an up-to-date-looking fire station, the men in blue uniforms with brass helmets, lolling about in front of several small trucks. The square was the oldest part of Katmandu. On it fronted the King's Durbar Hall, a huge structure of white stucco with columns in the best "Georgian cum Louis Philippe" style replete with Corinthian capitals and overdecorated cornices. This was the one modern note. The rest of the buildings were very old, mostly temples in the Nepali style which at first glance seemed Chinese. The square brick buildings had very wide overhanging eaves supported by elaborately carved beams and rafters. The roof lines went up in a graceful sweep only to be broken again by more eaves and a second smaller roof above. This usually was repeated a third time with another still smaller roof, so that the effect was like a pagoda. There has been much argument among archeologists about this form of structure, some claiming that it was Chinese influence brought to bear on the Hindu style of building, while others have asserted that actually this Nepali style has descended from the earliest extant Buddhist architecture at Sanchi in western India, where similar pagoda-like roofs have been found in stone.

One temple, smaller than the rest, on the north end of the square, had only one extra roof above the main one. Under the eaves of this roof was a window out of which leant two of the gods, Mahadeo and Parvati, realistically carved in a pleasant pose as if to survey the activity in the square below. But most of the carvings were not as decorous where the human form was concerned. Nepali temples have always been noted among foreign visitors for the orgiastic riot of fertility symbolism portrayed in their carvings. I was interested to notice that when some of us stopped spellbound beneath a particularly lurid and fantastic copulatory pose, our Nepali audience would invariably be puzzled to know what we were staring at or having a discreet chuckle about. It never occurred to them, quite naturally, that the grotesque little human forms were funny or smutty as they seemed to Western eyes. Finally it would sink in, and the people around us would begin pointing and discussing among themselves. Then they, too, would start smirking and giggling shyly. It always seemed a bit sad to me that foreigners have had to come to Nepal to create the idea of pornography, as such, where it had not existed before.

All around this square the old town pressed in about us. These were the old houses and these the crooked mediaeval streets which had witnessed the whole pageant of history in Nepal, the conquests, the massacres, the plagues. Nothing had changed, neither the houses nor the people. The market place was still thronged with the sellers of vegetables, fruit, and firewood, sitting about on the steps of the temples, and the crowd of buyers and hangers-on. Sacred cows and odds and ends of other animals wandered about munching among the rubbish. Here a bull glutted himself on a heap of discarded pepper leaves from the stall of a betel-nut vendor. There a starved pariah dog nosed among an odorous pile of dusty trash. A fat chubby child squatted by the curbstone grimacing and chuckling happily as it relieved itself. The chuckles turned to lusty squalls when a hen left her chicks and ran out greedily to peck at its buttocks. Children, especially boy children, were spoiled industriously in Nepal. The mother hastily emerged from her booth, rescued the baby, shooed the hen, and patted her child into chuckles again.

We walked home by a roundabout way through the narrow twisting sixteenth-century streets. Here we were a spectacle, and men, women, and children pressed in upon us from all sides. It was a relief when a file of coolies came by carrying enormous fagots of kindling and baskets of charcoal. We could follow them freely for a time in a sort of eddy in the wake of their passing.

When we arrived at the guest house, Maniram was waiting impatiently to greet us. He had news. There would be much to do in the next few days. In the first place, we could have an audience with His Highness the Maharajah the following day. Then word had just been definitely received that the new American Ambassador to India, who was also Minister to Nepal, Mr. Loy Henderson, was coming to Katmandu with his party of assistants and would be in the valley in a very few days.

"There will be much to do to make the American Legation ready in time," he bubbled.

There would indeed be much to do for everyone concerned with the guest houses. Normally these houses remained quite empty and devoid of furniture, but when a guest appeared, something had to be done, and so each time furniture would be temporarily borrowed from one of the palaces of the Rana family. Only a bare minimum was actually available to the guest department. The rest had to be rounded up, and of course varied according to the rank of the guest. Compared to our first visit, Ed and I knew we had done well and had risen in rank when we first saw the plush Victorian settee and chairs.

We heard more of all this at the Kilbournes' that night at dinner. Mrs. Kilbourne was the charming wife of Roy Kilbourne, the Englishman who had so capably run and supervised the Nepal Government power and telephone system for a number of years. He was the only foreigner in Nepal Government service in the valley. Mrs. Kilbourne had been urged to help the guest department wrestle with its decorating problems. She was coping valiantly.

"I do wish that the Mir Subha would just leave the furniture in the principal guest house once it is all installed, rather than drag it all out again after each visit," she sighed.

"But then there would be no way of gauging the importance of each guest," someone put in.

"Rubbish!" she snorted in her best twentieth-century vein. "That's all gone by the board long ago."

The next day Maniram came to take us to the Singha Durbar, the official residence of the Maharajah, for our audience.

The Singha Durbar was a vast white stucco palace across a causeway that opened onto the east side of the Tundi Khel. There was a huge gate like an arch of triumph, then a divided avenue on each side of a mirror pool with ornamental planting and a Victorian bandstand, and finally an entrance door under an archway with masses of brass pots full of ferns and orchid plants. A huddle of retainers clustered on the steps dressed in jodhpurs, tweed coats, military caps, and heavily armed with bandoliers, pistols, rifles, and "kukris," the national knife of the Gurkhas. These bodyguards, so characteristic of the palaces of the Ranas, always made me think of Sicilian brigands, perhaps because of their droopy mustachios or the almost ludicrous weight of arms that they carried.

We were met at the door and conducted inside by the Maharajah's Secretary, Sirdar Dikshit, a capable, pleasant man with a somewhat more elaborate gold seal than Maniram's on the front of his beaver cap, to denote his higher rank. The Sirdar conducted us through a rather low dark hall, hung with cut-glass mirrors, to a double marble stair. Here a small museum was pointed out to us — stuffed rhino and tiger heads, a cock Impeyan Pheasant in a glass case, and two stuffed Lesser Pandas, devoid of most of their fur. Up the stairs we went to find that the whole upper part of the large stairwell was ornamented with murals, done very realistically by an English artist, of hunting scenes of the Maharajah's father, Maharajah Chandra, and his younger brother, Maharajah Juddha. The hunting shown was the Nepali royal sport of tiger shooting performed in the center of a great ring of tame elephants which beat through the grass and scare out game.

On we went into a huge audience hall complete with

Tharu children inside a hut at Tikapur. The huge earthenware jars are for mustard oil.

There were lots of Tibetans at Boddhnath, mostly ragged-looking men and women who had just come down from the high passes.

The Goddess Tara in brass at Swayambhunath, the finest piece of sculpture in the valley.

throne chairs at the end on a dais. The color scheme was pink even to a dry pink marble fountain in the center decorated with pink sea shells. There were enormous mirrors everywhere, glass chandeliers of giant proportions, a large crystal-glass grandfather clock, glass sunbursts along the wall containing electric light bulbs, and a single monumental tiger skin on the floor. Beyond was a small sitting room, rather dark, filled to bursting with overstuffed chairs, with a chromium and enamel finish.

The Maharajah, His Highness Marshal and Supreme Commander-in-Chief, Mohun Shamsher Jang Bahadur Rana, rose to greet us, accompanied by his youngest brother, the dapper and twinkling Commanding General Shankar Shamsher, and two of their sons, Major Generals Bijaya Shamsher and Shri Dar Shamsher. We all shook hands and sat on the blue sofa and chairs while Dikshit and Maniram sat behind on small gilt chairs against the wall. The Maharajah and his family were wearing frock coats over their white jodhpurs — new and very handsome frock coats they were too. It would be interesting to know what firm of tailors in the world is still busily making frock coats. On his head the Maharajah wore a visored military-style cap made of beaver, on the front of which was an ornament, the coat of arms of Nepal in diamonds. The stones were glittering and large, the center a marquise-cut stone of at least twenty carats. With his dignified and commanding bearing, his sweeping gray mustaches, and the great stones, His Highness looked every inch the part.

The beginning of our audience seemed to me strained and stiff. I suppose it was partly that we were all on edge, solemn and constrained in our business suits which were still unpressed from their sojourn in duffle bags on coolie-back. I presented the Maharajah with two books of National Geographic maps which had been bound and suitably embossed with his name in gold. I showed him a copy of the *National Geographic Magazine* in which there was an article by Wentzel about Rajputana, the legendary home of both the King and the Maharajah's ancestors. There were a few remarks about the weather and other general subjects. It did not seem to me that the atmosphere was propitious. In the silence that ensued, I thought back with a sense of frustration over the months of planning, the letters, the question of funds, the arrangements, the trip out. The trip out! In desperation I embarked on the story of our midnight arrival in Paris. At the word Paris everyone sat up. The twinkle in General Shankar's eye brightened. I told of our troubles finding rooms, "les Maisons de bon accueil," and finally my girl friend paying the bill.

"So you see, Your Highness," I concluded, "on our first night in Paris the dignified scientists of the Expedition found themselves being 'gigolos' and ended up in a house of ill repute."

There was a pause, and then His Highness smiled and the Generals at the signal burst into hearty laughter. Another pause, and then the Ruler spoke.

"Well, Doctor Ripley, now that you have come all this way, where do you wish to go and how long would you like to stay?"

Our luck was still with us! I took out a life-sized crayon drawing which had been made for me of the Mountain Quail, one of the birds I hoped to find somewhere in the hills drained by the Karnali River in West Nepal. The Maharajah became interested in my story of the seventy-two-year disappearance of this beautiful little bird, and requested copies of the picture which could be circulated among the Districts. Wentzel readily agreed to photograph the picture, and it was arranged that prints would be sent to the Durbar for distribution.

During the ensuing conversation, the Maharajah would call one or more of his officials into consultation from time to time about some point in the discussion. A General was sent for who was the Governor of Dhankuta District in the east and who happened to be in attendance at the Court at the moment. Major General Mahdub appeared, tall and splendidly turned-out, with rather a mystic's face and a long drooping mustache. General Mahdub was one of the exiled members of the Rana family, dating from the rearrangement of the Roll of Succession. Presumably his mother or his father's mother had been of a caste not high enough to eat rice in her husband's presence. However, he was a trusted member of the Government service even if he did have to spend most of his life in virtual exile in far-off Dhankuta. The Maharajah proceeded to shoot a series of terse commands at the General, who folded his palms together in front of his chest and murmured respectfully, "Sirkar, Sirkar," after every sentence. This was always the formal pose of an inferior being spoken to by a person of exalted rank. Whenever General Mahdub addressed His Highness, he used a stylized mode of address, again with the hands together, a sort of apologetic tone of voice, and a way of saying everything as if "Of course, Your Highness, I know you know what I am going to say anyway, but allow me please, just to mention this in passing." It seemed to be protocol. I was very glad to meet General Mahdub, as I knew that it would make a great deal of difference in East Nepal that we had met him in the Maharajah's presence.

After this we stood up to go and His Highness vouchsafed that it would be nice if I called on his next younger brother, the Commander-in-Chief, General Baber, who had unfortunately not been able to meet us today. I hastened to agree, and said that I should like to call also on the next brother, General Kaiser, who was the Senior Commanding General, and who had been Minister to the United States the previous year. All of this passed off very agreeably and we parted in a fine aura of co-operation and cordiality.

General Shankar, who was acting as the Household Minister, along with his son, tall General Shri Dar, who at twenty-one seemed rather young for his post of Chief of Police of Katmandu, escorted us to the stairs. General Shankar was a merry person whose reassuring twinkle had prompted me to tell the story of our first night in Paris. He had an emerald jade bracelet on his left wrist and told us, with no little pride, that he had shot thirty-two rhinos on shooting trips in the Terai, a disturbing confession for a zoologist to hear.

General Bijaya, one of the two sons of the Maharajah, also came with us to the stair. In his post as Foreign Minister, Chairman of the Development Bureau, and Head of the Guest Department, he was particularly concerned with all foreigners' visits. He seemed to us an outstanding man, who already in his early thirties had a remarkable command of affairs of State and a vision for the future. I arranged with him that we would meet His Highness again before we left and that we would communicate to him a proposed schedule of our visits to western and eastern Nepal, and receive letters addressed to the local Governors, the Burra Hakims of the Districts through which we would pass.

Sirdar Dikshit bowed us out at the front door, and we swept away from the grand entrance and down the long avenue in our decrepit Ford, the same ancient vehicle which had met us below the Chandragiri Pass on arrival. Maniram, who had sat on the edge of a side chair in the audience room, drinking in everything reverently, was agog with excitement. The audience had gone off very well, and he was obviously pleased with his foreign charges and delighted to have been in on the affair.

When we arrived home, relieved and excited by our visit, Ed picked up a note on the table from the Kilbournes inviting us across the street for a drink before dinner. As there were only two or three British families living in Katmandu, calling cards and a supply of formal notepaper were, of course, a necessity, far more so than they would be in a large community. I hastily sat down and dashed off a note of acceptance, having learned my lesson in such things on our previous visit. It was just what we should like to do. We could blow off some steam. Besides, I wanted to ask them something.

The Kilbournes were delighted to hear of our successful audience and wholeheartedly wished us well on our forthcoming trip into the interior. After twenty years' residence in Katmandu with only two side jaunts out of the valley during the whole time, they could have been jealous of these brash young Americans who arrived, asked, and were given permission, just like that, to visit previously unknown territory, but they were good-hearted, generous, and friendly instead.

"By the way," I said, after we had told our news, "I wanted to ask you about that room next to the one we sat in for our audience, a small room on the other side. I got only a peek in there, but I couldn't believe my eyes."

"What do you mean?" Mrs. Kilbourne asked.

"Well, there seemed to be tall mirrors all along the walls, the kind that you see at Coney Island at home, or at Madame Tussaud's wax works, you know. One mirror makes you into a dwarf, the next a long string bean."

"Oh, yes, the funny mirrors." Mrs. Kilbourne sounded as though they were the most natural thing in the world. "Maharajah Jang Bahadur brought them back from his visit to England. He saw them when he went to Vauxhall Gardens, the London Coney Island of the time. We often go and stand in front of them when I have to see the ladies. It's always useful for conversation and a laugh."

The next morning we went out for a collecting visit to Gokarna, a wooded and walled-in preserve about twelve miles from Katmandu. It was crisp and clear and so cold that our fingers were numb on the safeties of our shotguns. Gokarna had a wall of brick eight feet high all round enclosing perhaps two hundred acres of grass-clad valleys, hillocks covered with jungle, and heavy scrub. A small herd of axis deer lived in the park and rhesus monkeys were numerous. It was said that leopards often holed up here for the day on their excursions from the hills down into the Katmandu Valley in search of an appetizing pie dog or a goat.

In the grassy spots pied chats perched on the tips of reed stalks and a handful of larks swung up and away before I had a chance for a shot. The chats were singing faintly, or trying to, and I wondered if perhaps they were breeding for a second time, a fall breeding season in which some birds in India indulge. I collected a fat male bird who proved on dissection to be in breeding condition, but the females taken at the same time showed no indication of a parallel state. Perhaps the male was in a kind of pseudo-breeding condition associated with the deposition of fat and the migratory urge. This would be a fascinating line of research in a subtropical climate where mixed migration and breeding instincts may be inducing a variety of responses in an individual bird at one and the same time.

A flock of tree-pies flew over, and I followed them into the jungle. In a clearing I found a small party of rose finches, refugees from the wintry weather at high altitudes, who would make their winter home in the valley. There were numbers of migrant species beginning to come down now in November, species that we had not encountered on our previous visit. This sort of comparative collecting, visiting a locality at two different seasons, was extremely valuable in order to round out the picture of the fauna as a whole.

Farther on in a thicket, the undergrowth was full of small birds feeding on a variety of fruits and berries, small bitter yellow fruits like miniature crabapples, and a sort of blackberry growing on excessively thorny stems. In the midst of the flutter and commotion, I spied a pale yellowish bird of warbler size and fired, bringing it down. The rest of the flock melted away like magic. Crawling under the bushes, I found my trophy, a pretty little thing, greenish-yellow above and white underneath, with a stout yellow bill. It was a babbler, *Erpornis,* a bird that had no business being in the Katmandu Valley according to all the books. In Stuart

Baker's monumental eight-volume work on Indian birds, he writes of the little *Erpornis* as a bird of the foothill jungle, found from the beginning of the hills up to about three thousand feet. We had gotten three specimens along the slopes of the valley on our previous trip at about six thousand feet. I had thought at the time that perhaps the birds were partially migratory, moving upward with the advance of spring, but now here it was still in the valley at the beginning of winter. So evidently the birds were resident after all, and another fact would be noted down about bird distribution for inclusion in bird books of the future.

An hour or two later, we reassembled and rode back into town in our doughty little Ford. We had a medley of birds that would keep Toni and John busy for hours. It had been a worth-while morning. Now that we were going into the west and the east, I was more than ever keen to collect here in the central valley, to identify the subspecies to which these little warblers and babblers belonged. Would the birds of Central Nepal be more like those of the western Himalayas, or those of the east? Where did the break come, and would we be lucky enough to find it? And if we did find the area where there seemed to be a division between the bird populations, would we be able to find out why? What could serve as a barrier in this continuous welter of mountains and valleys? My mind was a jumble of unsolved, half-answered questions as we rolled by the Tundi Khel, past the Gurkha soldiers drilling and the boom of the midday gun.

V

A Panoply of Plumes

LAVIRAM conducted us about the valley. Laviram, with his white peaked hat, his white shirt hanging down to his knees, his white jodhpurs and tennis shoes, always looked to me as if he were a Chinese in mourning. There was something about the Nepali dress, like the Nepali cast of countenance, that reminded me of China. There were lots of things in Nepal to remind us that the country was halfway between India and China's ridgepole, Tibet.

Maniram arranged for Laviram to take us to Swayambhunath, a Buddhist shrine west of Katmandu on a small projecting hill. It was one of the two most important Buddhist holy places in the valley which must contain literally thousands of Hindu shrines, but even here in this ancient spot, venerated in Asoka's time, Hinduism has penetrated. Next to the processional way about the central stupa was a small ornate Hindu temple dedicated to Sitala, goddess of smallpox. Roundabout the stupa were a number of Shivaite shrines and "lingams," some of the latter disguised as Buddhist stupas. The old Buddhism has been constantly on the decline in Nepal for centuries, surviving now only in such pilgrimage spots as this one which have been gradually permeated with Hinduism. At least the two have lived together peaceably, in a relationship probably unique.

The central stupa consisted of the usual white stucco-covered hemisphere of brick, surmounted by a small square brass-gilt tower painted with two strange heavy-lidded eyes set on each side of a question mark for a nose. The little tower served as a base for a spire or finial of thirteen rings topped by a parasol, all in shining gilt. Round the base of this great monument was a series of small shrines let into the brickwork. Between these shrines was arranged a tier of prayer wheels, foot-high containers of copper, set on spindles so that the touch of a pilgrim's hand would start them spinning, automatically saying thousands of prayers written on coils of paper and placed inside. We photographed several pilgrims going around the processional way, turning the prayer wheels as they went.

All the while monkeys darted in and out of the shrines looking for offerings of flowers, rice, or sweet cakes which they could eat. There were hordes of monkeys here, another Hindu incursion, which seemed to live off the offerings left by pilgrims. Each time a new set of offerings from a tray held by a devotee was carefully arranged about the base of a shrine, and the little oil lamps lit or refurbished, there would be an abrupt halt by the monkeys to the endless searchings in each other's shaggy coats, and dozens of beady eyes would be fixed on the scene, measuring, calculating. At last the pilgrims would wander far enough away for the boldest to move. Then would come a sharp chattering as a big male monkey circled in for the first bold swipe. Sometimes he would be threatened en route by a rival male, and there would be a violent discussion in monkey language about the whole affair. As far as I could see it was a bluff business and there were few enough actual fights, merely a sudden crescendo of whistles, hisses, suckings of indrawn breaths, and "kkkkkkkks."

Swayambhunath was on a small hill which rose from the flat floor of the valley. Legend has it that the whole valley was once a lake and the Boddhisatva Manjusri himself struck the surrounding hills with a sword and made a gap through which the Bagmati flows today, to drain away the waters. Swayambhunath was one of the first points to appear above the surface and there Manjusri built himself a dwelling. Whatever the truth of the story, the hill has been venerated since the earliest times. The finest thing at Swayambhunath was the brass statue about half life-size of the goddess Tara, as beautifully executed a piece of sculpture as I saw in the whole valley. It was a reminder to the Tibetans that Buddhism was introduced to Tibet through the efforts of this Nepali Princess by her marriage to a Tibetan King in the seventh century.

The other Tibetan pilgrimage spot we visited was Boddhnath, an even larger stupa a few miles east of Katmandu. This was the traditional center for visiting Tibetans. Roundabout the stupa there was a whole village of houses for the pilgrims. Laviram pointed one out to us, better kept than the rest, as the residence of the Chini Lama, a dignitary of somewhat uncertain status, who was titled the Tibetan representative in Nepal by some, by others the chief Lamaist priest. Whatever his position he seemed to have some sort of diplomatic or secular immunity, for we were told later that he and his family had been causing no end of trouble to the municipal electric power authorities in the valley. Apparently they overloaded their circuits in the beginning, but having found that this would get them into trouble, they had now learned to tap the wires before the meter, so that they could get extra free power. The Nepali who was telling us all this did not seem to find it surprising that the Chini Lama should know about such things as meters and tapping electric light wires.

"After all, he is a very holy man," he said, as if electricity was a property of omniscience.

There were lots of Tibetans here, mostly very ragged-looking men who seemed to have just come down from the passes. As they filed in from the road beyond the houses, they would pause to bow reverently and long before a shrine at the base of the stupa, their foreheads touching the stone, then finally move on around the processional way. Numbers of them were basking in the warm sun, naked from the waist up, minutely picking over their ragged robes. They seemed to have little curiosity about us as we wandered around with our cameras. I wondered whether some of these people were so "jungley," as the phrase is, that they had not even heard of white people, let alone having ever seen any.

We did not sight-see every day, however. Although I wanted to show the others all the sights of the valley, particularly Wentzel and Leeson, who were anxious to photograph everything they could for the *National Geographic Magazine*, I also hoped that we could get in some collecting. The valley has changed critically since Hodgson's time. Today the population of the thirty-mile-long valley stands at about half a million. Every inch was now farmed, with the exception of the groves of trees around the holy places and a few enclosures which belonged to members of the ruling families. When Hodgson was in Katmandu in the eighteen-thirties, there must have been jungle right up to the edge of town in places. At that time the Durbar assigned the East India Company's Resident a small plot of land about a mile outside the capital, which was of poor quality, swampy and malarial. It was not long before the British, with their ingrained sense of gardening, of making a home away from home, had turned the area into the best-tended part of the valley, the garden a neat and beautiful place that confounded the Durbar. However, the old grounds were now all very open and park-like with tall pines and cleared, open stretches of lawn. The birds which Hodgson described in his accounts of the bird life of Nepal as having lived in the Minister's garden were species to be found now only in dense patches of scrub forest or thick shrubbery immediately alongside jungle, only high up on the few jungle-clad ridges surrounding the valley, or, occasionally, in the preserves belonging to the ruling family.

Laviram, who had been much interested in our excursions so far, was less enthusiastic about trips to these small bits of forest. He was a camera fan and our antics with our various still and movie cameras fascinated him. He was also town-bred, and the still glades of the forest did not seem congenial.

"There might be bears," he said.

We reassured him as best we could and went out early the next morning. The Maharajah had given us permission to hunt for birds on Naggarjung, a long spur rising from the floor of the valley about two miles north and west of Katmandu and continuing on back to the surrounding ridges. The valley side of Naggarjung was surrounded by a high wall and we entered on a motor road which ran up through an old gate. On one side was a gatekeeper's lodge from which peered several old men who salaamed as we drove past. The road ran along the flank of the hill for a time and then stopped at an abrupt curve where there was a small garage. There were two paths from here, one of which doubled back up the hill at an acute angle and finally came out on the lower slopes of the ridge, where, amid pines, the Maharajah had a small chalet fronting on a superb view of the floor of the valley. The other path continued on around the flank through ever-thickening bushes and trees. Ed and the others had gone up the hill. I set off along the overgrown path, closely followed by Laviram. I did not want him to think that I was not glad of his company, but in fact I was not. No bird collector likes to feel a warm breath on the back of his neck. Not only that, but today Laviram had discarded the tennis shoes and was equipped with dark hard-soled creations that were apparently made out of wood judging by the noise of our progress.

I had hoped that Laviram would trail along with the others. It was my fate instead to have him follow me. I wished that I could have shooed him away politely. The morning was bright and clear and if I had been alone would have been very pleasant. Down the hill, below the wall, I could see fields and cultivation and one or two men beating clods with wooden mallets, an antique Nepali way of harrowing the land which reminded me of a farming landscape in mediaeval tapestry. In spite of being the Maharajah's private preserve, the forest had not been protected. There were numerous paths across broken parts of the wall and the sound of chopping above announced that the eternal quest for firewood was being pursued even here. In course of time I learned that the Nepal Government had promulgated a law that no living tree should be cut down, and that only dead wood should be used as firewood. Considering the decline of the forests, this was an excellent conservation scheme except for the natural ingenuity of the people. Their solution was to lop off branches gradually from a tree until it died of its own accord. In this way no law was broken and a continued flow of kindling and logs assured.

In spite of the commotion, birds and even animals were everywhere. A flight of red-billed blue magpies, long blue and white tails streaming behind them, sailed across from one tall isolated tree to another. A smothered twittering and scuffling in a flowering bush announced activity. The branches were alive with brilliant small scarlet sunbirds, almost the color of the flowers. Farther on, a tall tree was full of black bulbuls, slate-colored birds about the size of a thrush, with thin red bills, carrying on a busy subdued conversation with each other which would burst out loudly as soon as they flew. I stopped, listening to the birds and eager to bring a halt to the crunching behind me. There were all sorts of twitterings and chirpings in the surrounding thickets. Suddenly around the corner of the path ahead a form came leaping, intent on its own affairs. It was a Himalayan yellow-throated marten, a beautiful mahogany-colored beast almost as big as a fox, but far thinner and more lithe, with a curious undulating gait. The animal was so close that I brought my shotgun up thinking that I would not need to put in a heavier load. But the marten was incredibly fast. It turned even in midair as it caught my motion, and simply flowed off at an angle into the bushes so that I fired behind it.

There was a hush after the shot.

"Was that a bear, sir?" came a breath behind me. Laviram pronounced it "beer."

"Sorry, Laviram, that was a marten, an animal that has probably been eating all the eggs of His Highness's pheasants."

We had been given a pheasant from the Durbar as a present the previous day and I had heard they were common on Naggarjung. This species was the kaleej, the only pheasant that we saw in Nepal, a lovely dark purplish-blue bird with gray lanceolate breast feathers and a brilliant red wattle about the eye. This was the same pheasant mentioned by Colonel Kirkpatrick, the first Englishman to set foot in Nepal, who journeyed there on a mission for the East India Company in 1793. There was a colored plate of the bird in his volume on Nepal and a remark that "they are far from abounding" and "I cannot say much in commendation of its flavor." I would agree with the former statement, but not with the latter. Wherever the marten occurred, the kaleej was sure to be threatened. Whenever we had a chance to eat these pheasants, we found them delicious.

We went on. Occasionally I was able to get in a shot at some small bird before it was scared away by the apparition of Laviram and myself prancing in step down the path. As we went farther into the fastnesses of His Highness's preserve, I found Laviram treading ever more nearly on my heels, like an old-fashioned act in vaudeville. The path finally worked around into a small valley full of low bushes, with woody thick stems, some sort of *strobilanthes*, just over a man's height. A couple of tracks branched off into the underbrush, and I paused here, wondering if perhaps Laviram would be willing to stay by himself on the path. A man quietly appeared from the bushes beside one of the paths.

He was soberly but cleanly dressed. There was a rapid-fire exchange, sotto voce, between him and Laviram.

"You must not go farther, sir," Laviram said finally. "There are 'beers' here."

This was a bit exasperating.

"I can't think of a more unlikely place for bears, Laviram," I said. "You stay here with this man and I will be back shortly."

I turned up one of the tracks.

"No, no, sir," Laviram hissed excitedly.

I sauntered up the path as quietly as I could. Both of the wretches were now following me. Thirty or forty yards into the bushes, I suddenly heard the "kutttttrrr!" of a cock kaleej pheasant, rather low and rolling, not far off. I couldn't believe that a pheasant would really be so silly as to sit there in the bushes and call, but I persevered and went on until I stumbled into a small clearing in the middle of a thicket.

I could not think afterward which of us had been more embarrassed or sheepish, I or the other hunter. In the center of the cleared space in the bushes sat a very large plump man, expensively dressed in tweeds and gaiters. Near him was a wicker cage, half-hooded with a cloth, containing a captive cock kaleej. Ready to hand were three clean and highly polished double-barreled shotguns and a small rifle. Farther behind crouched a second servant. Evidently I had interrupted his game. The big man did not look pleased. Probably I had scared away any pheasants which might have been decoying in to his captive bird's calls. I should have been polite and apologized. After all, I was a guest on land of the Rana family. Instead I stood looking, taking in the scene.

"I had heard this was a dangerous place," I said finally, smiling.

"Yes," he said, not smiling. "You should have gone around the other side of the mountain."

"Yes," I agreed. "I *was* told by your servant there were bears here," turning away.

I wondered as I backed out if he realized he looked rather like a bear himself.

Laviram was not pleased and neither was I with the morning's episode. I had interfered with the pleasure of one of his bosses and he had spoiled my morning's collecting.

Fortunately, it was not necessary for Laviram to accompany us to Godaveri where we went in a truck to stay for several days before the awaited visit of the American Minister. Godaveri was a small summer house of the Maharajah built beside a spring and a temple on the side of Phulchok, the highest of the hills surrounding the valley. We camped out for three days in a bungalow belonging to one of the Rana family, hunting for birds and trapping small mammals. The trapping was not too successful as the small rats and mice that evidently lived thereabouts were indifferent to Howie's traps. However, the birds were abundant on the tree-clad slopes above the temple and we managed to get a sizeable number of forest species which were now rare about Katmandu itself.

We left the last day of November, after a raw rainy night which had coated with snow the eight-thousand-foot slopes of Phulchok above us. On the way back in the truck we seemed to coast most of the way down the slight slope toward Katmandu. It was late afternoon and we had a superb view, the city in the distance with Bhim Sen's Tower rising over all, mist and smoke blurring the outlines. Then came the circle of surrounding hills, the higher ones, Sheopuri and Mahadeopokri, powdered with snow. The tones were bright, the grays and browns of the city and its surrounding fields overlaid with orange in the slanting light.

Above the lower hills rose the mountains in a long serrated row, so vast and spreading that perspective was quite lost. It was impossible to say which was which, which nearer, which farther. No wonder most Nepalis spoke of the "Himal" a sort of blanket name for the mountains. We had had Gosainthan pointed out to us, a huge hogback lying north of Sheopuri. Far to the northeast rose ridge on ridge of sheer upended masses of ice and snow, among which one, higher than the rest, was said to be Gauri Sankar, and a small pointed peak, a good hundred and fifty miles away, Kanchenjunga. There was one place on the road where a snow point, rising between two others, was said to be Everest. The whole elevation is impressive, the whole cyclopean Himalayan Range, rather than any one peak. Nowhere else in the world could there be such a spectacle. As we moved on toward Katmandu, the sunlight slanted more and more, sunset came nearer and the unbelievable mass gradually became overlaid with rosy pink, the color of a finch's breast. It was hard to believe that it was true, that the panorama was not a vision, hard to believe that you could not reach out and touch it and find that it was all just bright raspberry-pink icing. Then the guns began to boom out the salute to the visiting American Minister. No, it was true. We were in the valley, and those mountains that looked so incredible, so beautiful and terrible, were true and securely inaccessible.

The next few days were a jumble of activity and social

gatherings. Never had the valley had so many Americans in it at once, our party and Mr. Henderson and his aides.

"It's a shame the Falconers aren't here," said Mrs. Kilbourne. "The British Ambassador simply shouldn't take his holiday at the time when your Ambassador — I mean Minister — comes up. What a lark we could all have together!"

Just the same, the Indian Ambassador arranged a dinner. The Kilbournes had installments of the American invasion together, and the Prouds, the British First Secretary and his wife, entertained various groups of the Minister's party or ours at different times. It was all rather dressy, dinner jackets for the men, long dresses for Mrs. Kilbourne and Mrs. Proud. The Nepalis mostly did not appear. Their orthodoxy reached heights which are now found nowhere else in the Hindu world. In Nepal no ranking Nepali can possibly eat in the presence of an unbeliever, be he Christian, Mohammedan, or Sikh. A few of the Generals came in afterward to some of the evening functions. Most of the younger ones were not averse to a highball or similar concoction, and one of them was even remarkably good at dialect songs in the best Harry Lauder tradition.

The official functions, however, were the high point of life in Nepal. There was nothing to match them anywhere else. Certainly nowhere else today would a diplomat be handed six legal-size pages of closely typed instructions about the protocol of a medal-giving ceremony. The American Minister had brought along the decoration of the Legion of Merit which President Truman had awarded to the Maharajah as Head of the State for Nepal's part in providing troops in the recent war. Mr. Henderson was a model of a modern diplomat, full of efficiency, charm, and one of the most capable men in the foreign service. Never in his career, however, had he had to face quite such an ordeal of protocol, not even with the desert Sheikhs in the Middle East or the Titans of the Kremlin.

The first ceremony was the medal-giving. The principal guest house had by this time been prettied-up inside with rugs, lighting fixtures, overstuffed sofas, side tables, and assorted doodads until there was barely room to turn around. Apparently all the palaces had been raided of electric heaters, for the air was brisk at this season. Heaters and fires were burning in all the rooms to give that necessary hothouse atmosphere which Americans with their steam-heat complexes are supposed to like. For the medal-giving, the Maharajah himself, with an escort of lancers, driving in a State landau drawn by six horses with postillions and runners all in uniform, made a formal call on the Minister at the guest house, by now bedecked with bunting and homemade flags. The Nepali version of the American flag had only eight stars and six stripes as if we were all back in Revolutionary times, but fortunately no one noticed in the general excitement. Later, the Minister and his retinue in morning coats and top hats was driven in carriages to the Maharajah's Durbar Hall, where the formal presentation ceremony was to take place.

The Maharajah's call went off beautifully. First in the bright sunlight of early afternoon came a company of household troops in red winter uniforms. Along with them came a platoon of very smart-appearing Gurkha troops in full battle dress. These men lined up in front of the guest house, a red-coated band appeared, and began playing light airs in that deceptively gay and insouciant manner that only military bands can achieve. Finally there was a clatter-clatter of hooves on the road and a magnificent troop of "sowars" or lancers appeared in red with blue-and-gold turbans and high black boots, their fine horses prancing and capering. In their center rolled the open landau, its six horses pulling it evenly and splendidly so that the shining wheels seemed to spin backwards with an hypnotic effect. Before the carriage ran brightly dressed men with golden fly whisks like a Gérôme painting of the days of the Mamelukes in Cairo.

The Maharajah in the center of his aides was also the center of attraction. Atop his military uniform of scarlet-and-gold lace besprinkled with orders and a wide blue ribbon, the Ruler wore the Nepali style of crown, unlike any other known in the world today. The base was of tightly fitting inverted basketwork covered with seed pearls. The rim all round was adorned with a design in pearls, a ropelike affair to imitate the twist of a turban. The whole was set with large flatted diamonds. From the rim hung pear-shaped emeralds. On the right side there hung a great cluster of these emeralds like a bunch of grapes, of the most perfect color. Above the cluster was a famous carved emerald which had belonged to Nadir Shah, the eighteenth-century pillager of Delhi, and later to the Nana Sahib, the Indian General in the Mutiny of 1857, who was responsible for the massacre of the British women and children at Cawnpore. The center of the crown on top was ornamented with an enormous ruby spinel bead, memento of the Imperial Chinese Order of the Double-eyed Peacock Feather, accorded the father of the present Ruler, Maharajah Chandra. In front of the crown there was a circular ornament, a parure of diamonds, above which from a jeweled holder spouted an enormous plume of flank feathers of the Greater Bird of Paradise, the New Guinea species which has been an article of trade and a badge of royalty for centuries in the East. The plumes arched up and over and down in back, shimmering in the sun. These glittering jewels and plumes stirred the imagination with thoughts of the ruthless and violent deeds of which they were the witnesses.

The Maharajah descended from his landau and walked hand in hand with the Minister in the antique fashion into the guest house. After introductions all sat stiffly in the sitting room and engaged in stilted periods punctuated by silence. Finally the agonizingly long time appointed by convention was over, and again the Maharajah grasped the hand of the Minister firmly and departed. The next episode would take place a half-hour or so later, when the State carriages arrived for the American party.

Meanwhile all our group had hurried off to the Durbar Hall beside the Maharajah's Singha Durbar Palace to take pictures of the scene. The Durbar Hall was a rather squat building, with columns and an ornate porte-cochère, which looked like a baroque Italian opera house. Its distinctive style was enhanced by the fact that a large part of it was painted a rich warm brown. In front beyond the driveway was an ornate bandstand in which the band, having hastily tramped over from the guest house, was again rendering bits of Victor Herbertiana.

We set up our cameras and proceeded to watch fascinated while all the Generals in the Roll of Succession arrived and milled about outside, chatting and trying on their crowns. Each General drove up dressed in red uniform and a fore-and-aft cocked hat surmounted with yellow cock's plumes. This was removed and a brace of servants undid a box for each one in which reposed his crown. All were on the same pattern as the Maharajah's, varying each from the other according to the taste or finances of the wearer in the number and kind of precious stones woven into the general array of diamonds and emeralds. All had the curving panaches of Paradise Bird plumes. These last were carried by two more servants in a separate sickle-shaped box, made to fit them. After each General had had the plumes fitted to the crown, he put on the whole affair and gazed into a hand-mirror which was produced by one of his retinue. Overhead the windows of the Hall were thronged with the ladies of the Court, who, although not in strict "purdah," as the shutting-away of the womenfolk is called in India, were still kept very much in the background.

Finally there was a salute of cannon and the American Envoy and his party appeared in their open coaches. The Maharajah and his next older brothers and cousins were lined up in formal order and received the party on the steps, after which each was conducted hand in hand, starting with the Maharajah and the Minister, into the Durbar Hall. As the carriages pulled away, one of the horses had been guilty of an inadvertence on the paved roadway in front of the steps, and a small ragged man darted in among the gold-braided legs of the Generals to remove the offending objects with his hands. The throng sought the entrance, and soon all were in, some of us drawing up the rear with our cameras. The band swung into "Tell me how much you love me."

Inside, the Durbar Hall was long and vast with a line of gilt chairs down each side on which sat the Generals in order of their importance and succession. At the end were two ornate gilded thrones on which sat His Highness and Mr.

Henderson. Overhead were chandeliers, along the walls portraits. Over the floor were strewn gold-embroidered red velvet rugs and all about were scattered stuffed tigers, gigantic brass lions spouting electric lights from their mouths, ornate furniture of a hundred styles making a panorama of splendor and dissonance. As the ceremony went on, Court criers, stationed near the doors, in red and white with gold staves of office, called out the turns to the imaginary populace in glissading tones like nothing so much as tobacco auctioneers in Carolina or Georgia, with the same nasal twang. The figures of the Generals glittering with stars and jewels and swishing plumes, the two High Priests sitting near the thrones in orange-colored gold brocade, the two Subhas in black and gold, wearing turbans surmounted with aigrettes, who appeared carrying golden trays set with boxes and goblets of attar and "pan," rosewater and betel nut — all of this together made a sight unlike anything else to be seen in the world.

The next day, much the same ceremony was repeated in the King's Durbar Hall in the square of the old city. This hall was all white, picked out with gold inside, with lovely chandeliers, and portraits of European royalty along the walls done in a languishing Winterhalter tradition. It had grace and light, and the single figure of the glittering King on his huge open velvet throne, rather like a precious stone set in a jeweler's window, made a focus at the end to draw the eye. Occasions like this, when the King received Mr. Henderson's credentials, were virtually the only ones at which he made a public appearance, for since 1867 the Kings of Nepal have been without power, although the titular head of the State. After this second Durbar ceremony, I was fortunate enough to meet His Majesty as the Maharajah led him, hand in hand in mediaeval style, from the room. His Majesty, Maharajadhiraja Tribhuvana Bir Bikram Jang Bahadur Shah Bahadur Shamsher Jang, was a handsome man of forty-three in red with silver lace, who did not speak directly to the visitors, but waited patiently until the Maharajah had translated what was said. This was merely custom, for the King spoke good English, and seemed somewhat fretted by the delays, an augury possibly of the fact that almost two years to the day after our meeting His Majesty made a dramatic flight to Delhi by plane to remain for a time as the guest of the Indian Government. During our whole stay in Nepal, we failed to receive any clear impression that the power of the Rana family was receding. Indeed, my impression in 1951 is that, newspaper reports to the contrary, the Rana family, having made certain concessions to popular sentiment by bringing representatives of the King and the Nepali Congress Party into the Government, are still in the driver's seat in Nepal.

After these ceremonies the rest of our stay in Katmandu seemed an anticlimax. We visited the beautiful old cities of Patan and Bhadgaon, former capitals of outlying kingdoms of the Newar times before the Gurkha invasions from the western provinces. We finished our sight-seeing and photography and had our farewell audience with His Highness. There was no stiffness on this occasion and we found the Maharajah cordial, interested, and charming. Together we planned for our coming six-week visit to the western Karnali River Valley to be followed by a similar period up the eastern valley of the Kosi. It was arranged that we should leave in a couple of days going back down the trail to Raxaul, and from there taking the Oudh Tirhut Railway to Kauriala Ghat, the nearest station in Uttar Pradesh to the Nepal border and the Karnali River. Now that we were planning our route, I only wished that we had more time and funds, for His Highness seemed keen to let us go as far as we wished.

"And let me know about the Mountain Quail," he said, twinkling.

When we returned to the guest house, we found Maniram, his eyes gleaming with excitement and reflected glory, waiting for us with two servants, their arms full of bundles. His Highness had showered us with gifts, a stuffed rhinoceros foot topped with teakwood as a stand for a potted palm, trays of rhino hide, ornamented and gilt-covered "kukris" for us all, jeweled boxes, and large and elaborate confections of brass consisting of an acrobatic pyramid of gods from the Hindu pantheon, all balancing on top of each other the while they sprang from a lotus flower. Such largesse overwhelmed us, for we knew it was not seemly to give presents to His Highness in return. We thanked Maniram profusely so that tears of affection came to the eyes of that good courtier, while little Laviram stood in the background dipping his head in the familiar sideways gesture.

A round of farewells took up the next day, along with the ever-present paying of bills for our stay and the hire of coolies for the trail, and finally we were ready to leave the valley. It was early morning, but clear, and already the air was warm when we reached the base of the Chandragiri Pass, left our cramped Ford, and saw the ponies and coolies waiting. This time we had a minor official along with us who helped to get the loads arranged and started us off in good time. The climb up the hill seemed easy. It was cool under the rhododendrons and oaks when we reached the top. A breeze was blowing from the north and the clouds were still off the tops of that incredible panorama. There they stood, Dhaulagiri, Anapurna, Himalchuli, Gosainthan, smiling now in the sun, wreathed in fleecy clouds above the valley which they guarded so well. There below rose the smoke of a thousand wood fires in the city, blended into a morning haze that reached as high as Bhim Sen's Tower. It was a wrench to turn away down toward the plains, one of those final gestures that one makes in life.

"There will never be anything else like that again," said Ed.

VI

Toward the Karnali

FORTY-EIGHT HOURS and over four hundred miles of bumping and shuttling along the spider-web tracks of the Oudh Tirhut Railway in our "Double First Tourist Car" from Raxaul, and we were nearing Kauriala Ghat. It was early morning, bright, dewy, and exciting. Since dawn we had been craning out of the windows in the cold crisp air, looking at the scenery. This was good country — high grass in the open stretches, mixed with real jungle and occasional winding streams. The endless cultivation and villages had disappeared, raising our hopes about collecting.

In the solitary silk-cotton trees which stood out above the high grass we could see the hanging gourd-shaped abandoned nests of last summer's weaver bird colonies. They had now migrated somewhere in their own unexplained way, one of the Indian bird mysteries. There were lots of peacocks in the grassy areas along the tracks, and in one high tree I spied a whole family of Indian Gray Hornbills, a dun bird about the size of a crow with a clumsy, bulging bill and a long droopy tail. As we passed, they set off one after the other in single file over the grass toward another big tree, alternately flapping a few half-hearted flaps of their small wings, then stiffly gliding. I was fascinated to note that each bird seemed to flap and glide at exactly the same place in the air as had the one in front of it. Farther on, we passed three spotted deer hinds cowering beside the tracks. They were crouching, "hiding," in the open when they could have jumped into the long grass easily. We were so near and passed so slowly that we could see their soft flanks rising and falling spasmodically.

Kauriala Ghat had been simply a name on a map to us. None of the officials in Katmandu could give us any real information about West Nepal. A famous fisherman in Calcutta had told us that he had worked up into the Nepal Terai along the Karnali River looking for mahseer, India's great river game fish. He had reported that Kauriala Ghat was simply a wide place in the road, but that there was a motor road from there across the Terai to the foothills, and even into the duns beyond, the inner valley along the Karnali River bank. This road was traversed by the trucks of an Indian lumber company. During his visit he reported that he had never seen any Nepal Government officials, and so far as he knew could have gone anywhere he wished without questioning. He said the place was jungley and full of game.

In Katmandu General Bijaya had assured me that he was writing to the Burra Hakim, the Governor of the District in which we would be. Fortunately I had a copy of that letter, but not securing any real information about West Nepal in Katmandu, I had decided to be on the safe side and write for aid to the Indian Government. Accordingly I had written post-haste from Katmandu to Mrs. Sarojini Naidu, the then Governor of Uttar Pradesh, whom I happened to know. I explained to her our predicament, our lack of knowledge beforehand about the area, and our interest in making a first exploration of the fauna of West Nepal by going up the Karnali from an Indian jumping-off point on the border. Perhaps the U. P. Government would intercede for us with the Indian lumber company so that we could hitch a ride on their trucks.

The station before Kauriala Ghat was Bellraien. Here on the little platform in the bright sunlight a deputation awaited us. An enormous husky gentleman with wrestler's shoulders bulging out of his gaberdine suit introduced himself as the Uttar Pradesh Divisional Forest Officer. Mr. Nandlal and his several assistants proceeded to get into our compartment with us, perched on duffle bags and bedding rolls the while welcome hot tea and toast were brought, and discussed the situation. They would ride up to Kauriala Ghat with us, having received several pages of instructions from the head Forest Office of the Province about our reception. Tents were awaiting us at the Ghat, a thoughtful provision, as it would save us opening out our own. It turned out, there were no houses, no station, nothing, at Kauriala Ghat. In truth, it was "just a wide place in the road."

We questioned the deputation about the road into Nepal. It appeared that there was a track, but that the branches of the river washed away any bridges each year and so it was quite impossible for trucks. The lumber company had a plan for trucks in the future, but not at present.

"But what about our man in Calcutta?" Howie asked. "He said that he went up to the foothills in a truck."

"During the war, one winter, they were cutting much lumber," replied Mr. Nandlal. "Not so much now, so the bridges are all gone."

Mr. Nandlal was resourceful, however. He had an elephant for us to ride on and some bullock carts could be secured for the heavy luggage.

"It is a good elephant," he remarked. "It is the Court of Wards elephant and we use it here for forest work."

Apparently the elephant had been included in the estate of some minor which was in litigation, and had ended in the Court of Wards, from whence she had been lent with her mahout driver to the Forest Department. We liked the name, Court of Wards elephant. It gave her dignity.

"What about the Burra Hakim of the District across the border in Nepal?" I asked.

"I don't know any such man," the Forest Officer answered. "But there is a Lieutenant Malla about fiften miles away in Nepal toward Rajapur. Perhaps he has heard of your coming."

As we moved slowly along through the grass and forest, Nandlal told us something of the U. P. District in which he worked, and its problems. It was a great forest area and full of game. There had even been wild elephants here up to about twenty years ago, but now they were all gone. So, too, was the Great Indian Rhinoceros, a vanishing species now confined to two small areas of the Terai in Central Nepal, outside of its main home, which is still the northeastern Indian State of Assam. Now the remaining game was being poached a great deal. It was hard to persuade people with guns and motor cars that deer, leopard, or anything else moving cannot be legitimately shot at night by jacking. I sympathized with him and assured him that there were plenty of Americans who were equally unco-operative with our game laws.

Kauriala Ghat proved to be a name on a railway station

The central stupa at Swayambhunath consisted of a stucco-covered brick hemisphere surmounted by a small square brass-gilt tower painted with two strange heavy-lidded eyes set on each side of a question mark for a nose.

The temple of the five stages at Bhadgaon, the largest in the valley. Each ascending set of carved figures on the terraces represents a power ten times as great as the one just below.

name plate, and that was all. A few grass huts some distance away indicated a small village. Other grass sheds sheltered three or four buffalos. I had been wondering all the morning why it paid the railway to run a train up here to this siding on the Nepal border. The few cars besides our own and the baggage car seemed to be empty. The answer came when we reached the Ghat. A sizeable crowd of Nepali hill men stood or squatted, waiting for the train. They wore ragged jackets of homespun wool, rounded caps, and loincloths. Many carried baskets. For a moment I thought that these were coolies waiting for us. They looked exactly like the men we had hired for the trip from Bhimpedi over the passes into the Katmandu Valley.

With only the most cursory glances at us, however, the coolies proceeded to swarm aboard the train. Meanwhile some of the Forest Department men rounded up a few to help unload our goods and chattels. After the usual delays we succeeded in finding the owners of the buffaloes and bribed them heavily enough to persuade them to hitch up their carts, load our gear, and carry it the two hundred yards to where the tents had been pitched for us. By about lunch time we were installed in several comfortable and spacious tents, complete with tables, chairs, and Indian string beds, all courtesy of the U. P. Government. Then an incident occurred which amused me. An Assistant Forest Officer appeared with a large file of paper tied together in the upper left-hand corner with a piece of reddish tape.

"Sir, the Department has a bill here for rupees ten and ten annas only, being the amount sustained by us in erecting this camp and taking it down on December first, for Your Honor and Mr. Salim Ali," he intoned solemnly, all in one breath.

"But today is December tenth, the day I wrote Her Excellency the Governor that I would arrive in Kauriala Ghat. You know that. You were all here to meet me," I cried.

"That is true, sir, but we received word to expect you December first from the Office of the Conservator of Forests, and that all costs would be borne by you."

"Certainly," I said. "Except that I wrote I was coming December tenth."

"Sir, this will be difficult for us, as we will be out of pocket. This is the second time we have erected camp here for you."

The Assistant Forest Officer was not half so bewildered as I was. To him the instructions of the Great Ones were taken for granted. Then, thinking back, I remembered that in my letter I had mentioned to Mrs. Naidu that I was planning an eventual book on Indian birds in collaboration with the well-known ornithologist, Mr. Salim Ali, of Bombay. So far as I knew, he was still in Bombay, but this was probably all that was needed to start the rumor going that we would be coming together. But December first — this was a puzzle. A great deal more talk ensued, but there seemed to be nothing to be done about it, and I paid.

Over lunch, which Abdul, having plenty of warning, finally produced toward teatime, we asked Mr. Nandlal about the coolies who had boarded the train.

"They didn't look as if they had the price of admission, let alone knowing where they were going," Ed remarked.

"You will see these 'paharis,' these hill men, everywhere from now on," the Forester said. "They come down like this in great numbers in the cold weather. They bring borax, ghee (clarified butter), or cloth, or sometimes fruit — any local product. These they sell at the market in Rajapur, a few miles north of here in the Terai. For this they get money enough to come here and get on a train."

"But where to?"

"Oh, Bombay, formerly Karachi, some big port. They work for three months. Others go to Dehra Dun or some such places in the hills to the west to work in the lumber companies. Then in the end they come back with their few rupees, go to Rajapur again, buy cloth, pots, pans, and salt, and go back into the hills."

"How much money do they make in the process?" asked Howie.

"When they reach the hills, they have no money left. They make only enough to buy a few goods that they need at Rajapur."

This seemed to be a real phenomenon, all these men going hundreds, sometimes thousands, of miles to make enough money to buy a few bits of cloth or cooking utensils for their families at the bazaar at the foot of the hills in which they lived, but we were to pass hundreds and hundreds of these men on our way in and out of West Nepal. At least the railway seemed to profit from this annual migration.

After lunch, in the gloaming Nandlal conducted us down to the stream, the Kauriala, from which the station took its name. The Kauriala is a branch of the Karnali and there was a ford here, hence the name "ghat." The warm orange light of the sun made everything orange — the dusty sand banks, the dead pale brown grass, the oily limpid stream. Stone curlews, big plover-like birds with staring eyes, ran ahead of us over the sand and flew up with mournful cries. A pair of Ruddy Shelducks in midstream took up the call, stretching their necks out low over the water, their throats distended, making a great series of rolling hollow notes that would carry for half a mile. Their normal color of dull orange was picked out by the sun until they looked as if they were made of molten coppery gold. The calls seemed to start everything else going at once. Wagtails ran along in front of us, long tails bobbing up and down, chirping on a sudden. Sand martins dipped back and forth across the stream, cheeping to each other. And then, drowning all the rest, came the wild rattle, the call of cranes high up in the air. As we strained our eyes up through the hazy, dying orange light, we could just make out the dark shapes in silhouette, sweeping majestically overhead.

Sitting round the fire later in front of our tents, warming ourselves in the chill marrow-biting evening mist, with a little hoarded rum, listening to Nandlal's tales of his youth near the forests below Dehra Dun, where tigers were a far greater menace than traffic accidents at home, we all felt a real thrill of satisfaction at being at last on the threshold of West Nepal.

The next day was a turmoil of preparation. In the morning we went along the bank of the Kauriala on the Court of of Wards elephant looking for peacock. A big flock of six cocks and a number of hens got away from us, running faster than a man could through the scrub and underbrush. On our return, Lieutenant Malla had arrived with his elephant, a small but fast cow about sixteen years old. Her mahout was a young Tharu named Sitaram, who seemed to be keen about hunting and would help us farther north in the Terai Forest. Lieutenant Malla was a bit diffident about assisting us at first. He had received no official news of our coming from his boss, the Burra Hakim of the District. Not only that, but even the jungle telegraph, or coconut wireless, which in the East according to the books is supposed to be ever-present and all pervading, had failed him. He had merely received a note from Mr. Nandlal the day before saying that six American visiting naturalists, the guests of his Government, had arrived. The sight of General Bijaya's letter, however, changed all that. Once I had satisfied the amenities by writing him a number of letters clearing him and his heirs from all possible responsibility for any actions performed by us, as well as writing to General Bijaya to say what a fine man he was, he agreed to cooperate. He would lend us his elephant indefinitely and send along a couple of minions to help us. He would even come along to the next halting place on the fringe of the forest and try to help us get a little hunting. Meanwhile six bullock carts were arranged for to start early on the morrow for our next camp, twelve miles in toward the foothills.

The next morning had that quality of quiet desperation which makes for insanity, or philosophical detachment. To the foreigner, particularly to an American used to things happening on time and getting done with a minimum of reiteration, the experience of running a group of buffalo or bullock carts can be unnerving, to say the least. The carts had all been loaded up the night before. Now, as I stood by the breakfast fire a few moments after six, rubbing my chilled hands and staring out through the penetrating mist, I wondered when the cart men would turn up. They had promised to appear by six. Abdul was now well trained. He had been told to have breakfast ready before light at five, which meant that we were likely to get it fairly promptly before seven.

Dick and Howie had gone off to collect their line of traps for mice and shrews which they had put out the night before. Ed, our most meticulous dresser, was shaving. Kurt and Francis were as usual efficiently getting their photographic equipment in order for the coming spate of pictures of our departure via elephant-back.

There was no chance of breakfast for a good half-hour, so I walked across a small gully a hundred yards to where Nandlal and Lieutenant Malla had been bunking in a separate tent. They were up and drinking their early morning tea. Nearby the two elephants were being saddled with their pads, the large straw-filled mattresses which become as unyielding, after a few hours of travel, as any torture rack of the Middle Ages. The Court of Wards elephant was stretching her huge legs, one after the other, buckling up her vast paunch and letting it go again, and emitting blasts of wind in all directions as is characteristic of elephants waking up. The other animal had the hiccups, and was shivering violently to boot.

"Has Sitaram been giving her strong liquor, Lieutenant?" I asked.

Sitaram himself looked rather bleary to me.

"Oh, no, sir. Too many chili peppers with her grain last night." He laughed. "If there was any liquor, Sitaram would not waste it."

"What about the men for the carts, Lieutenant?"

"They are taking food, sir. They will be just now coming."

These two sentences became a byword with us. For one reason or another, we seemed to hear them every day for the next three months. I retired to our tents after an expression of hope that we might see the men shortly. Breakfast finally came with the clearing of the mist, and soon our last preparations were complete and we settled down to await the buffalo cart men. The flock of cranes flew back overhead, quite low this time, and I saw that they were the large common cranes, a Siberian bird which winters occasionally in the Terai. In the distance we could hear the rolling calls of the Ruddy Shelducks. It was time to be off.

Relays of messengers departed at frequent intervals. Still no cart men arrived. It was after nine, nearly nine-thirty, before they came strolling in behind their beasts, whose grain-spattered muzzles showed that they had barely finished breakfast. There was nothing to be done but wait patiently while the buffaloes were hitched to the carts, nothing to do but wait while Abdul finished cleaning the utensils for the cook box, just wait while Kurt and Francis set up their cameras and made what seemed to me several hundred exposures of us all getting onto the patient elephants. I had given up seething long ago. It didn't seem to matter any more whether we made an early getaway or not. We did have twelve miles to go, the day's limit for an elephant. At the rate of one and a half miles an hour for the carts, it would take them a good eight hours to go the distance. With luck we might get some dinner that night — with luck. I gave up. I decided to acquire philosophic calm. The alternative seemed to be too horrible to contemplate. By ten-thirty we were off.

"On into West Nepal! Into the blue!" called Kurt gaily from the other elephant, hand to the visor of his hat in the best explorer's gesture.

The elephants soon outdid the buffalo carts. It was as

well, for the carts raised a great cloud of dust behind them which enveloped our boxes and belongings with a heavy layer. We came to the river bank and waded across, almost up to our feet as we sat on the elephants. I wondered what on earth would happen to our gear in the low carts.

The rest of the trip was a long-drawn-out affair. It seemed that we wound across the fields of the lower Terai for days, not hours. Our goal was Tikapur, a small clearing on the edge of the forest belt, which was much wider here, nearly ten miles across to the foothills compared to about six in Central Nepal. The sun beat down fiercely even in December. The elephants tired quickly. Their reputed four miles an hour soon lagged to two. Both mahouts had a curious rhythm in their behavior which fascinated us. For a time they would go along, bending with the elephant's motion, seemingly lulled by the regular swaying of the head of the beast. The neck is always, of course, by far the most comfortable perch on an elephant, especially when there is a sort of stirrup arrangement made out of coils of rope wound round and round the throat. This gives the mahout support for his feet, just as in a saddle.

Every so often, perhaps twenty minutes, our mahouts would subtly rouse themselves from their lethargy by degrees. This arousing began with a slightly more exaggerated bending and swaying in time to the animal's motion. Then the mahout would start whispering to his steed, soft little encouraging phrases. As this never took effect, the whisperings and the swayings would gradually increase until he was calling loudly to the elephant and rocking vigorously back and forth on the wretched creature's neck. Finally, like a conductor wielding his baton for the whole orchestra to come in fortissimo, the mahout would lift up his iron goad and with a final "eeugh" sink it into the top of the elephant's head. There would be a lurch and the beast would sway forward at an increased pace for fully twenty yards or so before she relaxed once more into her usual slow gait. The head of the Court of Wards elephant looked like a very large old moldy cheese, so large and old that it had sprouted a few black hairs. The surface was dotted with old wounds, and by the end of a morning there would be trickles of blood from a dozen more. Old Baban Khan would murmur to his steed after these paroxyms in a complaining "I told you so, it's your fault" tone. We cringed each time the blow fell and the point of the goad went into the flesh with a soft soughing, but it was no use protesting.

The other elephant was treated by Sitaram in exactly the same way except that he used a wooden mallet set with four nails instead of the iron "ankus," the same sort of mallet that is used to whack an elephant on the rump in wild elephant noosing.

Later on, I asked Sitaram if he had ever done any elephant noosing. He had the typical wooden mallet or flail used, and his elephant had the sore on her rump which is kept open for the hunting. When this particular sore spot is pounded with the mallet or a sharp stick, the tame elephants used in hunting run so madly that they can catch up with a wild one.

"No," said Sitaram. "Not now. Before a long time ago."

The sore on his animal's rump, however, looked as if it had been open not more than a few months ago. Maybe he liked to keep in practice.

I had read about elephant noosing in Lawrence Oliphant's book, written in 1852, after the young British surgeon had been taken on a hunting trip in the Terai by the redoubtable Jang Bahadur. Later on, I had seen elephant noosers at work in Assam State in Northeastern India. It is a weird and wonderful kind of hunting, certainly one of the most dangerous sports in the world. After locating a herd of wild elephants in the jungle, the hunters in Assam would dope themselves with a bit of opium and start off on their specially trained hunting elephants. When a herd has been sighted, the assistant to the mahout, who is perched on the tail end of the elephant hanging on for dear life to its rope harness, applies the flail and the chase is on. This was the position that had been assigned to Oliphant on his trip, and he describes graphically in his account how he thought he was going to be trampled on or else beheaded by the branches as they swept by. Nowadays in Assam a young animal is singled out from the herd, the lasso-like nooses of rope thrown over its head, and it is finally lashed to the tame elephant and dragged back to camp for training and later sale. The Nepal sport, however, included the chase of full-grown tuskers, and often there were real battles between the wild tusker and the mounts of the daring mahouts. Not since Jang Bahadur's time, however, has this dangerous pastime been indulged in by the members of the ruling house of Nepal. I never could find out how long it has been since it was last done in the Terai or when, for that matter, the last wild elephant was seen in the country.

About mid-afternoon we arrived at the fringe of the forest, large gaunt isolated trees appearing first in the fields. They grew thicker and the cultivation ended. These were huge trees. In the solitary ones eagles and vultures had taken up their post. Presumably they were good lookouts for the mice that lived on the open ground. A White-winged Kite sailed near us and I got him with a lucky shot, my first from elephant-back. Another half-mile and we turned off to the bank of the Kauriala, here the westernmost of a number of sprawling channels of the Karnali, miles wide. This branch was perhaps fifty yards wide in this season with a slight flow over algae-draped smoothed rocks in the center. Beyond were series of small narrow islands. River terns, silvery gray with orange bills and feet and black caps, flew up and down and hovered over the pools. A black-and-white pied kingfisher perched on a snag. The bank was open and park-like with occasional big trees and closely cropped grass underfoot. It looked peaceful and very inviting.

We tumbled off the elephants, stiff, and grimy from the dust. Soon we were all in the pools, the elephants unharnessed, being scrubbed busily by the mahouts, rolling over first one side then the other with sighs of bliss, and all of us farther upstream sitting in the water, possessed by its coolness. It was a luxurious time, completely and utterly relaxing. The kingfisher sat and looked at us. Wagtails didappered up the bank toward us, tails bobbing nervously. A flock of black ibises circled high overhead wheeling endlessly on the ascending air currents. The air was full of the buzzings of millions of drowsy insects, punctuated by a sort of rusty-pulley noise coming from the top of a hundred-and-fifty-foot tree. The noise nagged at me. Finally I saw the bird, a Pallas's Fishing Eagle, the Asian version of our Bald Eagle at home. All afternoon we lazed about waiting for the bullock carts. They straggled in finally after nine at night, our boxes covered with dust and mud from a mild wetting in the river. Meanwhile a nearby village of Tharus had produced wood and made a fire for us and even brought mounds of crisp freshly boiled white rice and curried vegetables. It was very late before everything was finally arranged.

The next few days we spent at Tikapur trying to organize a beat in addition to our collecting. The Tharu villagers nearby were recruited for beating. The Tharus were quite different in looks and style from the Nepalis. They were the aboriginal remnant, the tribe who have always lived in the Terai jungles. Originally forest nomad hunters, they had settled down for many generations as farmers and had done well with mustard, from the seed of which a cooking oil was made, food crops and animals. They were very dark and very skinny without much of a Mongolian cast of countenance. Their greatest trait was an inherited ability to withstand malaria. The summer monsoon rains make the Terai a steaming bed of malaria and have always closed it off to outsiders including the hill Nepalis. But the Tharus have developed an innate ability to withstand the sickness and so have been able to live the year round in the Terai, a source of envy to the hill people who covet the potentially rich and flat farming land.

Our beat finally was a very simple affair, lacking the dash or the certainty of one of the Maharajah's. We picked out a block of the forest running along the river bank, and went off on elephants, dividing up our party. Lieutenant Malla had by now produced another small female elephant, giving us three all told. He rode his beast with the fifty-odd Tharus that we had gathered together for the beat running behind. Three of us went on the Court of Wards elephant, three on the other smaller beast with Sitaram. We proceeded about half a mile ahead of the beaters, and threading our way silently through the trees, were dropped off one by one at vantage-points in a crotch of a low tree where we could get a good view. Then the elephants withdrew silently, and each of us was left alone facing back toward where the beaters would come.

It always seemed to become immensely quiet in these interludes of waiting. I could hear my heart beating, could hear the slightest motion, the scratch of my clothes as they rubbed along a branch rhythmically with the motion of breathing. No birds stirred. I hardly ever saw birds even as the beaters drew close. Just as the silence would begin to seem oppressive, the distant first shouts of the beaters would come, sounding so loud, even though far away, that I would think they must be very close, that they had made a mistake. But no, they would take ages to come up to a level with us.

There was always a moment when game, if there were any, would come. It would be at a certain distance from the beaters, and it was as hard to judge as the beaters' voices and hoots and calls were hard to judge. The noise of the beaters sounded menacing like a mob, rather chilling but also exciting. The men yelled in the beginning half-heartedly, but after a time they yelled with the excitement of it, spontaneously, and to protect themselves, too, for they could never tell what might go out of the grass ahead.

We could see from the fresh pug marks along the river bank that there were several tigers about, but we never encountered any on these beats: they were too open. A big cat could slip out to the side, or even past us, but we were always alert, never knowing just what we might see. In that time of waiting I felt that I memorized every tree, every blade of grass ahead. I knew each open space, each open alley through the brush, every place where an animal would come, but still I was often surprised. There would be the faintest of rustles and a pig would move slowly through the grass, along the edge of a bank where I had thought there was no space for a trail. Sometimes spotted deer, "chital," as they are called, would rush past unexpectedly just where I was not looking.

The second beat of the morning, some miles away from the camp, I was in a devilish position, one where I could keep my balance only with difficulty, so big and round was the sloping branch, and with so few handholds. A whole troop of the gray langur monkeys arrived, and, having seen me, began to scold violently, making a series of coughs like dyspeptic old men, their side whiskers standing out in grotesque tufts as they viewed me from behind trees. I tried not to watch them, but they were terribly distracting. I couldn't feel serious any more about the hunt, or wax excited as the calls of the beaters began to swell in the distance. There was a sudden rustling, and a mongoose, a big one about the size of a woodchuck, went scurrying past, loping, intent on his own plans.

I waited now tensely, hoping that the monkeys would give up and go away. At least they seemed a bit quieter. Suddenly there came a loud "bang" and then another and two more. I thought it was probably Howie and Dick who usually sat together. Maybe they had gotten some deer, maybe a leopard, maybe anything. I was very excited by now; and then gently and elegantly a buck spotted deer walked from the surrounding thickets straight toward me. He was a big fellow, but his antlers were just knob-like affairs in the velvet. He continued to walk toward me and I heard nothing — no monkeys, no shouts — just was conscious of his carriage, like a ballet dancer, his grace. And then he lifted his enormous limpid eyes and saw me. There had been no time to reach for my gun which lay across a crotch. As he saw me, he made a short rush to the side and stood, tail twitching, about thirty yards away staring. As he ran, I had eased the gun into my hands and I was now looking down the barrel at him. I thought to myself that I should shoot, and then just as I pulled on the trigger another shot rang out much nearer than the previous volley. With the sound my gun lifted as I fired, over the deer's head, missing him comfortably. I watched him run off, feeling a sense of relief. After all, one of all those shots must have secured the deer that we should need for food. To me then it was a much greater pleasure to have missed than to have killed.

The Court of Wards elephant, which had been waiting some distance away, now came up. The mahout had not seen me miss, or seen the deer. The monkeys, subdued now and quiet, after all could not tell. We picked up Ed, who had shot a mongoose, perhaps the mate of the one I had seen. Farther on, we found Howie and Dick with two does, already skinning them. Everyone was so excited about his luck that no one asked me about my shot. I had no intention of telling them about my pleasure at missing. Besides, we had more than enough venison.

VII

Birds Along the Trail

TAKING FOOD; just now coming." It was the same invariable refrain. We were off as usual much too late toward the hills. It was a lovely clear morning when we did get off from Tikapur at last, putting the cares and trials of organizing behind and just relaxing, enjoying our surroundings. Ed and I sent the elephants ahead and walked after them, through the aisles of the forest, listening. The buffalo carts were already far behind. Behind, too, were twenty-five coolies that we had taken on. They were a group, members of a party on their way down to India, that we had waylaid with promises of pay and work far more rewarding than the ordeal that they would have to go through on the trains and in a strange country, but curiously enough, so ingrained was the habit of this annual winter migration that we had great difficulty in persuading any of the men to stop and work for us.

From Tikapur on about fourteen miles lay Chisapani, so called, a common Nepal name. It would mark the end of our use of elephants, for it lay in the gap in the Siwalik foothills where the Karnali emerged. It took us two days to make it through the forest. The trees were very large here, although the biggest ones had been cut over the past few years. Most of them were the sal (*Shorea robusta*), but there were numbers of the huge silk-cotton tree, as well as a few others of the lumber kind. The silk-cotton tree (*Bombax*), towering, of mighty girth, and in the spring so beautiful with its scarlet flowers, suffers rather a come-down in being much in demand for matchwood. There were lots of them here as we went on that morning. Many were encrusted with vines if they were growing a bit in the open. There were numbers of birds in the vines, for they were in fruit, covered with small berries. Green pigeons sat very still and then went out with a burst if we got too near. At one tree I heard distinctly the call of a Serpent-eagle, a characteristic three-note whistle. It was some distance away and I turned off the trail and crept forward carefully, for we had not collected one of these birds in the western part of the country so far. With Ed watching, I hoped that I was stalking effectively. Some moments later, after a considerable and rather exhausting demonstration of the quiet approach, I was near enough to get a view of the bird amid the vines toward the top of the tree. To my surprise the imitation had been perfect. It was not a Serpent-eagle calling, only a Racket-tailed Drongo. In the same way at home, our Blue-jay imitates the Red-shouldered Hawk.

The drongo was about the size of a starling, all over spangled black, with a crest of black, recurved, lanceolate feathers which gave it a very dashing appearance. Added to this were two elongated tail feathers, nearly eighteen inches in length, bare shafts tipped at the end with spatula-shaped feather rackets. I fired, and the drongo tumbled out of the tree, but I used the barrel with number eight shot as the fours for the eagle would have been too heavy.

There were several drongos in this forest, the biggest, the Racket-tailed, then a miniature edition of it, complete to the long tail feathers and the glossy plumage but with a smaller crest, the Lesser Racket-tailed. A third species was the Hair-crested Drongo, a brightly spangled black bird, the size of the Racket-tailed but without the crest or elongated tail, and with two strange wire-like feathers growing out of the back of its neck. A fourth was the small Bronzed Drongo, the size of the Lesser Racket-tailed. All these species lived together, at least in the winter time, in the Terai Forest of West Nepal. Presumably they moved to slightly different altitudes in the foothills in the spring to breed, otherwise it would be difficult to imagine how they all parceled out the available insect food supply, for though these birds were found about flowering trees and vines, they seemed to be entirely insect feeders, living on the insects attracted by the nectar.

Farther on in the understory, the slightly lower trees and bushes which grew loosely at a twenty-foot altitude under the main trees, Ed spied a considerable commotion. It was one of those parties of birds which move through the forest together feeding in communal style. Here again were a pair of species, fantail flycatchers this time, little birds not much bigger than one of our warblers but with a fanned-out tail, rather long in proportion, and held high. Both species were a slaty-black color above, but one was all white below while the other species had only a white throat. Both kept their tails widespread while they pirouetted and danced ceaselessly, hopping from twig to twig wagging their long fantails behind them. I have invariably seen these fantail flycatchers showing off, dancing about waving their tails continually like punch-drunk hula dancers. It has always seemed strange to me that the birds could keep it up, that they didn't die prematurely of nervous exhaustion. All the time as they moved about they sang small jittery snatches of song, rather thin little phrases half under their breath. Ed and I both shot, collecting four of the birds, and the rest of the company fluttered on zigzagging through the trees, endlessly, hectically moving.

We didn't always shoot, however. We shot selectively whenever possible, trying to secure specimens of species which were really important, species which I wanted to study at home. Other birds like the junglefowl we stalked for the pot, but they were very sporting birds and hard to hit. I did manage to hear a rustle on this morning's walk, a rustle in the dead leaves at the side of the path, and, turning off quickly, got a view of a young cock junglefowl walking swiftly away, head and tail held low. That was one character of the wild Red Junglefowl which instantly separated it from the domestic bantam rooster of similar appearance, the habit of holding the tail low like a pheasant. Ed and I both turned off the trail and ran forward, hunching down, but still trying to keep a lookout ahead. We got into an area of waist-high, exceedingly uninviting shrubs. Junglefowl were all about, the hens cackling just like excited barnyard fowl as they scuttled off through the bushes. These bushes were "jhaveri" (*Zizyphus*), a frightfully hostile plant, rather like a wild rose, both in the amount of prickles and also in bearing large haws of a pretty orange color, beloved of the birds. I finally got in a shot, just as I tripped over a root and fell into a jhaveri bush. There was a call from Ed — "got him" — and I rose, covered with blood from a deep cut on the nose.

"Hey, what's the matter? Did he bite you?" asked Ed as we retrieved the bird.

Later in the day Ed got a peahen, so that with these and

our venison from the earlier game drive, we were well supplied with meat. We camped in the jungle en route and next day reached Chisapani fairly early. It had been just too far for the elephants to travel in one day. Chisapani was a beautiful place, a rather steep bank down to the Karnali with four-thousand-foot hills on each side of the narrow gorge. The whole mass of the river surged out here, a smooth oily greenish-blue torrent, flowing slickly down to a bar below where it broke in a series of ripples and then a long churning rapid. The air was full of a constant lulling roar from downstream. Because of the narrow gorge and the very cold water, there was a sharp breeze every evening and morning, which came up on a sudden and blew down the gorge violently, lashing the trees and filtering fine white river sand into everything. It was the only drawback to the place. Otherwise the sun shone; the air was crisp; the water glistened and sparkled like a clear but faceted emerald.

Our camp was in a small depression in the bank facing out onto the stream with our backs to the wind. For a fireplace we had a huge overhanging boulder which reflected warmth in the evening. It was a marvelous camp. From the bank we could look out and watch mergansers floating downstream fishing as they went, and then flying upstream again when they came to the rapid. Or there were otters, a whole party of them, playing in the water, floating on their backs like tiny seals, sometimes diving and playing tag with whistles, hisses, and a sharp cat-like "keeow" call. It must have been the mating season. Sometimes the game of tag would become so prolonged that the animals would dash out of the water, over the rocks of the farther bank, and up until we lost sight of them in the brush. These were the big otters, first cousin to our otter at home.

It was at this camp that we really began to find good birds. Here at the foot of the hills, numerous higher-altitude species had come down in a vertical migration for the winter. And here I first observed a curious thing. Nepal is in a transitional zone between the area of higher rainfall of the Himalayas to the east and the drier mountains to the west. As one moves west along the battlemented hills, the rainfall gradually becomes reduced. All rain comes in the summer from the annual monsoon winds that sweep up from the southwest over the Indian Ocean, but the western ramparts are somewhat too far west, too removed from the main rainfall, separated by too great an expanse of land from the sea.

For some reason as yet unexplained to me, a species of bird, let us say a barbet, which would winter at four thousand feet above sea level in the colder western Himalayas, and breed higher up still at eight thousand feet, would behave quite differently in a wetter zone to the east Here presumably the same barbet would winter right down to the level of the Terai at one thousand feet, and breed somewhat lower too, at say five to six thousand feet.

I found another interesting thing in this connection. If a barbet, again, had a close relative, another species of barbet, which was known to occur in the eastern Himalayas, replacing the first species in that wetter zone, we found that the two species did not replace each other vertically by the map from north to south, but rather diagonally from northwest to southeast. That is to say, that if we followed the western species toward the east, we would find it occurring at lower and lower altitudes, coming down to the Terai level, where farther west it was found only high up in the hills. So then we would suddenly find the next species beginning to replace it higher up in the same range, not descending to the same low altitude, and thus never occurring in exactly the same places. Still farther to the east again, the second species might occur lower down in its turn. All of these strange and unexplained phenomena of distribution, by which one species occurs in certain parts of a geographical range and other species in neighboring parts, still remain to be worked out. Most of it remains a puzzle and a mystery today.

Chisapani was where we got rid of the elephants. I was just as glad. It was one thing to admire elephants at a distance, as in a zoo. It was quite another to live with them. I think all of us would like an elephant, preferably a little one, as a pet some day, but only if we had a mahout and his assistant to take care of him, and if some inexpensive way could be found of feeding the creature, for he has a gargantuan appetite. At the moment elephants were selling well in India, but I think it was mostly for a long-term investment, or for prestige. Twelve miles a day was about the limit for our elephants, and their rate of speed was considerably slower than that of a determined man on foot. After their stint they had to be bathed and scrubbed with a brick in the stream, and then fed the most enormous quantities of food. A full-grown elephant will eat up to twelve banana trees in a day, or an equivalent amount of hay if any such exists, let us say a fifth of a ton. Or, if we were in a rice area, perhaps the elephants ate rice, or again flour. Our Court of Wards elephant would think nothing of putting down thirty-two pounds of flour at a sitting. Our bill for flour was staggering, since every bit of it had to be brought up from India on coolie-back.

In addition, it was hard to sleep near the ponderous pachyderms, as they munched all night, and in the intervals of munching their stomachs rumbled, or they produced violent blasts of wind, or the mahouts would curse them, or they would rattle their tethering chains. All told, camp was very noisy when elephants were around.

The mahouts didn't like Chisapani. Old Baban Khan complained that it was too cold, that there were too many stones for his elephant to ruin her feet on, and generally that he was miserable and wanted to go home. In fact, he was terrified to be so far away from home and the forests that he knew across the Indian border. The Tharu, Sitaram, said little, but he too seemed to want to go. I told them finally that they could go after one more day's hunting and a beat on the flats near the river where there were small acacia-covered sandbar islands in the dry river bed. There were deer here. We could hear spotted deer "chinking" in the evening, a sharp high call, more like a bird than an animal. Perhaps we could get another and make dried jerky meat for the trip into the hills farther on.

In the night, however, Sitaram and his elephant left, quietly, noiselessly, taking with them a whole half-sack of our precious flour, and, in spite of Sitaram's professed Hindu orthodoxy, a whole haunch of our venison. There was a commotion in the camp the next morning. Baban Khan said he had heard nothing. None of the coolies had heard anything, or the little subofficial, an hysterical little man that Lieutenant Malla had sent along. I called the camp out and before them all denounced Sitaram for being very disobedient, not only to me but to his master, Lieutenant Malla, who had promised me that he would stay with us for at least ten days. Having cast out Sitaram and committed him to the mercy of the powers that would arrange his next incarnation, I turned to other matters, paid off Baban Khan and the other elephant mahout, and told the subdued little official that all of this would be duly reported to Higher Authority, to the Durbar at Katmandu, no less, a mystic, wholly terrifying and unimaginable organization to these simple people who had never been outside their own district. For our coolies and for our hysterical little official, Katmandu was as remote and far more glamorous than New York was for us at that moment.

We little thought at the time that this small incident would have a sequel, but a few days later there was another commotion one morning as the little official ran wildly back and forth through the camp babbling to one and all some great and portentous news. I asked Rao to go over and find out what was going on. The little man was talking in Nepali. Rao brought him back.

When he was a few yards off, he stopped, drew himself up in an exaggerated manner, and saluted with great deference.

"What is it?" I asked in Hindustani.

With Rao helping, we finally got the story.

"Oh, sir, the news has just come from a coolie traveling along the road."

"What news?"

"Sir, you tell the truth and we are all in fear."

"Why, what has happened now?" I was curious.

"Sir, you said that something very bad would happen to Sitaram, and that he would be punished for his crimes."

I certainly did not remember saying all this, but thought it better to let the story come out. It appeared that Sitaram, having taken himself off to a village about fifteen miles away, had camped there. In the evening, being drunk, he had tried to climb a tree to cut some tender leaves for his elephant, and had fallen out breaking his neck. It was quite obvious to all present that I had put a curse on the wretched man and so had caused his death. I adopted a policy of dignified silence as the little official backed away from my presence in an awestruck manner. After all, the incident might do us some good in the end. It was certainly no use trying to persuade them that I hadn't willed the whole thing. It may have been only my imagination, but it seemed to me that things got done around camp for the next few days with a shade more efficiency.

Each morning we would be up at dawn, and off after an early breakfast. Not that breakfast was ever early enough, but Abdul was getting a bit quicker, especially if one of us took turns urging him on, or even trying to cook a dish of our own. Dick Mack was especially good at this, having quite a talent for camp cooking learned on fishing expeditions along the Oregon rivers. Our morning schedule would vary according to our jobs. Dick and Howie would go out over their trap lines. Some of the small mammal traps could be covered before breakfast as they were set in mouse or shrew runways near camp. Kurt and Francis would work out photographic projects, such as village life among the Tharus, portraits of various types among the coolies or the local passers-by, or pictures of life in the camp. Sometimes they would accompany one or other of us to photograph our hunting activities.

At Chisapani I was first able to use my Italian silk birdcatcher's nets which can be invaluable to a bird collector in certain areas, particularly in heavy jungle. Many species of ground-living birds scuttle along through the underbrush so effectively that they may never be seen by the collector. For these, a net was the only solution. Nets have been developed over hundreds of years, both in Italy and Japan, as methods of snaring small songbirds for eating. Even today in Japan it is a big business, although this activity has decreased in recent years in Italy, partly due to the pioneering efforts of Dr. Axel Munthe, author of that best-seller, *The Story of San Michele.*

My Italian nets consisted of a central fine-mesh silk net, rather loose and baggy. On either side of this were two stout, six-inch-mesh cotton nets. A small bird flying into this contraption would hit against the narrow silk mesh which would bag out with the impact, forcing itself through one of the large meshes of the outer net, there to drop down in a neat purse or bag. It was almost impossible for a bird to get out of a contraption of this sort, and very difficult even to untangle them oneself. My practice was to search through the forest for a spot which seemed to be an obvious passageway or corridor for birds to use in flight. One good spot was parallel to a trail and at right angles to it. I found birds reluctant often to cross open spaces, and likely to put off the crossing for a time by moving through the underbrush parallel to a trail. Sometimes in dry areas, a spot near a waterhole or pool was good. Quite often, though, disasters occurred. We would go out to the net and find a big rent in it. Once I could see junglefowl feathers where the bird had forced its way out. Other times the holes were mysteries.

The net was strung like a shower curtain by rings at the top, which slid along a supporting rope. Then weights, pegs, branches, or strings were used to tie the bottom down, and make the contraption fairly taut. The whole affair was rather tricky and tedious to put up, and maintaining it was a bother. If there was wind or rain, there were always sure to be dozens of leaves or twigs caught in the meshes the next morning, and of course this would tend to give the net away to the birds. It was, however, constantly surprising to me how effective the net was, how little it could be seen. Very rarely would birds appear to notice the meshes before they flew into them. Even bats could be caught, in spite of their various devices, including supersonic cries, for avoiding objects in flight. Bats, too, were the very devil to get out of a net, and it was a sad day for me on several occasions when I had to spend hours abstracting six or eight small fruit bats, hideous creatures and, besides, hard to kill. I have never understood how bird trappers can take birds, let alone bats, in any number out of nets without killing them. If a bird was alive and struggling, its delicate claws would grip quantities of the silk strands, almost certainly preventing any untangling. Such men as Charles Cordier of the New York Zoo must be wizards at the business.

The net was not always wholly secure. One morning I took Kurt out to get a picture of my net operations, and sure enough in the first net we came to in the jungle was a lovely yellow-naped woodpecker, a species that I had secured in Katmandu, but not so far in West Nepal. By the time the camera was set up, the flash gun and reflectors arranged, for it was dark under the trees, the woodpecker, which had been struggling continuously since our first approach, suddenly achieved his freedom and swept off in a graceful arc while we all stared dumbfounded. As luck would have it, we never saw the species again in West Nepal. Poor Kurt realized that we had had a real loss, and realized, too, that it is not always easy to make all the different phases of an expedition work together to the mutual advantage of each phase. There were always bound to be a few times when the demands of photography held us up or interfered with other work. There were undoubtedly other times when ornithology or mammalogy put a crimp in the style of the photographers. Just the same, it was remarkable how well all the different outlooks of all of us fitted together in the end.

During these days we were constantly on the lookout for more coolies. As I went along near the trail where the men were coming down from the villages in the hills on their strange annual migration to work in India, I would stop them sometimes under the pretext of buying some of their oranges — tangerines they were really — to see if any of them were interested in working as coolies for us for a time, rather than making the long trip by railroad into the plains. Most of the men would not even stop. They would scarcely talk to me or my gun coolie, but would hurry on as if impatient of any delay. It seemed to me that they knew only this, and that their minds were not geared to accept any deviation from the usual pattern. Most of them would not even sell us the tangerines, fearful that somehow it would interfere with the selling at the market town below.

Day by day as the season advanced, the men became wilder-looking. They were evidently coming from higher and higher up in the hills. Now these men were dressed, not in the loincloth and shirt and cap any more, but in strange hanging homespun garments made of wool from the fleece of their own goats. It was woven rather like coarse tweed, gray, with a black stripe. Curiously these western Nepali hill men often looked Aryan to me rather than Mongolian as I would have expected. They were tall and rather light-colored with black mustaches and beards. They looked more like Kashmiris than Tibetans.

Of course Tibetans were mixed in with the wanderers. We met several parties of them. One was led by a lama, a pleasant old man who said he had been down before and that he was going back to revisit Buddhgaya on the Ganges. He said that he had come from Shimbuling Gompa, a monastery at Mount Kailas, the sacred mountain in western Tibet, and that it was eighteen days' march from Chisapani. He said that there was a lot of snow and ice already on top of the passes. Although he was poorly dressed in patched red robes of different shades, these were obviously his traveling clothes, for when he saw we were willing to talk, he finally produced several articles of superior workmanship which he wanted to sell. One was a nicely made human thighbone trumpet used in the lamaist ritual, with bands of brass on the ends and decorations of turquoise. He also had two fine bells and a drum, the latter made of two inverted human brain pans, covered with skin. All of these he unlimbered from a pack which one of his lesser colleagues was carrying, and proceeded to give us a small demonstration, in the middle of the trail, of the way a prayer service was conducted in his monastery, punctuating his recited "om mané padme hum" phrases with bursts of weird and shrill cacophony from horn, drum, and bell. His performance was so effective that it drew quite a crowd of wayfaring coolies and caused them to stop. So while Kurt was bargaining for the thighbone trumpet, I used the opportunity to recruit ten more coolies for our onward journey. My promises of two rupees a day (about sixty cents) plus their food seemed to be acceptable. It would certainly be considerably more than they would earn after journeying such a long distance by Indian train.

The last morning of our stay at Chisapani was my best bird morning. Two of the previous days had been bad. I had a theory that it was a matter of the barometric pressure, that when it went up, the birds did not sing, and of course, not singing, could less easily be located. Whether there was anything in the theory I don't know, but this day it was calm and rather cloudy and the birds sang loudly. My first piece of luck, for it always seemed to me that bird collecting had in it a strong element of luck, was a good flycatcher in one of the nets. It was a small black-and-orange bird with a brilliant patch of blue on the head, a migrant from the hills, wintering down in the foothills.

Another piece of luck, although I hardly realized it at the time, was a pair of tree-creepers, inconspicuous little creatures like our brown creepers at home. The tree-creeper has a thin curved bill with which to ferret out insects in crevices of bark. It hitches itself up and down the trunk of a tree, clinging with its slender toes and supporting itself with the rather spiny long feathers of the tail, the two center ones of which act like a shooting stick. I found out later on in the Museum at home that these little streaked brown birds were of a Himalayan species which had never been recorded as far east as Nepal. The species was only known from the western Himalayas. In addition, it was one of the species which in the western Himalayas bred at about eight thousand feet and wintered down as low as four thousand. Now here I had found it in the lowest foothills at the edge of the Terai, no more than a thousand feet above sea level.

Unfortunately I never carried along all the books I would have needed to know enough about the birds I was catching or observing each day. Often I neglected to make as complete notes on a species as I might have had I known that what I was encountering was a rare or unexpected occurrence. Obviously, where a fauna consists of many hundreds of species, it takes years and years to see most of them, let alone acquire any real and detailed knowledge of them. It was not until I returned home and studied these little tree-creepers in the Museum that I realized that the three specimens I had gotten along the Karnali represented a very dark population, previously unknown from Nepal, and therefore a new subspecies. This was just one of a number of new records for Nepal which we made here in the west, where no one had had an opportunity to go before.

Another good bird of the morning was a little wren-babbler, a tiny creature with the look and the habits of a miniature mouse. I always wondered if they could fly, for one usually only sees them hopping about among low brush or mossy boulders close to the ground. I was still-hunting, just sitting on a rock and waiting and watching. There had been a moment when I thought I could get a pheasant, a kaleej. I had heard a scuffle and then a good deal of pheasant talk up a hill among some huge boulders, and finally got a glimpse of what seemed to be a fight between two cock birds with a hen standing by. The whole affair was so quick that I never did get a chance for a shot, and so I finally decided to wait and see if anything would appear. It was a good place. A rill of water tumbled down among the blackish-brown, lava-like boulders, stirring the air slightly. There was a sleepy buzz of insects and long slim fingers of dew-spangled fern waved gently over the stream. Then finally at my feet the little bird hopped out, quite soundlessly, from under a boulder. I held my breath, watching as he flitted about, dark-mottled, hopping with a flick of his wings, evidently a sort of nervous tick. Often his hops carried him back and forth sideways instead of forward, as if he were dancing. When he did this and flicked his wings too, it seemed as if sometimes the gesture was effective in starting up insects, for once or twice I saw him snap up something in his tiny bill with a barely perceptible gesture. I had to wait a long time until the creature was far enough away so that I could dare to shoot, even with the number thirty-two dust-shot shell. This was one of the smallest loads that could be used, but still it was powerful enough to blow such a bird to smithereens. Finally a moment came and I fired and got him, a mite of a bird to come all the way to the Himalayas for, but a valued specimen, unique in coming from West Nepal.

By the end of the morning I had seventeen birds, a big haul, one that with what Ed had secured would keep Toni, John, Ed, and myself busy the rest of the day, cataloguing, skinning, smoothing out, tagging, and wrapping away securely for the trials of the trail. For we were off the next day. There was a lot to be done, coolies to organize, boxes to be packed and sorted, our own gear to be packed for an early start, food to be arranged for, some of our stuff to be left behind in the care of an under-officer who had finally shown up at camp, an emissary from the District Burra Hakim. I would leave him behind, as he showed no willingness to come on into the hills with us, and so he could be useful, guarding our extra gear until we returned.

Meanwhile we had tried to budget our food carefully for the onward trip, not only for ourselves, but also for our thirty-six coolies. The hill men coming down had told us that food was scarce in the hills, mostly barely sufficient for the people who were resident there, and that we could get

Author showing hill men at Rekcha a drawing of the Mountain Quail. Most claimed to know the "salo kano titra," but during our stay there no one found it for us. The man in the center background made a special ten-day trapping trip without avail.

A panorama of Katmandu from Bhim Sen's Tower, a jumble of twisting mediaeval streets interspersed with modern structures. In the background lies Naggarjung Hill and the towers of Swayambhunath nestling on a hillock.

only limited supplies of rice, flour, or potatoes for our men. So we bought a quantity of rice and flour from the Tharu farmers below Tikapur, trying to estimate in advance just how much we could take reasonably and practically without having at the same time to hire so many more coolies that we would have altogether too many mouths to feed. This has always been a problem with expeditions using human transport. So many men could carry your goods, but then so many more men would be needed to carry food for these men. Eventually so many extra men would be needed to carry the food for the men carrying the food for the others, and so on in a vicious circle, until it seemed as if everyone was merely carrying food for someone else.

At last everything was done, the last bird packed, the last preparation made. We crawled into our sleeping bags tired but fairly well convinced that we would make an early getaway the next morning, on up the trail along the foaming river into the hills. Gone were the elephants, the buffalo carts. Surely the delays would not be great and we could make a good start.

Next morning dawned, clear and cold. A wind was sweeping down the gorge, driving fine sand before it. I had warned Abdul to be up at five, and we finally had our breakfast by seven. I had harangued the hysterical little official, and he, subdued a bit by my obvious supernatural powers, tried his best. Eight o'clock came and went.

"Well, what now?" I cried out to the wretched man.

"Coolies taking food, sir, but just now coming." It was like a refrain, a chorus. I thought suddenly that we ought to be able to work out a little pas à deux, the two of us in best Gilbert and Sullivan style singing, "With a hey nonny, hey nonny, just now coming, just now taking food, just now coming." But I suppose the whole thing would have taken too much trouble to explain to the little man.

So instead we went about and hefted packs and got each man onto his feet, and forgot about the delays in the struggle with the loads, and finally at long last swung out and off up the trail.

VIII

Rekcha and the Spiny Babbler

THREE DAYS out of Chisapani, between the Bheri and Karnali Rivers, we came to a place called Guttu. It was in the duns, the inner valley behind the outer foothill ranges. The Siwalik Hills here looked like mountains of the moon, eroded, dry, scrabbled-looking, but the mountains ahead were green, and the duns were rich solid jungle, full of enormous towering sal and other lumber trees, so thick, so packed, that once buried among them the horizon was lost to view. Guttu consisted of perhaps forty small wattle and daub huts in a meandering open space among the trees where rice and mustard were being cultivated in small patchy fields. From the clearing we could get a fine view ahead of what looked like a plateau towering up ahead of us to a good five thousand feet, very sheer and rather dry-looking, with a fringe of green and thicker growth toward the top.

We arrived at Guttu about ten in the morning after a three-hour walk from our camping place of the night before deep in the jungle. I was looking for the trail which would take us up to the top of the plateau ahead, a five-thousand-foot plateau marked on the map in a big bend of the Karnali River. The only map of western Nepal had been prepared by the Survey of India in 1924 after a rather brief reconnaissance of the general region by some Indian cartographers. A very large proportion of the information on the map had come from hearsay. The contours, the villages, the trails — all were there big as life on the sheets of the map. It was, however, a separate and distinct experience to start walking into these hills. The trails wandered about irrespective of the maps. So also did the contours. It was to be expected, though, and I was not too surprised.

My purpose in coming into the hills had been to get to a spot about five thousand feet or so and camp there, provided the surroundings were good for collecting. Continuous traveling would never lead to good collecting. There would never be a chance that way to get to know the area and the fauna. So we had picked out a place on the map where there seemed to be a plateau of the right altitude high above the river. The name of the place was given as Chauklé.

At Guttu we failed to talk to any of the local people. This turned out to be a mistake. The little official with us was a Terai man who had never been up beyond the last ford over the Bheri River. None of the coolies with us were local men either. They all came from villages in other parts of the hinterland. We saw very few people at Guttu, only a few women and children in the distance in the fields or on the verandas of the little raised huts. None ventured near us, and after resting a bit on the trail and scouting out the cliffs ahead, we started on, the coolies still behind. As it was still early and the plateau ahead deceptively near, it seemed to me that it would be possible for the whole party to get up on top before dark.

So we simply walked out of the village and toward the plateau to the north, following a broad well-marked trail. It seemed obvious and inescapable that this was our trail and that it would lead us to the top of the plateau to Chauklé as it was marked on the map, but just outside Guttu our troubles began. The trail forked. One branch went to the left, another to the right. We kept to the left as that trail looked more used. This must be the one down which the hill men come in the winter, I thought. There were marks of old camps and camp fires here, always a sure sign of the main trail. According to our maps, and verified by what the people waiting at the last river ford on the Karnali had said, there was a main trail down from the plateau, part of a route which went right on up to the Tibet border, via the village of Chauklé.

After a while the left branch turned and started up. We felt reassured. Dick and I were well ahead by this time, but we assumed the others would soon be close behind. We stopped to look at some grayish giant squirrels cavorting in a high tree. Then we went on again, climbing, as I realized afterward, much too quickly. Another mile of steady ascent and we came to a second fork. This time a trail went off in each direction, to right and left, and one straight ahead. I sat quietly, watching a mixed flock of small birds, while Dick tried the right-hand trail of the two. Among the birds was a small wren-warbler which I finally stalked and shot after watching the whole flock for a time. These hunting parties were always fascinating to watch. Sometimes really rare birds appeared in them if you were patient and sat quietly.

Dick came back and said that the trail seemed to meander off along the side of the hill. The left fork we looked at, and tried to shout to two children who were grazing goats nearby, but the children evidently didn't understand Hindustani, and the path seemed small. We left a branch pointing up the trail, with a piece of toilet paper stuck in a fork with an arrow, and on it the words, "We've gone up here," and went on up. I was beginning to wonder whether we were acting wisely, but it seemed as if we should soon come out on the plateau, and then we should be all right. I felt sure Chauklé must be somewhere ahead, but instead we went up and up. The trail got steeper. I was puffing and gasping, but Dick was forging steadily ahead of me, and I felt reassured by the sight of his back. I knew that I had to keep on making my legs flex at the knee joints, just keep on going and I should get there. The effort slowed down my thought processes. I should have contemplated the climb and realized that our coolies would never make it today with their loads. They were slow enough anyway.

Finally we came out on a miniature plateau. From the look of the sky, glimpsed through the trees up above, I had thought that we would be on top, but no, there was a rather horrifying-looking climb on up ahead. This little plateau was merely a step, a landing in a flight of stairs up to the real top. Dick and I sank to the grass, panting. We had some water and some dried jerky venison. I thought that surely the others would come after a while, so we simply lay back and rested in the sun. After a time the sweat dried out on our shirts and we began to get cooled off, even chilly. No sign of anyone so far. I went to the edge of the plateau and looked down the trail. Not a sound to be heard. I fired a couple of shots from my shotgun out over the trees in the hope that someone would hear.

By three o'clock we decided to go on. That would only give us about two and a half hours more of daylight. There were no inhabitants at this plateau, even though there were green fields, but the two little huts here were both empty and their doors fastened. We left another note on a prominent branch by the narrow trail. Fortunately our toilet paper was holding out. The well-trodden trail went straight on up again into light forest. There were signs of people about, one or two recent camp-fire sites in level spots. We came finally to a small house along the trail. A woman and child stood near the door peering out at the strangers. I asked them whether Chauklé lay ahead. The name didn't seem to register with them. "Chauklé, Chauklé," I persisted. No response. Instead, the woman pointed up the trail and murmured something that sounded like "rickshaw." Dick and I struggled on.

This part of the route was less steep than the last, but by now we were both pretty well winded. In fact, I was so winded that when we saw a group of scimitar babblers crossing the trail ahead, I had to sit down on a rock to get my breath before I could hold my shotgun steady.

"This is something," I panted at Dick. "I really feel bushed." For me it was a confession. I had always rather prided myself on my ability as a walker.

By that time the birds had evaporated in the bushes as they had a habit of doing, and so the interruption merely served as a rest period. It was beginning to be sunset time. We were on a steep slope now, with a superb view off to our left to the south over the Siwalik Range. The lower valleys were purple and dark, the hills above them shading into blue, tipped in places with a dusty yellow light which would intensify and turn to orange-gold later. We were in light forest, mostly oaks covered with moss and epiphytes, tiny ribbon-leaved ferns, clusters of yellowish-stemmed orchids, and wisps of the trailing moss. In places there were patches of tall grass interspersed with big pines. The whole landscape was exceedingly dry. There had been a few springs and streamlets farther down, but here the crevices and channels seemed to have recently dried up.

Finally we rounded a last bend and saw fields and cultivation ahead. A few more weary hundred yards and we came out on an open space on top of a flat plateau-like area. Neat arrays of trimmed paddy fields spread before us in a flat area a thousand yards long surrounded on all sides by narrow steep ridges of forest-clothed hills. In a gap in one of the small protecting hills, we had a sudden glimpse to the north of the snow mountains, unexpectedly near. To one side of the fields there was a cluster of small houses. With an overwhelming sense of relief, we pushed on across the fields. Each step seemed an effort.

"Well, thank God, we're somewhere, wherever we are!" Dick exclaimed.

Our first efforts were unsuccesful. The little cluster of houses seemed to be uninhabited. It was not until we came to the end of the village that we had any luck.

The last house was brick, a soft mellow orange-red color, glowing in the sunset light as if it were a heap of smoldering coals. We turned off the narrow dirt causeway made of the ridge between two paddy fields, and slowly, painfully, walked stiff-legged into the little yard around the house, through a break in the mud wall which had been half-fenced off with branches of thorn. We could see that the door in the center of the porch was open, and smoke was coming from the chimney. Already the air was chill in the fading light. Already we were cold in spite of the caked sweat.

"Hey!" I said in my poor Hindustani, sinking onto the porch. "Anybody there?"

There was a series of hoarse croaks and a veritable wrinkled crone appeared, head draped in a long shawl which hid everything except her bright eyes and tanned, seared face. She showed no sign of astonishment at the sight of Dick and myself in our dirty clothes, seated on her porch.

"We would like some food and shelter, Madam," I said in my most polite phrasing. "We are very tired, and," I added hastily, "of course we will pay."

The old crone looked quite cross. I realized that she must have thought we were low fellows, well beneath her notice. After all, there was no one with us and we had only our shotguns and light musette bags. We had long since given up the idea of the coolies catching us, and Heaven only knew how far back the rest of the party was. It was getting dark too. We must act or we should be in trouble. I pulled out some Nepali and Indian rupees and waved them at her.

"But I am a big Brahmin," she said. "I cannot give you food."

"We are big people too," I boasted. "Our coolies are behind, but there are many of us and we have tents and food in plenty. However, they are all behind now. You must give us something, and some shelter too. We will pay well." I waved a five-rupee note in the air in front of her.

The old crone backed away. I could see into the dark kitchen beyond. In the firelight there was a little girl peering at us.

"No, no, you can't come in here," the old woman said hastily. "I am a Brahmin and this is a Brahmin house. You will have to stay out there."

A good deal more palaver went on, during which we could

see that she was getting food for us. Finally it came, two enormous platters of rice, two heaping mounds of crisply cooked grains, each standing apart from the other and snowy white. The platters were made of round green leaves neatly sewn together. With these were two smaller platters containing a glutinous heap of dark green stuff, evidently a sort of spinach, and a tiny leaf plate of seasoning. All of this delectable fare was dumped onto the porch in front of us.

"We must have a fire. We must go inside somewhere," I said.

After more talk, we were led around to the side and shown a sort of lean-to room, built against the main house. It was getting dark now, and cold. We sat in the room and the crone brought us a burning log which was placed in a depression in the center of the floor and one or two sticks added to it. I explained meanwhile to Dick what a Brahmin was, the highest Hindu caste whose whole being would be defiled by the presence of an unbeliever in his house.

A young Nepali hill man appeared, evidently a traveler like ourselves, and presumably of a lower caste than our hostess. He too was given some food and proceeded to demonstrate the proper method of keeping warm in Nepal. Every wooden window shutter and the door, all were closed tight against the piercing cold air. Once the place was well sealed up, for there was no chimney, our new friend began to work on the fire. His technique was to blow, long hissing inspirations followed by long, even blows. The effect was staggering. We were soon in imminent danger of suffocation. Dick and I lay on the floor, our faces as near to it as possible, tears rolling out of our eyes, gulping mouthfuls of the welcome rice and spinach all the while. To make matters worse, I mixed some of the condiment in with the spinach. It was incredibly powerful stuff. It seemed as if patches of the inside of my mouth were being torn away with red-hot pincers, but still, I was so hungry that I kept on eating. We had long ago used up the water in my bottle, so I staggered out into the cold chill air and beat on the door of the main house.

"Water, water! Hurry, hurry, please," I mumbled, my mouth on fire.

A brass water pot was produced, taken back and set to boiling on the fire. In spite of Dick's protests and my mouth, I was determined to boil the water before drinking it, having seen the village well on the way in.

At this juncture there came a knock on the door and our hostess appeared. Leaving the door ajar, she proceeded to sit on the lintel. Gradually the smoke cleared. I started to question her, hoping to find out if possible where we were and just how far off base. My Hindustani was creaky, but after a time things began to come out.

First of all, there seemed to be no such place as Chauklé. That town was a figment of someone's imagination. Then I discovered the name of the village where we were. It was Rekcha, the name that had sounded like "rickshaw" along the trail. The old lady added that some distance farther to the east along the top of the plateau-like ridge there was a place called Chapré. Perhaps that was what the map-makers had meant. According to her it was a village about the same size as this one.

I asked her about the people, and she said that most of the men had gone down below to look for work. Probably we had passed some of them along the trail near Chisapani on their way down to the Indian plains. It seemed extraordinary to me what little influence these trips had on the mountain villages. Perhaps because the men moved about in tight little groups of their own kind and did not mix, they returned with few impressions of the outside world and with few enough goods or money. The women who stayed behind seemed to have no idea certainly of the big world below into which their men had ventured.

I asked the old woman what her impressions were of us. Who were we and where did we come from. She looked at us quizzically.

"You must be Punjabis," she said.

People from the Punjab in northern India are tall and light-skinned. She knew of them, and that there were Punjabis employed by the lumber company which had a concession to cut timber in the duns below.

"No, we are not Punjabis," I replied. "We come from across the sea."

This would be the "black water," as the Hindus term it, to cross which in the orthodox Hindu mind is to brave the terrors of purgatory.

The old woman thought a long time about this. Finally she said, "I have heard of the people called the "Angreez' who live across the black water. They have a flag."

"No, we are not 'Angreez.' We are from even farther away across the sea. We are from a country called 'America.' We have a flag also."

This seemed to please the old lady. She said that when our people came she would show us where to camp. She presented us with more wood and departed.

Dick and I lay down in the stifling atmosphere and listened

to the young Nepali's snores and cogitated at intervals what to do. There seemed to be no point in moving now. Besides, it was too cold outside. We had no idea where the others could be. We had no flashlight to guide us, and it would be hours before the moon was up. I felt worried about the day's events. I thought now in retrospect of all sorts of alternatives that I should have adopted during the past twelve hours. We should have waited until the coolies caught up with us in Guttu. We should have tried to locate a guide. We should have stopped along the trail. Any number of things should have been done, but there was no use crying over spilt milk. The others would have sense enough to arrange things even if I hadn't. We both sank into a series of troubled naps, our eyes weeping constantly, our mouths caked and dry.

In the middle of a cat nap, I woke up. The fire was almost out and it was very cold. There were movements outside, stirrings, and I saw a stab of light under the edge of the door. Then there was a call. Someone was trying to arouse the house. I sprang up, tripping over Dick in the process, and stumbled and groped for the door. Outside three of our coolies were wandering about with a flashlight rapping on doors and giving vent to occasional and tentative "view halloos."

"Okay, here we are," I called. "What's up?"

The men rushed over to us, jabbering with excitement, and one of them thrust into my hand a note written on the inevitable piece of toilet paper. I read it by flashlight. The first part was from Ed saying that he and Kurt were with the coolies and had made camp just outside of Guttu. The men had been incredibly slow and had been unable to get beyond Guttu by afternoon. He was sending up three coolies to follow the four of us carrying our bedding rolls and some food. He would ride herd on the coolies in the morning and they would hope to reach us wherever we were by then.

At the bottom of this there was a postscript by Howie. He and Francis were somewhere in the village of Rekcha. They had arrived after nightfall and had only just heard that we were there too. They were comfortably fixed and they had all our bed rolls and the food. Would we join them? We certainly would! Dick and I picked up our shotguns and musette bags and sallied forth into the frosty night leaving our snoring companion, who had never waked up, to his own devices in the smoke-filled room. There would be time enough tomorrow to thank the old lady; or rather today. It was one-thirty A.M., December twenty-fifth.

The sky was clear and the stars sparkled brilliantly. It was so cold and clear that we could almost hear the frost crackle in the stillness. The stars seemed to be just overhead. There was an old moon hanging on the edge of one of the little surrounding hills. We could see perfectly as we walked along the little ridge between the paddy fields with a new spring in our step. In a moment we should have some food and our own bedding rolls — in just a moment. Back on the outskirts of the little village we could see a fire. It seemed to be burning in the open, and as we came near we could see that the house was a sort of open-sided manger. One of the coolies said that the Sahibs were there.

The moment seemed appropriate. As Dick and I neared the fire, we broke into "Silent Night, Holy Night." From the fire Howie and Francis caught up the refrain. It was a welcome tune. Francis spread before us biscuits, chocolate, and a tot of whiskey each to drink a Christmas toast. We clustered about the fire which was built here on a three-sided porch. It warmed us and at the same time the smoke could escape. Our bedding rolls were spread out on the floor of the porch and in no time we were as snug as could be. Howie's and Francis's tale was simple. They had merely followed us up the trail, but more slowly, not hearing my shots or finding our notes, but like us they had persevered and had come to Rekcha just at dark, to find this first hut which we had missed. The man of the family was there and had welcomed them with a place to sleep and the fire and a plate of rice. The three coolies, following behind much later with the flashlight, had somehow picked up the information that we, too, were about and had finally located us in the old crone's house. It was a great relief to be even partially reunited. I felt as if someone had just handed me a surprise Christmas stocking.

The next day was spent in reconnoitering. I was anxious to find a good hunting and camping spot. We walked about in different directions, and Dick, with incredible energy, set off on a jaunt towards Chapré along the trail to the east. It took him several hours, and when he returned he reported that he had walked until he came to a very deep cleft in the plateau through which the main trail from Guttu apparently ran. It was, of course, not marked on the map. There was no sign of the missing village of Chauklé. The main problem up here we soon discovered was water. Except for the wells at Rekcha, there was no real body of water on top of this whole plateau. There were a few tiny pools and one or two trickles of streams, but there would certainly not be enough for us to camp. We would have to stay right in Rekcha. At this point the old lady appeared and urged on us a camp site near her house. It was on a flat raised area in the midst of the paddy fields which we were told was a shrine. There was a small enclosed shrine at one end, a wooden frame with two bronze bells hanging in the center, one or two wooden posts, crude lingams, the Hindu phallic emblem associated with Shiva, and an amusing iron swing, an unexpected note in this far-off place. Here the old lady said we should camp, and here we could put up our flags. It was not until later that we realized that all our talk about flags had confused her and that she was associating them with prayer flags, the customary decoration for a shrine used by the Tibetans.

Late in the afternoon the first coolies appeared, and finally, at the end, Ed and Kurt, who had spent the day urging on the men. We had just time to get the tents up and a fire lit in our new camping place before nightfall. Again it was bitterly cold, and our light unheated tents seemed clammy and dank, but we had two pressure lamps and these soon warmed up the main tent, our ten-by-twelve-foot dining tent. We put on all our long woolly underwear and heaviest socks and shirts and clustered in the dining tent to read or work until dinner time.

Meanwhile I opened up a Christmas package which had come along with us all this time and discovered in it some tins of smoked turkey, a plum pudding, and a flask of brandy to go over it, pâté de foie gras, and other dainties, and even a bottle of champagne. I had wondered why the package seemed heavy. Dick decided to make hard sauce, using tinned cream and butter with sugar and brandy to taste, and

I instructed Abdul in the making of creamed smoked turkey. With so much supervision Adbul for once was fairly prompt. We eventually dined sumptuously in festal spirit, drinking our champagne in tin mugs and vowing it was the best dinner we had ever had. Outside, the ice was already forming in our washbasins and there was a coating of rime on the grass half an inch thick.

The next days were busy and highly productive. Each morning we were off by seven from our camp, some to check the trap lines, others to hunt. The afternoon of Christmas Day, before the coolies arrived, I had been presented with what at first I did not recognize as an extraordinary present. It was a piece of the sort of luck that makes one feel that a collector has to have luck on his side in addition to everything else. I had been high up on the side of one of the hills which surrounded Rekcha. I was coming back from a reconnoiter. The hill was rather steep and full of scrub. It looked as if goats were grazed there, and there were a few semi-abandoned fields at the bottom. Blackberry-like bushes, stinging nettles, and small scrubby thorn trees made progress slow. There were no trees on the whole slope, only one rather high bush near the little path which wound downward. But it was hard to see birds with all the low shrubs and heavy grass.

Halfway down the slope and near the large bush, I heard a series of low chuckles and "querr" noises. I stopped short. There must be a flock of laughing thrushes or babblers about, the sort of birds that go around in small family parties, constantly talking to each other. After waiting carefully, stock-still for several moments, I saw a group of birds hopping about, half on, half off the ground, at the base of the big bush. They were dark and bulky-looking, as big as a big thrush, and they flicked and flirted their tails as they hopped about, in the characteristic manner of the noisy nervous babblers or laughing thrushes. I waited again trying to get a clear sight. I could not advance or I would frighten them off. It was a long shot for my number thirty-two cartridge in the auxiliary barrel of the sixteen, but I took the chance finally, sighted and fired. The flock dispersed, evaporated rather, as I rushed forward. A few moments of searching and I found my prize. It was a brownish bird the size of an American robin or an English blackbird. The throat and upper breast were white, the rest streaked brown. The feathers of the upper side, particularly the forehead and crown, had stiff wiry shafts as did those of the throat. As this bird lay in my palm, I could think of no species of laughing thrush known to me which it remotely resembled. I brought it back with me to camp, and in the excitement of unpacking and arranging our camp and getting Christmas dinner ready, I gave the specimen little thought.

It was not really until the next day that I began to ponder seriously over my new bird. Meanwhile Toni had skinned it the night before, and I had written up the label very carefully, noting the flock and the open situation where I had seen the birds. Holding my prize and thinking about it, I began to turn over all the Indian species in my mind. What could this bird be? In the field a problem like this was not an easy one when books were not ready to hand, when there were several hundreds of species to choose from. Finally the stiff wiry shafts of the feathers gave the bird away. Although it was as big as a thrush, it could only be the Spiny Babbler. But I had never seen the five extant specimens. I knew

Acanthoptila nipalensis, the Spiny Babbler, only by reputation. It was a species that had defied scientists for years. None had been collected for one hundred and six years, since 1843 or 1844. At that time Brian Hodgson's Nepali collectors working for him in the unknown fastnesses of Nepal had secured several specimens. He himself had never seen the species in life. There was a record, too, of a single specimen taken in Kumaon, the neighboring Himalayan area under British suzerainty, by a certain Captain Stackhouse Pinwill, a British officer who sent his bird collections to the then dean of British ornithologists in India, Allen O. Hume. But the Spiny Babbler had remained a mystery ever since, one of the five species of Indian birds, which, along with the Mountain Quail, had apparently vanished from the face of the earth. But not quite, for if my guess was right, here it was hopping about large as life on the wooded slopes above Rekcha.

The rest of our days in Rekcha I combed the hillsides looking for the Spiny Babbler. But fate was against us, and after the single specimen which proved beyond a doubt that the species still existed, we saw the birds no more. I could not believe from its behavior that the species was particularly rare. Rather the Spiny Babbler appeared to be confined to western Nepal. That alone would account for nothing being known about the bird. Furthermore, it was a species found at about five thousand feet, a critical altitude. The hills at the five-thousand-foot level have been perhaps the most devastated of all. The farming or the lumbering operations have hit them badly. The topsoil has drained away wherever the original ground cover has been tampered with. The ground water has run off and the streams and springs have dried up.

Any species confined to this sort of zone is bound to suffer severely from the radical change in the environment. While we were in and about Rekcha, I got the impression that the local birds must be always on the move in order to survive. Like the sheep in parts of the western United States, they have had to keep on the run in order to find enough grass to eat. Probably the single flock of Spiny Babblers that I saw had a huge territory to cover in order to survive. There may have been quite a number of the birds altogether, but in a few days' time we might never see the same flock twice, so widely would they range.

All this time we were also looking for the Mountain Quail. This should be its home land. The only records for the Mountain Quail, the last dating back to the eighteen-eighties, had been in nearby parts of the Indian hills, in the area of Dehra Dun and Musoorie, two hill stations in the Himalayas near the western Nepal border. I had hopes that the non-appearance of the Mountain Quail near these places might be due to the increased cultivation, burning of the grass-lands, intensified grazing, and other changes in the environment in the Indian hills. I had hoped that the nearby and similar parts of western Nepal would be untouched, but our experience in Rekcha showed me my mistake. The adjacent Nepali hills were just as developed, as opened up to cultivation, as any in India. Nearly a century of prosperity and peace in Nepal under the Rana family had apparently boomed the population tremendously. The annual recruiting program of the Indian and British armies, drawing in thousands of young Nepalis for training in the famous Gurkha battalions, had brought prosperity and wealth to the country, both in the money sent back by the troops and also in the yearly stipend paid to the rulers by the Government at New Delhi. The obvious result had been a great population increase. Nepal now had a population of over seven million. The greatest increase had been in the hill tribes who, being unresistant to malaria, must stay in their hills away from the Terai, and who must cultivate and scratch food and sustenance out of the steep slopes. The result had been a tremendous impoverishment of the soil at altitudes between two and seven thousand feet, where some of the most interesting bird species occurred. We found what must be a fairly recent and drastic change for the worse at these altitudes. Local specialized species must suffer as a result.

Day after day we would go out, sometimes with coolies, at other times just hunting or with local hill trappers. I produced my picture of the Mountain Quail for all to see. We had hired several men along the trail who said they were bird trappers. All claimed to know the "sano kalo titra," as they called it. Several times we staged drives in what I hoped were suitable localities, mostly scrubby hillsides. Thirty or forty coolies would scramble down through the bushes toward us, shouting and beating the boughs and brakes with their long staffs, but no Mountain Quail flew out. For a whole twenty-four hours I was convinced that we had found them in one place where our drive had netted three small birds that flew over my head in a narrow rock cleft where I couldn't get a shot, but a careful stalk the next day produced the only possible bird in the undergrowth there, the common Red-throated Hill Partridge, a bird which in the air overhead looked deceptively small and quail-like. If the Mountain Quail were to exist at all in these hills, I am inclined to feel that it must be very rare and local, for none of our bird trappers secured anything except the same Hill Partridge. Perhaps a well-trained hunting dog might produce something, but a good bird dog was a rarity indeed in India.

My troubles identifying birds were not confined to the Spiny Babbler. Another day Ed came into camp at the end of the morning with a good haul including a tiny tailless warbler, not much bigger than an ordinary spool of thread. He had spent an interminable time hovering around a thick thorny bush before he had finally been able to secure his specimen. One glance at the bird and I became very excited. I was convinced that we had something really new here. With its soft brown upper-parts, chestnut cap, and grayish breast, it seemed to be a good new species of the small wren-warblers, little-known shy birds, the smallest and most difficult to see and study of their kind, but there was no known wren-warbler of just this color scheme. I complimented Ed highly and assured him that we had made a great ornithological coup. It was not until days later that looking over our specimens I realized that my tailless wonder was indeed merely a tailless wonder. Ed had shot the bird's tail off without knowing it. We simply had collected one of the rarer of the widespread small bush-warblers which were shy and hard to find, but otherwise common all up and down the Himalayas. This one was notable simply because the tail happened to be missing.

The days passed swiftly and withal productively in Rekcha. Our camp prospered on the shrine site, our two prayer flags, the United States flag and the National Geographic's insigne, waving happily over all.

IX

More About Hill Birds

EACH EARLY MORNING at Rekcha was a voyage of discovery for us. It was penetratingly cold in the dawn. We would throw on our heaviest clothes and get out of the tents to stand about warming first our fronts, then our backs, at Abdul's cooking fires. One or two coolies would be there, too, crouching as near the flames as they could get, shivering and drawing in long sucking breaths in the cold. Abdul would be bending over his pots, tending our oatmeal as carefully as any alchemist his mysterious brew. Sometimes for variety Dick would cook up some of yesterday's rice, mixed with dried raisins into a sort of rice cake which we would eat with golden syrup. Food, of course, was a constant preoccupation, and most of us felt the lack of fresh meat keenly, but there seemed to be very few if any deer at this altitude and our meat brought up from below soon ran out.

After breakfast we would separate, some to the trap lines, some to photograph or sketch, and Ed and I out in different directions to hunt birds. I soon set out several nets, so that each morning I would have to start off in the same direction, past the village and along the trail up which Dick and I had almost tottered that late afternoon of Christmas Eve. Now it all seemed familiar and well known, but in the early morning it would still be very cold and my bird coolie and I would walk along fast, over the muddy path, ridged and heaved where the frost had frozen it during the night. Just beyond the village was the gap to the north, and here each morning there would be a slightly different vista toward the snow mountains. Some mornings dawn-tinted clouds would be making rapidly around their summits, wreathing them in lengths of pinkish wool mufflers. Other mornings there would be a heavy sullen bank of cloud, dark with bluish and purplish reflections, lowering, foreboding. Then we would know there had been a change of wind and we were in for a cold blow from the northeast. Again the dawn would still be on the peaks, open and clear-cut in the palest of ice-blue skies. Only the lower valleys would be full of cloud, down below us, like a billowy snow field, soft and downy. Then we would be in for a good clear mild day with a warm sun and no wind to speak of.

Just beyond the gap there was an abandoned field full of weeds, and here each day I would flush a party of rose finches, Hodgson's Rose Finch, named for Brian Hodgson. Each day when I flushed the birds, I would look intently to see if any males had appeared. When we first came at Christmas time, there were only females, dull olive-brownish birds, the size and shape of a house sparrow, lightly streaked with brown. But finally on the last day of December, the migrant males had arrived. Two brilliant rose-colored finches flew up into a dead tree along the path as I came by. They were shy and kept a bit separated from the dun-colored females. Evidently the females in this species come first, down from the Siberian steppes and the higher mountains, and the males come by themselves later. Taxonomists have named several geographical subspecies of this Rose Finch, based on the brownness or rich redness of the color of the males, and I was interested much later in the Museum to find that these two males which had flown together into the same tree, which had apparently come together to Rekcha over the hills the night before, represented two different subspecies, the one a resident of the higher mountains of Nepal, the other a winter visitor from Turkestan over a thousand miles away to the northwest.

Farther on, the path became thickly overhung with bushes and scrub, and here I always waited a bit, hoping to hear different bird calls. The dryness and the lack of jungle seemed to force the birds to wander. The same species never turned up two mornings in a row. At this season there were few songs, only chirrups and clucks, for the birds were on their wintering grounds and not thinking yet of breeding. In a hedgerow one morning I waited patiently for half an hour, moving a little at a time, and finally got a glimpse of what, from its tiny size, its erratic movements, and its sharp "tsick" call, I thought must be a wren. But no, it was only another of the little bush-warblers, like Ed's tailless wonder of a few days before. Evidently we were not high enough for the true wrens to appear. Being birds of temperate climates, the wrens in the subtropics are found usually well up in the mountains.

Farther on, I would often hear the same series of chuckles and "teeup, teeup" calls, rather harsh and carrying. This was a flock of Rusty-cheeked Scimitar-babblers, the commonest bird of Rekcha. The scimitar-babbler occurred in a variety of species throughout the Himalayas. The Rusty-cheek was a bold, noisy bird about the size of a thrush, brownish with a dirty whitish throat and underparts and a slash of pale cinamon on the cheeks, neck, and flanks. The bill was thin, yellowish, about an inch and a half long and curved like a sickle. But even though we had collected several of these birds in Rekcha, I always watched the flock anew each time, as the birds hopped about and scratched on the dried leaves, sounding as loud as a family of pheasants. Every so often a strange bird of another species would be in the group, sometimes one of the other smaller scimitar-babblers, sometimes a relative, one of the laughing thrushes. The laughing thrushes were not really thrushes at all, although they were much the same size. They belonged to the family of the babblers, found in Africa and Asia and the East Indies, a great medley of species of all sizes and colors. The laughing thrushes were some of the prettiest and best songsters of the family. Every morning in Rekcha there would be a big flock of the White-throated Laughing Thrushes out on the open fields of the village, wandering about and searching for insects among the shoots of the young upland rice as casually as starlings at home. Then in the thickets I would sometimes hear a series of "churrs" and chuckles, and if I were lucky, be able to stalk a Variegated Laughing Thrush, a brilliantly patterned bird of grays and rusty tints with bold black spots all over.

Each day these thickets would seem to contain something different, sometimes in the underbrush, sometimes in the medium height trees, sometimes in the huge dead snags which rose above the living trees. One day it was a flock of slaty-headed hill parakeets in the dead snag. Another day I saw a single pair of Brown Bulbuls. Again it was a hurrying flock of Black Bulbuls, of which I managed to drop one with a lucky shot as they swept over me. All of these species were most desirable, for we were bound to try to get as great a variety as possible during our brief stay in the western hills.

Finally without further ado we would come to the first bird net, and here each morning there would be suspense and surprise. More often than not there was nothing in the net, but sometimes we would be lucky and find a shy fly-catcher or a tiny warbler, something that I would not be likely otherwise to see. One day there was a hole clean through my small Japanese single-width silk net. Looking carefully on the ground, I found one or two warbler feathers, and decided that some bird of prey, perhaps a falcon or hawk, had dived at the captive bird and carried it off, straight through the meshes. Just as I was examining the net, crouching near the ground, a whole mixed flock of birds came over, traveling through the trees together. I stopped to watch them. Higher up in the tops of the light open pines were minivets, slim long-tailed creatures, the males scarlet and black, the females shades of yellow. With them were white-eyes, little warbler-like fellows, greenish-yellow with a tiny feather eye-ring of white. Also in the party were a pair of small black-and-white woodpeckers, hurrying from tree trunk to tree trunk, swooping down to land fairly well down each one, then swarm up it as fast as possible, so as to hunt for food in the crevices of the bark, but also not to get left out of the flock. A number of green willow-warblers were in the group, a nuthatch or two, and even a dark brown tree-creeper, which, like the woodpeckers, had to hurry twice as fast as the rest in order to get any foraging done in the bark crevices. There was a burst of twittering, with snatches of song, insect-like buzzings, and assorted chatterings and calls as the whole mixed array swept by. For a few moments all was bustle and hustle. Nervous energy was distilled all about. It spilled over in places. The air seemed to be electric with the discharge of so many small dynamos buzzing and bustling through the trees. Another moment and they were gone. The sudden medley of calls stopped as abruptly as they had started and all was silent once again. Such was the progression of a mixed hunting flock of birds, and once gone they seemed to leave a vacuum in their place.

Bird nets were painstaking to man and operate. They should be changed frequently in order to assess the locality. Some places were good, some bad. Only trial and error could tell. I was reluctant, too, to let more than a very few of the coolies know where my nets were placed. It has happened before that bird nets have been robbed in the night by the coolies for food, or sometimes for the reward that usually came when a specimen was brought in by a trapper. In Nepal, however, most of the men seemed to abide by the orthodox Hindu custom of vegetarianism, and furthermore, perhaps because of this, most of our men seemed to be uninterested in trapping for us. So I probably had little to fear from the coolies even though I was very careful. The only birds that were trapped were a few Hill Partridges which were taken by our men as possible Mountain Quail. No smaller birds were ever produced, and only small birds could be caught in these nets.

Finally by eleven o'clock I would turn back toward camp. The heat of the day would be upon us and few birds were still singing or calling or moving about. Only an occasional hawk or serpent eagle could be seen, usually far too high to shoot, or perhaps one of the long-tailed Red-billed Blue Magpies, would sail out from a higher tree across one of the miniature valleys to another tree equally high.

The return to camp was always exciting. There was always suspense to see what others had found, whether birds or mammals, but mostly it was birds. Rekcha was a poor place for small mammals. I supposed it was the dryness which had forced them down to somewhat lower altitudes, or perhaps they didn't fancy the baits of the traps. Much research went into the business of proper baits. In some areas rats and mice would take only fruit. In other places seeds mixed with peanut butter would be acceptable. Dick and Howie were not really experienced in this, especially in Far Eastern rat and mouse foods, and their ingenuity was severely taxed. My experience was limited, for I had never been a mammal collector, and so I was merely the blind leading the blind. Ed would often find quite different birds from mine, wandering over different paths, encountering different species. Sometimes, though, we would both come back with identical new birds, birds that so far neither of us had seen around Rekcha, showing that we were both catching part of a "wave" that had come in during the previous night.

Then would come a busy hour before lunch, cataloguing and going over specimens, checking over some photographic plan of Kurt's, perhaps discussing food. Food was a never-ending problem. Mostly it was the coolies' food that I worried about. Even though we were short of meat, we at least had plenty of tinned vegetables, soups, biscuit-mixes, pudding desserts, and similar sorts of dried stuffs. We could after all survive, but the coolies' food was a continuous burden. The villages of these hills were so impoverished that there was very little if any food for sale. We had brought up rice, dried split peas, "dal," as it was called, and flour, "atta." Our little Gurkha boy, Bagam, from Calcutta, was the official dispenser of these three staples each evening to the hungry line. In spite of his stern ministrations, we soon found our precious hoard, so laboriously carried up, so carefully apportioned and estimated in advance, dwindling seriously; and here was the nub of our logistic problem. Having arrived at Rekcha after so much effort, we knew that we should have to camp for at least a week before we could find out whether the place was really suitable collecting country. Meanwhile we could not let all our coolies leave us for fear of being stranded. There were no men to spare in the hills, no extra coolies to replace the ones we might release. As a result, we had to pay and to feed all our coolies every day full rations even though most of them were doing nothing for us. After a few days we realized that, though Rekcha was not an ideal collecting station, it was probably as far as we should be able to go. Our coolies traveled so slowly that it would take us days to go down the deep declivity that Dick had seen east of Rekcha, reach the bank of the Karnali again, cross it once more, and climb up to the next range of hills which might well, from the look of them, be just as dry as the one we were on; and all the time we should be on the move, unable to do any proper collecting.

Meanwhile what to do about our dwindling supplies for the coolies? They seemed to eat far more than even our careful estimating had indicated. The available surplus food for sale in Rekcha was exhausted in one purchase. We could get only enough for one full day's supply for the men. The old crone supplied this herself, telling us at the same time that, by order of the Maharajah, these hill villages were allowed to sell only one day's food to visitors. If this was true, it was a wise law to prevent overeager villagers trying to make a quick profit to their own eventual detriment. With Abdul and Bagam I planned to send out small parties of coolies in two directions. Bagam should take one, our little subofficial the other. To each I gave a piece of paper on which I had first written in English my request that the Headman of the village to be visited should sell us food. Bagam would cover the rest of the sheet with his own free Nepali interpretation of what I had said. I suspected him of embroidering my words, invoking the wrath of the Maharajah and other fell devices to eke out his prestige on these jaunts, but I never inquired too closely. Abdul told me that Bagam was using these documents to exalt himself sufficiently in the villages to achieve certain conquests with the local ladies. I taxed Bagam with this, but he denied it so vociferously and blushed so deeply that I hastily dropped the subject. Off he would go with his men in one direction, and the other party in the other. Each would be armed with thirty or forty Indian rupees, for Indian money was at a premium in the hills away from Katmandu. The next day about evening they would come back, usually with nearly a day's supply of more food, sometimes of rice, sometimes of dal, occasionally potatoes. Flour was unprocurable in the inner hills and valleys. After two of these jaunts, the men had to go even farther, so that it would be an overnight affair. I could see that this was a scheme of dwindling returns. We could not continue to supply our men in this fashion.

As we began to use up our own food and ammunition, I could at last get rid of a few of the coolies. One man fell ill and broke out with sores all over his legs. Him I sent away with a little food and money, down to the lower villages. Neither Ed, the official medicine man, nor I could diagnose his trouble. It seemed to be a severe sort of ringworm. Ed was always taking care of minor ailments. Fortunately we had no major ones. Everyone seemed very healthy in the hills, and luckily none of us fell ill. In Katmandu there was a small hospital with an Indian doctor in charge. I had asked him once what sort of cases he treated mostly. According to him the majority of his patients had broken limbs. Some had tuberculosis. When I asked if there were not lots of other diseases he replied:

"Oh, yes, there are, of course. But we never get them. People with serious diseases naturally die before they get to a doctor or a hospital."

So in the hills we never saw any sick people, except the occasional man like my coolie with sores on his legs. The others with serious trouble had presumably died. That may be one reason why everyone seemed so healthy. There were no others in this sort of mediaeval life. Only the strong could survive its rigors.

Afternoons there would often be some picture project. Kurt was very anxious to take lots of portraits of the local people. Most of these were willing enough to pose, but the younger ones, especially little girls like the old woman's granddaughter, were very shy, giggling and wriggling behind their shawls. For cases like this Kurt had a puppet, a rubber monkey fitted like a glove which he could manipulate on one hand while he held his Leica with the other. Another effective stunt was a series of tricks, the best a big handkerchief which turned from pink to pale green as it was passed through the hand. Two or three passes with this and the crowd would be awestruck and standing close around.

Our coolies and the villagers liked my radio, too, a power-

Fording the Karnali River we used dugouts and crossed amidst a great throng of hill men on their annual migration to the plains.

The days passed productively in Rekcha. Our camp prospered on the shrine site, our two "prayer flags" waving happily over all.

ful short-wave receiving set, that I had thought would be fun to take along for occasional news. Actually I was in a minority here. None of the rest of the group seemed to enjoy the news at all and to a great extent I agreed with them. Most news seemed decidedly fatuous up here in the hills, in the shadow of the immense indifferent snow peaks. With the music it was different. Loud blaring Indian music with high nasal vocal accompaniment fascinated the simple villagers and the coolies. As far as we could tell, they knew the music was their kind of music, although far more sophisticated than the sort they could produce. Apparently they could not overcome the mental hurdle of deciphering the words issuing from the black box. They knew they were listening to a voice singing words, but they made no more effort to understand than most people do with opera. Once or twice I asked some of the crowd where they thought the music was coming from. Sometimes there would be no answer, just shakes of the head, twisting of the hands, and standing on one foot and then the other. Most of them apparently thought it was a trick, that as the box was too small to have a person concealed in it, perhaps there was someone hiding in one of the tents. One coolie actually said "Hindustan," India, when questioned, but I thought it was because he had heard the words of the songs and knew they were in Hindustani, not that he had plumbed the secrets of the other.

For the photographers we had to do a great deal of posing. Sometimes it was a group activity like eating. We would sit about at our little collapsible table in the sun, pausing over lunch, while Kurt or Francis staggered up and down a nearby hill, overburdened with cameras, tripods, and various impedimenta, trying to get us and the whole tent camp into an acceptable panorama. Another time it would be a bit of staged business. Ed would pose in a tent near his medicine chest ministering to the imaginary ailments of one of the coolies, wrapping his arm over and over with yards of superfluous bandage. One afternoon we staged one of the beats for the Mountain Quail, pausing first to line up the grinning coolies while I made vigorous pantomime to show them where to go after exhibiting the drawing that I had brought along of the mysterious little bird, then distance shots and close-ups of the men charging down hill through the brush. Each one of our activities was tabulated and recorded in this way, often at very considerable expense of time and effort in order to show readers of the *National Geographic Magazine* and movie audiences something of what we actually did on such a trip. I had not realized before, until Kurt and Francis demonstrated it to us, how engrossing and time-consuming this job of making a photographic coverage of the expedition could be.

In the early afternoon there would always be much writing-up of catalogues and labels to be done. In addition, it was usually the only feasible time for a bath, and one or the other of us would stand behind the little walled shrine away from the curious eyes of the village, and lave himself with hot water, heated in kerosene tins by Abdul and Rao over the fire. In the middle of the day it was warm, even hot at Rekcha, but by three-thirty a chill came into the air, and even before we went out in the late afternoon we would have to put on heavy underwear and an extra sweater.

The last part of the afternoon was a final hunt or sometimes a beat by the coolies. The beats netted us nothing but Hill Partridges which were welcome for the good curry they made. Twice we missed getting a barking deer, the only species of deer seen in these hills. The first of them came down right toward me on one of the beats, stepping gingerly, moving without a sound. It was a solidly built animal, about the size of a big Labrador Retriever with slender tapering legs. I had heard them several times in the forest. Their alarm call, a dog-like "grr-ow," snapping sharp at the end like a bark, would ring out often across the hills, especially in the evening. I didn't see the little deer until it was very close, so close that as I raised my shotgun to fire, it caught the movement and sprinted off before I could aim. The second deer treated Ed the same way on another beat. We saw no more and so got no meat.

The late afternoon, if the wind was not blowing, had an especial charm for hunting. Birds and animals were on the move, and if I could get far enough out from Rekcha and find some vantage-point, new species could often be seen. One afternoon I found a small hidden saucer-like depression on the side of the mountain. From the top the path looked down upon a miniature alpine valley full of coarse grass, obviously a swamp in wet weather. The sides were clothed with wild ginger, and ferns covered the talus of rock shale where one or two small landslips had occurred. Higher up there was tall grass and huge isolated pines, their ragged branches etched against the background of farther hills and sky. There was utter quiet as I crept to a rock and sat crouched at the top of the slope looking down; but even in the quiet there was a feeling of suppressed movement. Animals and birds were there, looking about, measuring every step with cunning caution, moving downward to water or fresh grass or insect horde for the evening feeding.

The first thing I saw was a female kaleej pheasant, dun brown, moving slowly step by step across the trail where a few momonets before I had stepped so carefully myself. She was out of gunshot, and any movement of mine would have revealed me to her. She went on down, picking her way delicately and with care. After a time I heard a lisping suspicion of a sound and another moment revealed a whole flock of miniature Red-capped Tits, the smallest of the tit or chickadee family, tiny buzzing creatures that traveled continuously, flowing like a stream through the low trees and undergrowth. They chittered by, making a series of small notes and calls, and were gone as quickly as they had came. Two or three Grass-warblers succeeded them, skulking about down below the path in the tall yellow grass. They came near and hiked themselves up to the very tops of the grass stems to get a better look, swaying back and forth, their warbler-sized bodies balanced by an impossibly long tail held at a rakish angle. Finally they, too, disappeared, dropping to the base of the grass stems effortlessly. A few "tee-up" calls came from above where a scimitar-babbler was scratching in the brush, and then silence, and I realized that already it was late, the sun had left the hidden valley and was turning the tops of the pines orange-red, lighting them like flambeaux.

I was about to stand up when I heard what sounded like the discreet cough of a character on the stage who wants to interrupt the speaker. I had heard such a cough once before at night in the hills of Ceylon and I knew what it meant. The noise carried some distance. I turned my head slowly and glanced along the edge of the farther ridge of the valley seventy-five yards away. Two of us had been watching the little valley. As I looked, the leopard left his vantage-point and moved soundlessly down into the bush, and now a barking deer in the grass below had evidently heard the coughing sound, for he gave his sharp "grr-ow" alarm call, stamped his hoof, and moved off down the slope rolling pebbles under him and calling at intervals. The whole little world below seemed to be aroused, and in a moment there was a chorus of bird calls that must have represented twenty species. For a moment they called, and then all was quiet again, and strain as I could, there was no more sound to trace the passage of the leopard and his quarry.

I picked up my shotgun and hurried back toward camp in the chill dusk, anxious to get to Rekcha before dark, but sunk in a sort of satisfied contemplation of that panorama of life in the little hidden valley. Such moments were in a way the most welcome, the most fulfilling, of our journey in these unknown hills.

New Year's Day came and went with the realization that we should never find the Mountain Quail in the West Nepal hills, but also with the pleasure and the accomplishment of having found the Spiny Babbler. By that day I decided that we must return to the duns and back down the Karnali. The daily trips to outlying villages by our coolies under Bagam were yielding less food than the effort of the trip was worth. Also I began to suspect that our small friend was profiting on the side from being entrusted with my diminishing stock of Indian rupees. The little official, too, seemed to have made off with some money, although these things were hard to prove. I did find him out in one item of two rupees, but having actually found this out, I had no doubt that more serious peccadilloes lay undiscovered. We had by now gotten several hundred important bird specimens and a good haul of mammals. We had all the pictures we needed. To get up to a higher altitude collecting station would take at least a week of travel, and we lacked the necessary food and supplies. We had done our task and might as well return.

These thoughts were passing through my mind when an event happened which would have forced us to return in any case. We were just finishing dinner on New Year's Day, the usual late Abdul-served dinner, and drinking a toast to 1949 in the last of our Christmas brandy, when a sudden unexpected glow lit up the inside of the dining tent. It was coming from outside. There was no moment for thought. We simply reacted automatically. We burst as one man through the tent flaps and round the corner. A dreadful sight met our eyes. The tent in which Kurt and Francis slept, the tent with all their film and camera equipment was a solid mass of yellow flame. It had happened so quickly that even Rao and Abdul outside by the cooking fire had not yet reacted. As one again we burst through the flames into the interior of the tent. The material of the tent itself was burning so rapidly that nothing in it was yet afire, although the heat seemed intense. We simply walked through the burning fabric and went on out the other side where by now there was no side wall, carrying with us the two cots and whatever boxes we could seize. We stamped on the stuff underfoot, putting out what was left of the ground sheet, and in a few minutes it was all over. The tent had burnt almost completely in under one minute except for the dew-damp parts of the ground sheet. Saturated as it was with its protective waterproofing, the light fabric simply went up like a piece of paper soaked in kerosene, and yet out of this holocaust we rescued everything, even the boy's clothes. One or two things, a sleeping bag, a sweater, and a few other odds and ends, were singed. The camera and films by a miracle were completely unhurt. It was a hectic few minutes before we were able to take stock of what the damage actually was aside from the tent.

Meanwhile their cots had to be moved into the dining tent and things rearranged for the night. The culprit was a naked candle which one of them had foolishly left exposed in the tent in spite of previous warnings. The affair taught us a lesson. We realized more than ever the problem of heat and light in these flimsy tents, which by their very lightness had become so inflammable. It was imperative now to go back to the Terai where we had an extra tent cached with our stock of food and provisions. We were a sober group when we finally turned in that first night of 1949. There was no use even contemplating what might have happened had that valuable equipment or our specimens been lost.

The next day we rose even earlier than usual, and packed up camp in what seemed record time. The coolies had been alerted the night before, and the fire had made them more prompt and willing. Perhaps, too, the sight of dwindling supplies of food had made an impression. They seemed eager to take their loads and set off. Even Abdul for once needed little if any prompting to get us breakfast. All our own men had hated the cold nights of Rekcha, and had complained of the frost and damp. We could certainly not blame them, for their tent, which was of the same material as ours, lacked a ground sheet and so was inevitably colder. None of them had ever been as high in the hills before, or had felt such cold. However, their lot was immeasurably better, with their woolen clothes which I had bought for them in Calcutta, compared to the ragged coolies who slept for the most part in the open under crude bough shelters around a fire. A few of the coolies had been allowed by the old crone to take over the outhouse where Dick and I had tried not to suffocate on Christmas Eve, but I hardly envied them.

Now, however, all this was behind us as we handed the rolled-up tents to the waiting coolies, and Abdul tied the rope around his box of pots and pans. By nine-thirty we were off westward along the ridge to where we had heard there was a good trail down to a village called Bajora at the foot of the plateau on the way back to the Karnali River. It was a clear bright morning as the last of us wrapped up our "prayer flags" which we had taken down from the poles over the shrine to which they had been fastened. The old lady of Rekcha and her little granddaughter smiled and waved at us from their porch as we turned away across the fields. A gathering of larks took wing in front of us and rose in a body into the sky with shrill "tseep" calls, then like a dust devil picked up by a breeze hurtled off toward some unknown group of paddy fields over the ridge. How I wished that they and all the other birds that coursed so easily over these ridges and hills could speak to me and tell me if the little Mountain Quail somewhere still scuttled through the long grass.

X

The Road Back

WE WERE A GOOD FOUR HOURS getting off the Rekcha plateau. We scrabbled down through the oaks, finally leaving them behind after two thousand feet of descent. Then we were in thicker deciduous trees, and little streamlets and springs appeared. The birds also changed. We left our friends the scimitar-babblers and came to a grove where I saw a Traill's Oriole, maroon and black, a lowland jungle bird. It always was an astonishing thing to me how swiftly one zone could be left and another reached in the course of a single day's march. Going up, the lowland jungle birds pretty well disappeared at three thousand feet and a whole new fauna came in along with the changes in the shrubs and trees. I found, too, that these changes varied with the locality. In the western Himalayas where the climate was drier, the altitudinal zones were more widely spaced. In the eastern Himalayas, where it was very much damper and the rainfall heavy, the zones were more condensed. Higher-altitude birds descended lower, and the lower-zone birds were more confined, less spread out in their range. Probably this was due to the richer and more varied environment in a humid area with its greater food supply.

Some species, however, spanned several zones. A barking

deer called just before we reached the long narrow clearing of Bajora. The village was like Guttu, an irregular rectangular space full of paddy fields on the flat at the base of the plateau from which we had descended. In the center was a cluster of thatched huts raised off the ground on high platforms. Each platform had an open porch in front to which a ladder led — a notched tree trunk. Clusters of people sat about on the porches talking indolently. They stopped as we came by, but said nothing, simply stared at us. The inevitable troops of little boys appeared and came near, staring. We looked for a head man or some elder in authority and one was finally produced. He came down backwards off the platform of a larger house, his bare toes and feet gripping the notches as easily as hands. When he turned about, I saw that he was wearing a ragged jacket with brass buttons. It was an old tunic of one of the Gurkha battalions of the Indian Army. He was short and bandy-legged, a typical Gurkha with wide-open round brown face and sparkling eyes. He marched over to us, drew himself up, and swung with a snap into the Indian Army salute. We shook hands and I asked him what regiment he had been in.

"Fourth Gurkhas, Sahib. I was a Havildar" (a non-commissioned rank).

"Where did you serve?" Francis asked.

It turned out the Havildar had been in Italy in 1944. Wonder of wonders, in 1944 he had been riding around the Italian front in jeeps and trucks. Now he was back in the jungle in bare feet and a breechclout, only his ragged jacket with its buttons left to tell the tale. Furthermore, he seemed to have no regrets. He was a merry soul, and only drew a long face when we asked about rice or other food.

There was nothing in the village, he said. The people had enough for themselves, no more. We would need at least eighty pounds of rice or potatoes for our men and there was no such amount to spare.

"Any chickens?" I asked. As usual, we were out of meat, and we were all tired of vegetable curries.

A good deal of questioning ensued, and finally it was announced that for four rupees we could have one of the scrawny roosters running about. The price seemed reminiscent of wartime Italy, and I wondered, but decided that it simply indicated the people didn't want to sell. After some further haggling, I paid. We rounded up the coolies who had a tendency to hobnob, and swung on out of Bajora into the surrounding jungle, Abdul carrying our prize under one arm.

The lowland jungle of the duns was full of huge trees. I measured one sal tree that was twelve feet in circumference six feet above the ground, and it was a clean straight trunk. These were the original, the primeval trees which must once have clothed the whole sweep of the Himalayan foothills from Sikkim to Kashmir, and now they were gone except for hidden places such as this, and no man would see their like again. It was in these huge groves that we found the Great Slaty Woodpecker, the largest and most impressive woodpecker in Asia. Their loud-ringing, yarruping calls had a tremendous range, but they were very shy. I have seen these birds only in the biggest forest, which means, I suppose, that like our Ivory-billed Woodpecker in America they will become increasingly scarce, perhaps extinct, as those patches of great trees disappear.

In addition to the sal, we recognized "sihsum," *Dalbergia sissoo*, and "jamun," *Eugenia jambolana*, all of them and several others too good lumber trees. We wondered how long it would be before concessions would be let out to the Indian timber companies to fell these forests. The Nepal Government has prospered mightily in the past from its lumber concessions, where nearly thirty dollars in tax is paid by the companies for each big tree.

Another hour brought us out on the shining white sand banks of the Karnali, running swiftly here without a sound, a limpid emerald green. There was no ford, and we followed a beaten path in the sand which wandered along the bank downstream. Another hour or so over rock cliffs and more stretches of yielding sand brought us, hot and tired, out through a patch of scrub onto the sand bank again. Here was the ford, an unnamed place, just a stretch of calm water above a long rapid. The men who made their living along the Karnali were a special subcaste of boatmen. It was said that during the off season they extracted gold from the sand, but now was the season for the migration of the hill men, and the northern shore was crammed with men waiting to cross on their way down to the Indian plains. As we came out, we were surrounded by a curious throng of these men, most of whom had apparently been waiting their chance for days to cross the river in one of the two long dugout canoes, made from single tree logs which the boatmen had brought to the ford. There must have been three or four hundred people on the bank or camping in the shrubbery at the forest edge, mostly men in small family or clan groups with a number of boys and a very few women. These were the men who would go on down to Kauriala Ghat at the Indian border, after exchanging for money whatever they could at some Nepali trading market in the Terai, board the train, and strike out for a three-month winter job with a lumber firm or at some port, and then return in the spring with just enough money to buy a few pots or pans for their wives or a length or two of cloth. This huge migration in and out of the hills was one of the two most surprising things to us about West Nepal. The other was the intensity of the cultivation up into the hills with the great clearing of the original forest land. Even in remote Nepal the Nepalis themselves were increasing at a great rate and opening up their own country to an extent as disastrous as in the neighboring Himalayan hills in Kumaon, Garwhal, and on up to Kashmir.

We strode forward and found the head man of the boatmen who was resting himself at a small thatched building which had been put up on the sand as a headquarters for these men. It seemed to be some sort of tavern as well, for bamboo containers of a rather dubious-looking liquor were being ladled out to the bystanders. After some conversation the head man agreed to ferry all our party including the forty coolies across the river for four rupees, the same price we had paid for the chicken dinner. We drew off a bit and sat on the bank to eat our Indian bread-and-cheese lunch and await the coolies, who as usual were bringing up the rear.

Meanwhile we watched the life of the river. Along the bank near where the dugout canoes would land stood a crowd of men fully prepared with packs on their backs for the next arrival of one of the canoes. As the dugout returned from the farther shore, the crowd would bunch up and we could hear the loud talk of the men even above the roar of the rapids downstream. When the canoe actually touched the shore, a great hubbub would arise. All the men tried to push each other at once, elbowing out those to one side and getting in the best position to step into the canoe. With their heavy packs this was not easy. The canoe men would spring ashore and try to hold the men back with their paddles. No actual blows were struck, but the altercations were violent, and I never could see how it was all arranged. Certainly this was no meek queuing-up system, but a rough-and-tumble catch-as-catch-can. Finally the canoe would be loaded and shoved off, often with great difficulty and straining as some of the bystanders were pressed into service, and would start back across, shooting downstream at a great rate in the process.

Where we had seen only female Mergansers on the way up the river at Chisapani, now in early January the males with their green heads and white bodies had arrived. A whole group of mixed male and female Goosanders, as the Common Merganser is called, swept upstream low over the water. I fired at them, but they were some distance away and my shot had no effect. The noise delighted the hill men, several of whom leaped up and down with excitement like children. Two kinds of cormorants also flew by, and these, too, we fired at, more for amusement than anything else, as they were out of range. The noise of the shots would bounce off the cliffs across the river and echo back from the forest on our side in a most satisfactory way. Each time the hill men would cheer and some would jump up with shouts of glee.

It was interesting to notice the clothes of these hill men. Those from only a few thousand feet up wore loincloths as did our coolies, with the round Nepali cloth cap, a shirt of sorts, and a shawl draped over the shoulders. Those from very high up, perhaps twelve thousand feet or more, had complete trousers as well as shirts, made from their own homespun goat wool, gray in color, occasionally with a simple dark brown stripe. In addition they had the caps and large woolen blankets thrown over one shoulder like a Mexican serapé. Some of the men even had woolen puttee-like strips wound around the legs and crude sandals with a skin sole and wool uppers. They were invariably ragged, but far more heavily dressed than our men. From still higher up, the Nepalis began to be dressed like Tibetans. These people wore wool clothes, dyed purplish-red in Tibetan style, often the loose tunic, full-length coat, and Tibetan cloth boots. There was a perfect transition in the crowd, from those in true Nepali hill costume to those in true Tibetan clothes. Grouped in with the latter were a number of real Tibetans, recognizable by their flatter more Mongoloid features as well as the fact that most of these were lamas. We questioned several of the lamas, and found that, like my friend from downstream, they came from monasteries in the vicinity of Kailas, the sacred mountain by Lake Manasarowar, the great shrine of western Tibet, somewhere between twelve and sixteen marches north along the Karnali and over the passes. They reported that the passes were already covered with snow and ice and that travel was difficult and would be impossible after the next storm.

As we stood talking to some of these men, I heard a murmur and laughter behind me and turned around. There was a crowd of Nepalis behind me and they had pushed forward one of their number who was unusually tall. He was standing as close to me as he dared and comparing his height with mine. The top of his head came up to about my chin, and as I am six feet three and a half inches, he was a very tall man for one of his race. I turned around, lifted my arm from the shoulder and passed it over his head, at which there was a great shout of laughter, and he retired somewhat discomfited. Just then another shout came from near the river and we all turned and ran down to look where a boy was pointing at the water. On the surface twenty yards out, we could see two huge backs of fish finning just under the water. They were mahseer, the famous fighting carp of the rivers of southern Asia, huge fellows, probably running upward of sixty or seventy pounds. Howie ran for his fishing kit which he carried with him near the rivers. We had met Colonel Macdonald, the famous authority on mahseer fishing in Calcutta, and he had lent Howie some of his spoons and thin wire leaders. The fish sank below the surface and disappeared, but Howie went off downstream and cast into the head of the rapids, a favored spot. Meanwhile the rest of us waited for the coolies to arrive. After half an hour, as the first coolies began to come in, Howie returned definitely chagrined.

"There went the Colonel's spoon," he said, ruefully holding up the severed wire leader for our inspection. "I never felt a thing, except the line got lighter. It must have been *some* fish!"

By this time the afternoon was waning and I was anxious to get our men over the river. We loaded up the canoes with group after group of our men, six to a canoe, and Ed and Dick went on ahead to walk along the trail with the first coolies and pick out a camp site. Finally we got them all across, and Kurt and I came last in the gloaming. We plunged into the trees on the farther bank and hurried along the trail, here trodden into dust by many feet. Another mile and we glimpsed the twinkling fires of our camp, snug in a glade among the trees, the tents already going up and water heating for tea. It looked welcome and inviting. The air at this altitude seemed positively balmy after the chill of Rekcha in the hills above. We could hardly believe that we had walked through such a transition in one day.

Abdul fiddled over our dinner as usual, but after all he had a fowl to fiddle over. We would have a good curry by the time he was through, but when it came to the coolies' food, we were faced with a dilemma. There was a half-day's ration of rice all round, no more. I suggested that the men try some of our dehydrated vegetables, but the spokesmen who came for the rations every evening refused. As Hindus, they were not in favor of eating the food of casteless persons. For all they knew there might be a bit of beef or at least beef grease in it. The Indian Mutiny of 1857 had started with just such a mix-up between Hindu soldiers and the grease-coated bullets of the Englishmen from across the sea, the "Black Water." In those days the soldiers were trained to nip off the outer jacket of the bullet with their teeth before loading. I did not press the point when the men drew away.

"Well, tell them I am very sorry," I said to Bagam. "They know well that we have tried to get rice and potatoes and other food at these villages. There is no help for it. Tell them to divide up all the food that is left. That will have to do until we can get down to the Terai and get more."

We had enough rice for our own men, a small amount that I had bought for our use. All of them, even Bagam the Gurkha, would eat tinned stuff as well. I lectured them about conserving food. Our own supply now consisted of one small wooden box with a residue of all our tins in it. We had run out of sugar and jam and meats long ago. We had no more butter, and our powdered coffee was running low. We would have to give up coffee except for breakfast. No one grumbled. The example of our coolies, with their simple fare being down to half rations, was too much in the foreground. I thought to myself rather grimly that tomorrow would be a tough evening for all of us when the coolies gathered over their cooking fires to boil water and nothing else.

The next day dawned mistily as it so often did in the jungle. There was a constant dripping from the trees onto the tents as if it was raining. At first everyone thought it was rain, but it was just the usual heavy dew. We all coughed and choked with the damp in our throats, and at breakfast it sounded as if we had heavy head colds. Our rather discreet coughings, however, were as nothing to the coolies, who had chosen to settle very close to the tents. They had talked late into the night as was their custom. Then some of them always seemed to be waking up during the night and calling in loud tones. Their sleep seemed to be far less continuous than ours, more like that of a dog or even a bird which will sleep for a while and then wake again, then sleep, then wake. In between there were great snorings or the yells of sudden nightmares, and of course they all woke far earlier than we did, and started laughing and talking as they lit their fires and went off for water. I vowed we would make sure that our two camps were well separated the next night.

In the dripping mist we sat still over our precious coffee at our folding table while the men packed away the wet tents all around us.

"Let's get the show on the road," I said, for with our example the men would never start. I felt in that moment the rest hated me for it. So at times it must be. Someone has to take the initiative. Someone has to hurry the rest on. I felt often like one of those bullying top sergeants and I realized, too, how much bluff went into the business. No one would rather dawdle of a morning than I.

We set off at last, myself at the rear, having waited until the final coolie struggled off under his load. I liked walking at the end of the line. Only far at the end or far out at the beginning of the coolies was there any chance of seeing anything, and in a way it was better at the end of a line because no one would catch up with you if you stopped for a spot of hunting.

In the early morning the mist along the river was particularly fascinating. It lay heavy among the trees and along the banks, softening the angular lines of the branches as in a snowstorm. Overhead there was no ceiling. We were solidly bedded down in one of those blankets of cotton wool that we had seen every morning looking down from the plateau at five thousand feet into the Karnali Valley below. Skeins of the mist snaked along the surface of the water where it ran smooth. The water seemed to steam. All color was gone. There were simply tones of white and gray and black. The coolies walking ahead of me along the trail or along the sand by the river seemed to dance in and out of the mist like wraiths. A faint, a very faint, breeze came through the trees, whispering softly in die-away tones, and carried on the breeze I could just hear the mournful "kee-ow, kee-ow" of a Hill barbet somewhere above us and far away. It was the cry of a lost soul, lost in this world of grayness. We seemed to be in a spell, halfway between sleeping and waking. There was no reality to this world of mist. We were enchanted.

We plodded on through the sand. We were out on the bank now and the sand was white like snow and very soft. It was tiring going. No more birds called. No birds flew. Only the rushing of the river, the faint noise of the wind and the crunching underfoot broke the utter stillness. I wondered if we had ever waked at all this morning, or if I were dreaming all this.

Then shouts came from ahead. I went forward quickly to find a log jam among the coolies where they were stopped by the narrowing of the bank and a short piece of steep cliff down which they would have to climb. Packs were lowered first, then handholds made with sticks driven into holes in the soft mixture of clay and rock, and the men went down one after the other. The place was slippery and treacherous from the damp mist. The loose soil quickly turned to mud after a few men had gone down. We all slipped and slid without a fall, and went on across the sand once more.

Meanwhile the sun had pierced through the fog. The mist vanished, rolling up along the top of the water as if it were being swept away with an invisible broom. The sun sparkled on the water, blue now and tipped with patches of white foam in the rapids like a meringue. The trees stood out green and glistening. We strode on into another mood, another world of color and brightness. In a moment we were all chatting and smiling, and it seemed to me that suddenly the thickets were full of bird calls.

So it often was in the jungle. There were mornings when everything seemed to awake slowly, in a trance. Then, when the sun finally broke through, there would be a glorious fresh interlude for a measurable time, when everything twinkled and was dewy and the birds sang, but after this interval, the sun waxed too strong. The life went out of everything. The birds stopped calling. The trees hung lank and limp in the dry air, or else a breeze came up, fresh at first, but soon hot and dry with an insistent burning quality. Then the brightness was too bright, and so for the long hours until late afternoon everything slept, except ourselves, that is, for we plodded on through it all feeling hot and tired. Only near the river, near the actual water's edge, did it seem cool. Here the hot breeze had a tinge of moisture to it, and so by lunch time we would sit on the rocks, often with our bare feet in the chill water, drinking in the freshness and coolness of it all, watching the water cascading down the long flumes of the rapids, rippling over the shallow stones, or sweeping with a smooth ribbon-like flow down the deeper channel. Occasional birds shared the rocks with us, a greenshank or common sandpiper sometimes, more often a White-crowned Redstart, a thrush-like bird black and dull red with a silver crown. Sometimes a smaller Blue Redstart would perch on a rock near us, watching for water insects, bobbing its tail up and down slowly with an intense, compressed preoccupation.

After lunch we rested, then walked on again, leaving the bank and striking inland through heavy jungle. We were well along when on a sudden I heard a great noise of chopping and saw some light ahead. To our surprise we came out on a clearing where a group of Indian workmen, Punjabis by the look of them, were busily sawing the branches off several huge trunks of sal that had been felled. We had reached the outposts, the edge of the lumber invasion. The workmen looked at us in a measured, sullen way which suddenly reminded me that we were in Nepal where the Nepali people tend to smile and laugh. I had already forgotten how glum Indians could be. We walked on. I hated to see the coming of the lumber people. Year by year they would reach farther up the river valleys above the Terai, spreading and filtering northward along the river bottoms like an incubus, and yet nothing could stop their advance. No hint of future disaster could prevent the destruction of the forests. "Après moi, le déluge," said Louis Quinze. "These things will not happen in our time," said the Great Ones in Katmandu.

At least the presence of the workmen meant that somewhere ahead there might be a headquarters and a storehouse. We hurried on. Three or four more miles and we came to a clearing in the forest where two large newly constructed thatch huts stood. Outside, looking rather incongruous in the jungle, were three charpoys, the Indian string beds, covered with carpet, and here several industrious babus in dhotis, dark jackets, and white Gandhi caps were busy inscribing long rows of figures in huge ledgers. The Dhansing Lumber Company was alert and functioning even at its farthest outpost.

An elegantly laundered gentleman in a crisp white dhoti approached us buttoning his fitted tunic and adjusting his cap. We felt like ragamuffins by contrast, but our new friend smiled and greeted us warmly, saying that he had heard of the American doctors who had ventured into the hills. He was from Lucknow, he said, from the office of the lumber company and what could he do for us? I explained our need for food for the coolies. Mr. Datta was most helpful, and in no time a full "maund" (eighty pounds) of flour of good quality was produced, which I bought on the spot for forty rupees. Although the coolies usually made a fuss and balked when presented with a heavy load, there was no such problem this time. Several coolies rushed forward to redivide their loads and compete for the pleasure of carrying the eighty pounds of their night's dinner. The relief was tremendous. We all swept on down the trail gaily, delighted at the thought that there would be food for everyone tonight. As a parting present Mr. Datta gave us some oranges, small tangerines from the hills, of delicious flavor. It had been one of our disappointments at Rekcha that none of this hill fruit was available, although there were trees about. The local season had been just over, and these fruits must have come from a good bit higher up.

After that we were never far away from lumber people all the way back to the Terai. We passed small groups of the Punjabi workmen on the trail, marching north with their axes and huge hand saws. Occasionally we passed groups of supervisors or spotters, engaged in surveying the forest and picking out especially fine trees. Most of this lumber, the best in Asia, would go for railway sleepers, we were told. It seemed appalling waste to use this wood for sleepers, the way fine mahogany is often used in Latin America for the same purpose. That night we slept in the forest, this time with full rations of food for all. The next day we climbed over the last few outlying hills and reached Chisapani safe again. There was no food for us here, and no elephants or bullock carts, for that matter, but in another day's march we had come back again to Tikapur on the lower edge of the Terai Forest. Here a Nepali subedar or minor official was waiting for us with two elephants and the bullock carts and our precious cache of food and extra gear. We got out a small tent for Kurt and Francis and an extra cot, for one of theirs had been broken during the hasty exodus from the burning tent.

The elephants were welcome. With a few Tharus to help, we staged a beat and luckily Ed shot a small sambhar, the Indian representative of the elk family. Now we could feast on meat. In addition, we shot peafowl and junglefowl so that our larder was well replenished. There were tiger about and it was reported that one had killed the bullock of a Tharu not long before. All of us were keen to see and perhaps have a shot at a tiger, but here we ran into a snag. Foreseeing the possibility of coming across a tiger or leopard during our hunting in the Terai, I had made a point of saying to General Bijaya in Katmandu that we should like it stated in our letters to the Governors of the outlying districts that we were free to shoot such beasts should we meet them. It seemed well to be specific in a country where tigers were reserved for shooting by the family of the King or Maharajah.

For years past it had been the custom of the Maharajah to stage a winter shoot in some part of the Terai to which the current Viceroy of India with his house party would be invited. For these royal shoots fifty or sixty young buffaloes would be tethered out ahead of time in a wide area of the Terai jungle, with Tharus to watch them. A huge tent city would be erected in the vicinity to which special roads would be constructed, and a large stable of elephants assembled. As soon as a young buffalo was killed, the elephants would be off to make a ring around the nearby thickets where the tiger, gorged with his meal, would be lying up. Once the tiger was located and a nearly solid surrounding ring of elephants made, miles of white cloth would be brought up and strung around the whole party, making a white wall which scared the tiger and prevented his escape. Then at a signal the Maharajah and the guests would ride into the center of the ring, where in the space of an acre or more of thick cover, the quarry would be lurking. Specially chosen large male tuskers would go before to flush the game. Finally one or more tigers would appear, often a mixed bag with a bear or two, a leopard or sometimes a rhinoceros in addition, and all would swiftly fall before the massed array of high-powered rifles. Sometimes fifty or sixty tigers would be shot by a month's hunting party of this sort in addition to quantities of lesser game and a few of the ponderous Indian One-horned Rhinoceros, now so nearly extinct.

This was the traditional tiger hunting which the Nepalis, even the minor officials, understood. When they read our letter they interpreted it literally. "Coming across" a tiger or a leopard was different from the elaborately prepared shoots. Consequently, afraid of the wrath of the Maharajah, and convinced that there must be some double meaning to the instructions, they refused to help us search out a tiger in the vicinity, even when we heard of one near Tikapur. Tigers are remarkably elusive creatures, and so we never saw one during our stay, even though we often came across fresh marks of their pugs in the sand banks near the river.

Leopards were in some ways even more elusive, and we saw no trace of them while in the Terai. But leopards in the hills were more common, and even while we were hunting near Katmandu, one was reported as having taken refuge in an empty house near Godaveri when we were staying there.

So open has the country round Katmandu become that it was quite usual for leopards to hole up during the day in a shed or house if they happened to wander down from the surrounding hills in their search for a stray dog or goat. When the leopard was reported as discovered in the house near Godaveri, word was immediately sent to the Durbar in Katmandu, and one of the younger Generals who was keen about hunting was sent off in a car to dispatch the creature. We heard later that as there were no windows small enough in the house from which to take a safe aim, a hole was knocked in the wall and the General aimed his rifle through it. After sixteen shots the animal was finally killed and brought back in triumph to Katmandu.

None of this, however, was for us. We neither saw nor encountered any large cats in Nepal, except for my glimpse of a leopard near Rekcha. Nor did we see a snake. In all the days and weeks of tramping about in the thickets and scrub and jungle, we never saw a single snake, harmless or poisonous.

Now the time had come to leave. The Dhansing Lumber Company had meanwhile been busy on the trail between Tikapur and Kauriala Ghat and had constructed a temporary bridge over the one large stream that lay between the two. A letter of request dispatched by runner to the company's headquarters on the railway line below the Ghat brought the answer that we could have the loan of a jeep and a truck for a day. We were glad to be free of our delightful but tiring friends the elephants and the bullocks, and sped down to the railhead in style. On the appointed day we heard the all-but-forgotten noise of a motor approaching, and finally the jeep and truck hove into view. All the Tharus ran out from the village nearby in amazement. Even we found ourselves looking at these strident metal vehicles wonderingly.

At long last everything was done, the coolies paid off, a staggering sum it seemed to me, that would more than make up for their not having gone off to India with their fellows. The bullock cart men were paid off, the Nepali officials tipped. Letters of thanks were written to the Burra Hakim. Messages were dispatched ahead, elephants given a last feed and a last pat on the trunk, and we were off, the Tharus from the village assembled with the coolies in a large staring throng. We were off. The jeep and the truck coughed into life and we started up in a great cloud of monoxide gas. Back to India, to civilization, to trains, telephones, telegrams, mail, hot baths, restaurant food — the whole prospect swept up on us like an engulfing wave. All went swiftly and in order.

We reached Kauriala Ghat late in the evening after one or two minor breakdowns to find our railroad car waiting and all in readiness. About twenty hours of travel would bring us to Lucknow and a day in the city for shopping, laundry, banks, and all the other necessities. From there we would head on another twenty-four hours by rail to Jogbani, the Indian railhead for East Nepal and the last phase of our trip. Already in the throes of planning, Rekcha seemed a thousand miles behind us, the village, the people, the hills a warm memory.

XI

East Nepal: First Impressions

OUR ENTRY into East Nepal was less ceremonious than into the west end of the country and far more depressing. In West Nepal I had not been able to get in touch with the local District Governor, but at least I had an ally in Her Excellency Mrs. Naidu, the Governor of the adjacent Indian Province. Her Forest Department people had met us at the railhead and provided tents, furniture, a fire for cooking breakfast, and other facilities. The Indian railhead in East Nepal was a place called Jogbani in Bihar Province of India. Unfortunately, I had no friends among the Great Ones of Bihar. Jogbani was on a branch line of the tedious and dirty Oudh Tirhut Railway. We pulled in late at night and were forced to debark from our car by seven in the morning.

It had been all right at Kauriala Ghat. Even if there had been no one to meet us, we could have simply sat down on the clean grass and started a fire going and made breakfast. There was no town, no one to stare at us, plenty of free and open space. Jogbani, on the other hand, was a ghastly place. The grassless clay soil was baked and dry, inches deep in dust. There was an open brick shed of a station with freight yards, piles of lumber, and rusting pieces of machinery, and the village of clay and bamboo houses lay nearby. Not a tree or a blade of grass were to be seen. The heavy dust lay everywhere or blew about in careless eddies. Swarms of sullen fly-blown children hovered about us with an outer fringe of squalid elders.

After considerable picking and choosing to avoid as much as possible the refuse which lay among the piles of lumber, Abdul and Mohammed made a fire in the lee of some planks, opened up the cook's box, and began preparing pancakes, eggs, and bacon. Mohammed was a new addition from Lucknow. He was a pleasant-looking man with a jaunty air. He had an upcurling mustache and decidedly bowed legs which made him walk with rather a swaggering gait. He admitted to having been a jockey in his younger days. He was quiet and clean and conscientious, and he turned out to be an excellent cook.

Abdul, Rao, Bagam, and I had had a series of heart-to-heart talks in the hotel at Lucknow. As a result I decided that Abdul's trouble was that he was basically windy-headed. He just could not keep track of time, and besides he really didn't like to cook. He promised to be all that we would need in the way of an assistant cook, bearer, waiter, and bottle-washer for the rest of the trip, but principal cook he would not be. He said, however, that he knew a good man and would bring him to see me. This was Mohammed, and after a brief interview he was hired and some warm clothes purchased for him.

When it came to Bagam, I decided that we could do without him in future. He was more trouble than he was worth really, inclined to boast and swagger with the country-bred Gurkhas. Besides, I suspected that he was taking a regular cut out of the money for rice and flour. I paid him off and sent him home by train to Calcutta with a letter of recommendation which stated that I thought Bagam was a fine fellow but a little young for a position of primary responsibility.

The technique of writing letters of recommendation has always been a tricky one in India. Cooks, bearers, and bottle-washers all have them, but the days have long since gone when a bearer was simple enough to parade about showing a warmly enthusiastic letter from a former employer saying that he was "as clever as the fox," or some similar veiled hint. The present generation of servants either know English too well, or always rush off to a letter-writer with their new "chit" to have it translated. In any case I had nothing very serious on poor Bagam. He was just a bit young for the job.

So now we would try to get along without a Nepali speaker, but with what I hoped would be a really good servant instead. Meanwhile I looked about the station for some way of getting in touch with the local authorities. The dust and the ubiquitous crowd of dulled faces had taken away any appetite I had had before. I was anxious to find some place where we could camp or stay. Inquiry from the clerk in the station elicited the fact that a mile away in the Nepal town of Biratnagar across the border, I might find someone who knew the whereabouts of the local Governor. I started walking along the dusty road. It was very soft, and as I walked the dust was so thick and fine that it lapped up to the edges of my low shoes. I began to feel depressed.

There was a steady "put-put" behind me after a while and a jeep came up alongside with a merry-faced Gurkha gentleman at the wheel. He drew up, and speaking excellent

English, introduced himself as Mr. Bim Bahadur and could he help me? At first I was inclined to be a bit short, I am afraid. It had been such a singularly unpromising day so far, and I had not even had any coffee, but Mr. Bim Bahadur had a persuasive smile. Soon we were bowling along in his jeep into Biratnagar. It turned out that the local Burra Hakim was off in the countryside being attentive to a General, one of the ruling family, who was down on an inspection trip from Katmandu. However, Mr. Bahadur, who was the manager of the jute mill, came to our rescue, arranged for us to stay at the jute mill guest house, and before the day was out had us well started on our plans for journeying on into the hills.

We had time to kill in Biratnagar as Kurt had gone to Calcutta to pick up a new tent. We were waiting also for a temporary addition to the party, Gertrude Legendre, who had decided to come with us after all. Meanwhile we settled in at the guest house, a pleasant stucco bungalow in a compound surrounded by a high wall, which shielded one from the stares of the curious and kept out the cattle. Assiduous irrigation had managed to produce actual grass in the compound and there were even a few beds of straggly African daisies and roses rearing their heads up from the exhausted soil. Our time passed pleasantly. The local Government, having been unaware as usual of our coming, had made no provision for our getting across the Terai to the base of the hills, but there were roads here, and so, if we could somehow secure some gasoline for our trip, we could have the use of a truck and a command car (old United States Army surplus) which were among a number of items that had found their way into this little Nepali boom town. I set about writing letters to all the local business people, to the Indian District officer at Purnea, a few hours below Jogbani on the Oudh Tirhut Railway, and to the engineering camp in the foothills where a dam survey was being conducted. Mr. Bahadur was a tower of strength. He was bound that he would help us for the honor of Nepal, the local Burra Hakim being absent.

Biratnagar was in truth a boom town, a squalid dusty boom town, no more attractive than any other in that category, but fascinating no less for being the only one of its kind in Nepal. Jute was the principal magnet, and we spent some time being shown through the jute mill, from the first operation where the sugar-cane-like stalks of jute were being unloaded to the final roller, out of which was coming a continuous series of neat burlap bags. Bengal and Bihar in India had always had the monopoly on jute production, but now Nepal had attracted Indian capital, lured by the lack of income and other taxes, and one jute mill was in the twenty-ton-a-day category of production and another mill a-building. Eighty per cent of the labor was Indian, hired at eight to fourteen rupees a week, but Mr. Bahadur was confident that over a period of years Nepali labor could be educated to come into the mills. In addition, a sugar mill with a twelve-ton daily capacity had just been opened, Nepal's first, and a cotton-spinning mill with a daily output of 12 bales was in full swing. There was a thousand-kilowatt power plant also, and a considerable number of smaller, cottage-style industries had started up. It was astonishing in a way to see all this activity. Of course, it was only a mile across the Indian border and so hardly seemed to be Nepal proper, but it represented the first real rent in the veil of Nepal solidarity, that barrier formed of reluctance to change, to compromise with the modern world.

Mr. Bahadur was one of the few modern-minded Nepalis

An old Mercedes limousine being transported over the hills from Katmandu down to India to be sold, one of the "sights" of the trail up to the central valley of Nepal.

On the steps of the Singha Durbar Hall after the ceremony. In the center stands Mr. Loy Henderson flanked on left and right by the Maharajah and his next oldest brother, the Commander-in-Chief, Commanding General Baber.

that we had met. He was in the same group of younger men led by General Bijaya in Katmandu. He had served on one of the committees which had been formed two years before to modernize the Nepal Constitution. To him Nepal was a land of opportunity, of endless possibilities above and beyond the limitations of caste and religious orthodoxy which bound most of the population. He had been to Europe on a business trip the year before. His eyes had been opened by it.

"How did you make good when you came home?" I asked.

I was wondering what he had done about the problem of crossing the sea, for which orthodox Hindus have to do a certain amount of penance. In the old days when Maharajah Jang Bahadur had returned from his famous visit to Queen Victoria, he and his suite of family and retainers had had to spend six months in pilgrimage to the holiest Hindu shrines in India before they were absolved and the gods propitiated.

"Oh, that's mostly over now," he replied a trifle vehemently. "I went to Katmandu and paid seven rupees to old Guruju, the Chief Priest, for a paper giving me absolution. It just goes into his own pocket." He shrugged impatiently.

The old superstitions, the old traditions, lingered, and the thought of them rankled a bit. I wondered.

"Besides, all of that is mostly for show these days," he went on. "The Great Ones do it for the sake of making an example to the poor people. In their homes they do not regard most of the old observances." He shrugged again.

To us the contrast was startling. It was so different from the restraint, the etiquette, the reverence with which the old customs were at least outwardly observed in Katmandu. But in Katmandu we had had no opportunity of seeing into these sequestered homes.

Mr. Bim Bahadur was much interested in our trip into the

hills. We would have to go up to Dhankuta, the capital of the hill district governed by General Mahdub, whom we had met in Katmandu, and from there on up the ridges to the north. He had never been into the hills himself, and in line with his expansionist ideas he wanted us to look out for natural products which might be of value to the Government. I asked him what he had in mind.

"Oh, any sorts of minerals you may see. Anything of that sort."

I assured him I had no talent as a geologist, and that my interests lay along other lines than those of industry, but he seemed unconvinced. Like other officials of Nepal in Katmandu, he could not really credit that a grown-up man could be an ornithologist. It sometimes gave me an uncomfortable feeling that all the intelligent Nepali people must have thought we were some sort of spies, the industrial kind, come to their country to seek out their potential riches and get concessions. I hoped that the fact that we did nothing of the sort did not depress them too much, did not mean in their eyes that we saw nothing to ask concessions for. But perhaps that just meant to them that we were fools. In any case I promised to inform Mr. Bahadur of whatever economic possibilities we should see in the hills.

Meanwhile we had cast about for gasoline in all directions and finally secured forty-five gallons. Bihar State had gasoline rationing still in force, and very little got up to Biratnagar at the end of the line. Dick made a one-day excursion to Purnea carrying one of my letters, to plead with the local magistrate. He managed to secure twenty-two gallons. The rest we got from Bim Bahadur and his jute mill staff.

By the end of two days we were champing at the bit to

get away from the dust of Biratnagar and into the hills which we could see standing up above the horizon every morning in the dawn, pink tips of snow and ice above the clouds. The third morning Kurt and Mrs. Legendre arrived at seven on the morning train, arrived and found us all still abed, luxuriating in the relative comfort of a bungalow after so many weeks of the tents.

There was one patch of woods about two miles off from Biratnagar, a small patch which was being hacked and chopped down daily before our eyes. The bird and mammal collecting was so limited as a result that we had taken to dawdling about getting up. Twenty years ago the Terai Forest came down nearly as far as Biratnagar, but now we were told there was only a strip six miles wide at the base of the hills. Lumber had originally built the town and had brought the railroad to Jogbani, but that had all been finished before the recent war, and the Indian labor imported for the forest-cutting had stayed on to plant jute and cotton.

A busy day of repacking and last moment arrangements ensued. We could leave some of our boxes with Mr. Bahadur, specimens from West Nepal, some extra ammunition which we did not need, a miscellany of trunks and crates. Everything else would be loaded in the truck and command car the following morning and we would drive the thirty miles across the Terai to Dharan Bazaar, a town on this side of the hills where we were told General Mahdub had a winter camp, and where we could hire the coolies we would need for the onward trek.

By the next morning early everything was ready and for a wonder so were Mohammed and Abdul. We had a prompt breakfast and loaded up the trucks swiftly. Mr. Bim Bahadur supervised and with great efficiency ordered everyone about, including ourselves. He seated the whole party in the command car finally and then took the wheel himself informing us that he would give us the pleasure of having him as chauffeur as he had business in Dharan Bazaar.

We rolled off gaily in the cool morning air, clouds of dust streaming behind us. The road was moderately good across the flat land, between rows of fields, interspersed with small villages, Duhbi, Golaprosi, and Shitpur. We were never out of sight of cultivation. There were few trees, only an occasional towering silk-cotton in flower at this season, crowned with brilliant scarlet blossoms. After a time we came to the edge of the forest, rather gaunt and open-looking at first, but soon closing in about us. We stopped in the road once or twice with filter trouble. I looked about among the trees near at hand. A small bird flew out of a dead tree, circled swiftly and came back to a branch nearby. It was a pygmy falconet, the first that I had seen in Nepal. These beautiful little falcons, about the size of a starling, were fast and graceful on the wing, a veritable miniature of the peregrine, the bane of crickets, grasshoppers, and other large insects. Once I had found a nest of the pygmy falconets in Sumatra in a hole in a dead stub, lined with grasshopper wings. This Nepali species was brilliant metallic blue-black in color with a white front and rusty streaks on the feathers of the thighs; but now the motor coughed to life and I hurried back.

At the upper edge of the forest there was a thinning-out and Dharan Bazaar appeared, surrounded by its own fields. The village was a long dusty street headed up toward the hills above, with a succession of frame huts built irregularly along the side. Mr. Bim Bahadur stopped in front of the principal merchant's shop, where the cotton thread from Biratnagar was being sold. We sat on a board bench in front of the shop and had our lunch, helped along by a large gift of fresh tangerines from the proprietor. Meanwhile word was sent along to the local Government office that we would like shelter for the night.

After lunch we wandered around the corner and down a side street to where we had been told that the weekly market was being held. There was a regular warren of smaller streets off to one side with a narrow square shaded by big old trees. Here the market was going full force. The streets and the square were crowded to bursting with people, most of them from the hills. A few Tharus had come in from farms in the Terai with potatoes, peppers, radishes, mustard oil, small, very rank dried fresh-water fish, and a variety of powdery stuff, some apparently ground saffron, some a sort of curry powder. In addition, there were innumerable sellers of salt, most of them Indian traders who had come up from Jogbani by a ramshackle bus. Barbers were busily plying their trade, there was a cobbler or two, and in one place there was a whole row of jewelry booths. The jewelry for sale was about half and half silver or plastic. The plastic stuff, which was in great vogue, was mostly gaudy red and blue bracelets. The silver, all of it apparently made from silver coins, consisted of huge round anklets, and a variety of necklaces, many made merely of the coins strung together, others made of silver chains. Odd coins were being sold individually, and thumbing through one collection I came across several Indian rupees dating back to the eighteen-fifties. The older coins were of course more valuable, being pure silver.

Next to the food stalls the busiest part of the market was

the row of shops selling cotton cloth by the bolt or piece, almost all of it a local product being patterned by hand before our eyes. The verandahs in front of several of the shops were ornamented with rows of youths busily stamping patterns on the plain white cloth with hand-carved wooden blocks. Some of the designs were bold and striking, and with the bright colors used, red, orange, green, or blue, the flowered patterns were gay and cheery.

The street leading up toward the hills had a constant stream of hill men and women coming down, all with the big carrying baskets on their backs. We noticed at once that here in East Nepal the baskets were better fashioned and larger than those in West Nepal, many of them nearly four feet high and rather wide, perhaps three feet at the top, tapering to a narrow base of a few inches. In West Nepal the baskets had been more like cubes in shape, nearly as wide at the bottom as at the top and as deep as they were wide. Here the baskets, in addition to being tapered and wide at the top, were also not very deep, not more than eight inches from front to back. The larger baskets had a string fastened to the top edge so that the man or woman carrying the basket could hold on to the string with one hand, stooping forward and leaning in to the weight with one arm in addition to the tumpline that came up across the forehead from the base of the basket. In the other hand everyone carried a T-shaped stick of just the right length. When a man carrying one of these loaded baskets wanted to rest, he would thrust the stick behind him, fitting the T into a notch on the bottom of the basket, the other end of the stick just reaching the ground. Then he could lean back, his two legs braced outward, and rest against the basket and his shoulder harness, his legs and the stick making a firm tripod, the basket a firm back rest. So the coolies would stop on the trail or in the middle of a village street, or almost anywhere, stop and rest, one after the other, until a whole line had accumulated, all resting against their packs, sometimes puffing on their little clay pipes, sweat streaming down their faces, laughing and joking with passers-by or the vendors of food in the street, gossiping until the time came to move on again.

The people coming down from the hills into Dharan Bazaar had two main staples with them for trade, oranges or tangerines in great quantity, and wool. The wool-growers were from high up, twelve thousand feet or more. The men were of the type we had seen on the Karnali, dressed in heavy homespun wool garments with woolen puttees or close-fitting long trousers. One of the other two main products was a weed (*Swertia*), bundles of which were being carried down, looking like miniature fagots. It was called locally "infusion," presumably from the English word. This grew at fairly high altitudes and was an herb which, when brewed like tea, was used in the Indian indigenous homeopathic medicine. The other product was Nepali paper, which was made from the bark of a number of small bushes belonging to the genus *Daphne*. We saw them later on at high altitudes in the hills, just bursting into blossom in February, a bush about the size of an azalea with pink or purplish waxy blossoms and a sweet smell. This paper was a little reminiscent of Japanese paper, rather coarser, but with the same sort of texture, with thicker pieces of the soft shredded bark running through it making it uneven and a tough writing surface. Almost all Nepali documents or letters were written on it, however, and we were intrigued by its consistency.

The wool was being measured out by Indian merchants

on huge balance scales, and in return the hill people were receiving mostly salt. As far as we could see this was largely a barter market and relatively little money was passing from hand to hand. Everyone was busily occupied in getting the goods in exchange that they had come for, and no one seemed to pay much attention to us as we pushed about among the crowd, staring in our turn rather than being stared at.

After a time a rather well-dressed Nepali, with the black round cap and the Subha's gold badge on the front of it, came toward us. He nodded and bowed.

"His Excellency General Mahdub Shamsher would be pleased to have you come now to see him," he said softly. "His Excellency has finished his prayers."

We followed the Subha out through the throng and back to the main street. A jeep was standing by for us, and we all piled in and went bumping over the ruts and stones of the street, up a long incline which led out of the village and toward the hills. Beyond the last houses of the town, there was just scrub, a rather miserable scrub, for the soil seemed to be almost nonexistent. The whole place had the look of a stream bed. Probably in the summer monsoon rains it was a series of open watercourses, stones, gravel, and sand. No wonder nothing but bushes and an occasional runty tree could survive. The answer was to be seen in the hills above. Scars of old fields covered the steep slopes showing where shifting cultivation on hillsides, too acutely angled to resist the wear and tear of the monsoon rainfall, had taken its toll. The topsoil gone after the first two or three years, there was nothing left to hold the rain, and gradually the whole hills were being eroded out and the lower slopes and stream beds covered with gravel and silt.

On this inhospitable terrain the General had pitched his winter camp. Winding through the bushes we came upon some leaf huts where his military escort lived. A few lank and limp soldiers sprang to attention as we rattled past. We drew up at a small tent town. A cotton wall, a "pandal," had been spread around a square perhaps two hundred feet in each direction. The wall was six feet high. Inside were the living tents of the General, his wife and daughters and his staff. Beyond the wall was a sort of audience tent, lined with embroidered cotton and floored with colorful rugs where we were asked to take our seats on stiff wooden folding chairs. Outside, a crowd of hangers-on and functionaries stood, and bending down, peered in at us through the low doors of the tent. We sat about and made light conversation for a time, ignoring our audience. A few moments later, they all drew back and stood at what for the Nepalis was attention, a half-bowing stance, the right arm flexed, the hand bobbing back and forth toward the mouth as if gulping in handfuls of rice. I have had the gesture explained to me in two ways: one that it signifies the act of throwing dust in the face in the presence of a great person, the other that it means something to the effect, "Oh, Lord, I am starving and you give me food." Whatever the derivation, it is an act of homage performed by all Nepali men in the direction of a superior, presumably one of the Ranas.

And now the Rana arrived. General Mahdub and his son, tall, spare, and erect, the son the image of the father, swept into the tent. There was none of the obsequiousness that I remembered that day at the Maharajah's Palace in Katmandu. Then the General had stood in a stooped attitude, his hands folded as if in prayer, listening to the Maharajah and mur-

muring, "Sircar, Sircar," at intervals. Now he stood erect, master in his own District, handsomely dressed in a beautiful frock coat over an orange-pink shirt and silk scarf, fawn-colored trousers, and a jaunty Nepali cotton cap, made from a gaudy orange-and-magenta-flowered pattern. The son was a mirror of the father, except that his mustache was a straggly youngish affair.

The General was in good form, sat us down, did the introductions and the honors, and then ordered food to be brought. This emerged on trays from behind the "pandal," dishes of hard-boiled stuffed eggs, "puris," a kind of blown-up sweetish cracker, crisp from being fried in deep fat like a doughnut, sweetmeats, bananas, and tea. There was also a habit-forming stuff called "chura," made of nuts and blown-up rice husks, rather salty, the sort of thing that would be delicious with cocktails. All of this we ate and drank solemnly while the General and his son as solemnly watched, and the crowd of hangers-on outside peered in under the tent flaps. Between mouthfuls we made conversation. The principal question was one of arrangements for our march on into the mountains, but this had to be glossed over until the amenities had been fulfilled.

"How was your shoot in West Nepal? Have you had any hunting? Did you get elephants? Was it not dangerous, uncomfortable, difficult? Did you see any beers [bears]?" So went the questions.

In return we asked after the health of the General, his family, his wife, the Rani Sahiba. It turned out the son had shot a bear and was very proud. At this point the General said we should stay two more days at Dharan Bazaar and perhaps we should get some hunting. His forest men and subedars would arrange it. I protested that we were anxious to get on, but no, there was no moving him. It appeared that we could not get coolies for two more days. Whether this was a fact or not, we would have to possess ourselves in patience. There was nothing to do but accede to the General's wishes, even though I was anxious to leave this barren-looking place.

At this point the son arose. The General requested Mrs. Legendre to follow the boy into the "pandal" to visit his wife and daughters who were eager to meet an American woman. Our woman companion gone, the General felt more free to ask of matters in the outside world. What was our opinion of the Government in India? Good; well, then, did we think that India wished to take over Nepal? No; well, then, what would happen if the Communists took over Tibet, the northern neighbor? These and other posers were running through the General's mind.

He admitted that he could do nothing about the situation, shut off as he was in his rather lonely District, far away from the great world of events in Katmandu. Not for him the center of the Nepali stage. He was a virtual exile. His father, who was a Class B Rana, had been cut out of the Roll of Succession in the fiat proclaimed by Maharajah Juddha, the fiat from which there was no recourse. Senior members of the family who had been involved in this purge were not encouraged to spend too much time in Katmandu, but rather to live in what for them was "the sticks." They should behave, be loyal, do their job well, and be content. We never gathered any inkling that the General was not all these things, but being an active intelligent man, it was perhaps one reason why he had buried himself in religion. He spent much of his day in prayer and religious ceremonial.

We answered the politically tinged questions cautiously.

It seemed to me that these questions were ones in which simple zoologists should not show too much knowledge or interest. In the twentieth century we in America assume that everyone reads the papers at least, and usually has an opinion on the political topics of the day. But not so in the sixteenth. It was as well for us not to show too much familiarity with these matters. I had not forgotten that a left-wing Bombay paper early in November had headed an account of our forthcoming expedition, "U.S. Adventurers on the Prowl in Nepal," and had gone on to call us "Anti-Communist Propagandists" and to say that "a bird hunt will provide an excellent opportunity for making political contacts." In Katmandu we had been twitted about the article, but twitted in a way which showed that underneath it made people uneasy.

I evaded the questions and remarked that I hoped we were not putting the General and his staff to too much inconvenience with the plans for our trip.

"Not at all, not at all," the General assured us in his slow but good English. "I shall have sixty-five coolies ready for you in two days. You must pay them five rupees a day, and I shall also have a 'Munshi' [the title means a writer literally], and a Subedar to go along with you and make all arrangements for you, the Munshi for the coolies, the Subedar to assist you in your hunting. In addition, there will be a Havildar, and two or three sepoys to help with the coolies also. To all of these men you must give two rupees a day for their food."

This rather staggered me as I began to make mental computations of paying out two hundred and fifty rupees a day.

"But, Your Excellency, that seems a great deal," I protested. "We shall never be able to afford to go any distance at that rate."

The General smiled benignly and said that the times were difficult and the cost of food very high. I argued further, and he agreed that perhaps I could save a little by not paying so much when the coolies were in camp not working during the day.

"Otherwise on the march it must be five rupees," he concluded. "That is the official rate for this District."

The delicious "chura" and the "puris" felt like ashes in my mouth.

Mrs. Legendre came back from behind the white wall from viewing the ladies and we took our leave. She reported that the ladies had been a trifle exhausting as they spoke no English, and simply sat, dressed in their best Banaras saris and jewels, and stared at her. She had done as well as she could with the son, who spoke halting English. We returned to town a bit disheartened. Camp had been made for us in a small stucco house which was the Government Rest House for Dharan Bazaar. At least we would not have to set up tents, for there were three rooms, one for Mrs. Legendre, a sort of dining-sitting room where two of us could sleep, and a third room for the rest. In back there was a cook house, and Rao had hired two coolies to dig a privy in the back yard. Mr. Bim Bahadur had given up waiting for us and gone back to Biratnagar in his car and truck.

A wash, a sundown drink, and dinner would put everything right, I thought, but then the day became even more complicated by a revolt among the staff. Rao, who cultivated a plump figure and was afraid of losing it, was the ringleader.

"Sahib, you promised in Lucknow that we would have free food as well as our wages and fooding allowance, and now we have had to buy our own food."

"Why, I did no such thing," I retorted. "I said I would buy flour, but nothing else. You must buy the rest out of your food money."

An interminable argument ensued. All through it like a refrain came Rao's words, "What about ghee?" The phrase caught on like wildfire and we bandied it about camp in moments of confusion for the rest of the trip.

"What about ghee indeed," I replied. "Rao, you have chosen a bad time to talk to me of these things. I am tired and cross and with the Nepali coolies I shall have no money left anyway. I will talk to all of you in the morning when my headache is gone. Now peace until then."

Most of the night I could still hear Rao grumbling to the others. Over and over like a refrain came the inevitable "ghee," mumble mumble, "ghee," mumble, "ghee."

XII

A Little Hunting

IT WAS STILL DARK when the bells began ringing in the two temples nearby for morning prayer. We woke and dressed and had had our breakfast by six-thirty. This was a day for hunting. That would be something to look forward to anyway. I was still depressed about how far we could get into these East Nepal mountains with the exorbitant rates we should have to pay for coolies. Meanwhile we could hunt.

In the early morning even a place like Dharan Bazaar was beautiful. There was a dewy quality to everything, a rosy-dewy quality which lent enchantment to a squalid town like this. The dust had settled, the air was fresh and cool, the low hills round us, bathed in shadow, looked dark, indefinite, unravished. When the sun came up later over the nearest spur, we could see the scars of the landfalls, the broken, tumbled, stony watercourses, the devastation wreaked by the cutting of the jungle on the slopes, and the pitiful attempts at agriculture; but now the contrast of the purple shadows and the pink haze bathing the fringe of trees and brush along the crests refreshed the heart. It was good to be alive at that moment breathing the limpid air, so much like May at home.

The General had said that his Subedar and some coolies

would come at seven-thirty to take us out shooting. They would bring ponies: we might have far to go. Seven-thirty passed and there was no sign of the men. I took the occasion to get out my account book, call in Rao, Abdul, Mohammed, and John and Toni, our two bird skinners, and go over the food problem. In the fresh air of morning it seemed no problem at all compared to the sour looks and the mutterings of the night before. It was soon settled. I would buy flour, potatoes, onions, spices, salt, and the now-famous "ghee," used for shortening, and they would buy rice, dal, mutton, chickens, eggs, and any other staples for themselves. I acknowledged to them that the cost of living was nearly fifty per cent higher in Nepal than it was in India and that their food allowances, set on the Indian scale, could not cover the difference. Everyone was happy. There were smiles all round, particularly from Rao, who treasured his neat paunch.

Still there were no guides. Ed and the others were impatient. We had our shotguns ready and our three rifles for game, and it was past time to be off. Game would be on the move at dawn, and by nine-thirty would be holed up for the day. Not again until dusk would the grazing animals and the stalking animals emerge to forage anew. Meanwhile Toni, who had been off behind the back of the compound on some business of his own, appeared somewhat breathlessly to report that he had seen a few small birds that looked to him like quail.

Ed and I picked up shotguns and sallied out behind the Rest House. The place was surrounded with a wall made of planks set upright in the ground. The enclosed compound was thus a little more free of wandering goats and cattle and had been able to preserve a bit of grass. We climbed over a stile into a stretch of common land in back of the houses and huts making up the village street. It was an unsavory place of washed-down gravel where in the summer rains the floods would come from the hills. It was covered with weeds, strobilanthes bushes, and a very occasional gaunt tree, a perching spot for vultures and crows, for the pickings were good here. Cattle were left out here to die and be quarreled over by jackals and the scavenging birds. The bushes, too, were full of silent squatting villagers performing their morning mission. Ed and I had not previously found any quail in Nepal. The opportunity was too good to pass up. We proceeded to stalk carefully among the bushes trying not to disturb the silent figures.

Brown mynahs walked about on the open gravel pans talking monotonously to each other in metallic tones. A blue roller sailed from one tree to another in a flash of turquoise wings. Suddenly there was a whir exactly like a miniature Bob-white and a little quail buzzed up, flew over a bush, and settled again. Ed and I stalked the bush and got one and then another. I was delighted. These were the first Bustard-quail we had seen, curious little birds the size of half-grown Bob-whites. The female is the aggressor of the two, larger and more brightly patterned in contrast to most other birds. She is the dominant mate. She and several other females chase the male bird, and having settled on a mate, it is the lowly male who must sit on the nest and care for the young, a reversal to suit every suffragette's heart. The Bustard-quail was a bird of stony scrub land in the Terai, and Nepal boasted its own geographical subspecies named by Brian Hodgson over a hundred years ago.

Ed and I returned very pleased to find that our guides had

arrived. The General had sent us a group of rather skittish little ponies, each with attendant pony man, and two dignitaries, the Subedar, who wore his badge of office, a pancake cap of black cloth with a silver thread edging and a gold shield standing up from the rim in front, and a gentleman in white of uncertain status. We set off down the main street, making rather a jaunty cavalcade, through the deserted market place, and on into open country. The woods beyond looked ravaged. There were a few big trees left, and the dry watercourses wound through the scrub leaving tangled heaps of wrack, branches and tree trunks ten or fifteen feet high. The effect was desolate, sand and rocks underfoot, irregular jagged masses of vegetation above.

About three miles of this and we came to a village called Thengabari where an array of neat green paddy fields was welcome to the eye. A long tedious interval ensued while pony men were dispatched to the distant huts across the fields to scare up some guides. It was well after nine before two men were produced who were persuaded to leave their plowing and come to guide us. They reported that there were bear in the thicker jungle below the village. We left our ponies and walked swiftly into the jungle wondering audibly to each other whether it was all worth while.

Below the village we reached a dry river bed where the soft sand showed many fresh tracks of deer, sambhar, the medium-sized Indian elk, and smaller hoof marks, chital or spotted deer, and the still smaller barking deer. The forest was better here, tall trees, mostly the massive silk-cotton, a few remaining timber trees, and very tall second growth. The trees were dense enough above so that it was fairly open below and the visibility was good. Here and there where some mammoth tree had rotted and fallen there would be a huge heap of tangled vines and undergrowth and lower thicker bushes all around.

When we entered the forest, we spread out into a long line, each of us with a rifle making a nucleus. I tried to cut down the numbers of hangers-on, but this seemed impossible. I ended up in a train of three, a village guide, a miscellaneous and unwanted pony man, and the Subedar. The Subedar's shoes squeaked mercilessly. Fortunately the rest of the party had become so spread out that we lost sight and sound of each other, but I was already pessimistic. This looked like a wasted morning. I was glad that we had done well on the quail.

Bears seemed to be what the villagers expected to find. I was not sure that I wanted to shoot a bear. The sloth bear is the common bear of the low country all over India and into the foothills. They are big ugly slobbering creatures with pendulous lips, coarse black fur with a white chevron on the chest, and long sharp claws. They fear nothing and snuffle and shuffle about harmlessly in the jungle. Everyone including the tiger usually gives the sloth bear a wide berth. It seemed to me that it would be a waste of time to shoot one. Besides, we needed meat, preferably venison, for the onward trek.

The villager stalked ahead of me, padding along quite soundlessly on bare feet. I walked as carefully as I could on rubber soles, but there were quantities of dead leaves. The Subedar tramped behind me in his boots as determinedly as if on parade. The pony man scuffled along in the rear. I tried to remove the nagging irritation from my mind: this was the most hopeless sort of hunting.

Suddenly the man in front stopped and studied the ground. The soil was clayey and bare of grass. There were distinct claw marks and bear tracks. We moved on very slowly now scrutinizing the ground. The villager pointed with satisfaction. In the trail was a neat heap of grayish dung, still smoking faintly.

"Balu," he whispered, and to my annoyance the Subedar took up the refrain calling out "balu, bear," to me in stentorian tones, and pointing and talking as if I were deaf, dumb, and blind. I hastened on giving the Subedar a look which I hoped would shut him up. The villager proceeded on ahead, faster now, and we followed the trail quite clearly until we arrived at one of the huge piles of jumbled vines and bushes. The villager gestured to us to be quiet and cautious and we carefully proceeded around the whole mass, peering into it constantly, trying to see if the bear had holed up somewhere in the tangle. There being no sign, we went on to the next heap a few hundred feet beyond, and then to another and another, until we had lost the trail in a confusing complex of tracks.

In the midst of this there was a rustle, and a skittish chital ran out of some bushes ahead and streaked away through the underbrush before we could really get more than a glimpse of it. The Subedar looked at me in a sort of commiserating manner and shook his head. The gesture said that it was too bad, of course he knew better, and if he had had the gun naturally he would have been able to shoot the deer. I contented myself with looking daggers at him and we clattered on. Another mile or so of this and it was nearly twelve noon. We had paused at each fallen tree, and our noise had started up another deer and a pig, all far off. There were no sounds from nearby to indicate that the others were having any more luck.

We came to a large clearing made by the shade of two giant trees. I halted my three companions there and we stood silently for a time. I had heard a wren-warbler call, and I wished I had my collecting shotgun instead of the rifle. It would be something more worthwhile than these will-o'-the-wisp bears. The Subedar started to move after a time, but I stopped him with a curt gesture. It was far more pleasant to stay and listen awhile than the steady tiresome noisy progression. I enjoyed stopping the man and I hoped he was irritated by our wait. The little bird called and called again, hopping about in the knee-high undergrowth. The men with me seemed totally confused about what I was listening to and why I had stopped.

Suddenly there was the faintest of noises a good twenty-five yards off to the left and a sounder of five pigs walked out of some thick brush. I raised my rifle and shot the leader, shooting right over the head of the little guide. At the shot the pig dropped and the others turned and ran all ways at once. A striped baby came straight in our direction and then veered off when he glimpsed us. Right behind him was a huge boar. As the young piglet turned off, the boar apparently sighted me, for he put his head down and broke into a run charging straight toward us. I was conscious that the little villager had dashed to a slender tall tree growing in the shadow of one of the larger ones. Out of the corner of my eye I saw him swarm up it exactly like one of those toy tin monkeys which goes up and down a string when it is tautened.

I fired at the charging animal breaking his left foreleg.

It didn't stop him at all, but at least put him off course a bit. He automatically began to swing to the right as he ran. I heard now for the first time in my life the swift clickings as the boar grated his tushes in his rage. The whole front of his huge body swung back and forth and his head twisted and turned as he thrust and ground his tushes seeking his enemy. It was a demonstration of utter ferocity. I shot again, a body shot, and he sank to the ground a scant ten feet from me, his head still twisting from side to side, the tushes grating, until with a snort and a wheeze he fell back lifeless. It was the first time I had fired my new rifle, a .375 Magnum, and I was impressed by the power of this great boar and the way he came on in face of such a crippling shot. I was glad that I had a magazine rather than a double-barreled rifle.

After the crashing noise of the shots there was absolute quiet. I looked around. The little villager was coming down from his perch. The Subedar and the pony man were emerging from behind trees in the background. They were all grinning. I felt icy calm and a little tired. We stood around looking at the two animals until Dick and Mrs. Legendre and their accompanying cohorts came up. Then everyone started talking excitedly, and in no time the sow had been cut up and loaded onto poles for carrying back to camp. The boar meanwhile was taken in hand for skinning by Dick. He was a large one. We estimated he must have weighed well over two hundred pounds. His tushes were nearly four inches long. As we skinned, the villagers made away with various of his most important parts including the liver and the genitalia for some obscure and fell schemes of their own. As pious, albeit uneducated Hindus they should have been uninterested in any of this meat.

It was well into the afternoon and hot before we finished the job and turned back. It was evening before we finally got home. In the excitement I had forgotten my irritation of the morning with the extraneous officials who had been so much in our way during the hunt. Later, the next day when we saw General Mahdub, he took me to task for having hunted in that manner on foot, saying that it was very dangerous and had we met a bear we might all have been killed. He also said that in future I should modify my tone toward these officials and not upbraid them or scold them, as, "they are dangerous men when aroused and you might have trouble with them." I was astonished at his speech and attitude. I felt that I hardly deserved all this. The Subedar must have been a sensitive man indeed. Then it occurred to me that the General was probably adopting a stratagem. By attacking first, he was keeping me from making any accusations about his clumsy huntsmen. I thanked the General for his advice and kept quiet. Compared to the Nepali tradition of hunting on elephants with scores of retainers, our simple little adventure on foot must have seemed a risky undertaking to him.

The next day we made a digression, a side trip to the gorge at Chatra six miles west of Dharan Bazaar where the Kosi River empties out of the hills. I was anxious to see the site, four miles upstream from Chatra, where the Indian Government, working in concert with the Nepali authorities, hoped some day to erect a vast dam, the largest in the world. The walk up the river from Chatra was pretty and easy on a well-laid path which will some day be enlarged to include a standard railway bed, needed for transporting the vast amount of cement and equipment from India. The project was a mammoth one. In the nearly vertical gorge of rock, a tough blue quartzite, it was proposed to erect a dam about eight hundred feet high, higher than Boulder Dam. The engineer-in-charge stressed this several times. The main reason for the dam project was the uncontrollable state of the Kosi each monsoon season, when the floods simply rolled over hundreds of square miles of countryside in the Nepal Terai and beyond in India, sweeping away villages, killing untold numbers of people, and cutting new channels for itself. In addition, of course, there would be big hydroelectric power supplies to be derived from such a dam as well as irrigation potentialities from the barrage system of auxiliary dams to be built lower down below Chatra.

We went over the site with an Indian Colonel of Engineers who outlined some of the problems of the dam construction and its costs. What staggered me was the vast amount of silt flowing down the Kosi itself. The river has one of the highest siltation rates in the world. The watershed for hundreds of square miles upstream, as we were to discover later, has been cut over, and the topsoil eroded and destroyed. It seemed to me that there was little chance for such a dam succeeding in its primary purpose unless a vast long-range reforestation scheme was first adopted in order to control the washing-off of the land. Otherwise it would be likely that in a measurable period of years the dam would silt up to such an extent as largely to lose the effectiveness of having the dam at all. Dams, however, are a panacea in the new India. The dam is the great touchstone of progress, the symbol of the coming era of freedom and prosperity. The Government feel that only to build dams would bring food and wealth to the people, restore India's birthright, and herald a new dawn of prosperity and power. To build this dam will require a huge bridge across the Ganges River, a new standard-gauge railway for several hundred miles up to the dam site, the blasting and drilling of two-thousand-foot tunnels sixty feet in diameter through the rock, the erection of coffer and subsidiary dams, and finally the structure itself. The project will probably cost well over ninety million dollars before it is through, a staggering sum for India whose total annual Government budget is about five hundred and ten million dollars.

The Nepal Government had merely given the land for the scheme, as the project would be very far beyond their means. Watching the carpenters working on the wooden houses for the survey engineers' staff, using hand-powered lathes and holding the boards between their toes in age-old Indian style, I wondered; but then, the Great Pyramid exists, the Roman aqueducts, the Great Wall of China. Certainly the Kosi Dam could be built some day.

On our return we found that Dick had quietly shot a sloth bear. He had gone out in the morning to look over his trap line, and by some chance had taken his Winchester thirty-thirty instead of the usual twenty-two rifle. Rounding a large boulder in a stream bed up on the side of one of the hills, he had been surprised to meet an equally surprised bear. The bear had reared up and Dick had shot it, then spent most of the day having it brought down the hillside and skinned. For dinner that night we had a side dish of roasted bear's heart, a dish which Dick maintained was in great favor among the trappers in Idaho and Oregon. We all sampled it and so could have the satisfaction of saying that we had eaten bear's heart, but I for one was happy to leave it at that. We had taken the precaution of having pork chops as well.

At least we could all thank Fate for the fact that Dick had surprised a sloth bear with a powerful rifle in his hands.

The next day was set for our departure from Dharan Bazaar. It was the twenty-seventh of January. Early in the morning the Subedar arrived, the same one who had accompanied me hunting, along with the Munshi. Both were to come with us. The Munshi was a tall thin boy of perhaps twenty, dressed in ordinary Nepali style with a jaunty cloth cap. He had a merry expression and looked as if he would be a happy-go-lucky type. Behind them trailed a horde of coolies, each with his empty carrying basket ready to be loaded up with our gear. Meanwhile the gear was packed as quickly as we could get it ready, bedding first, then our personal duffle bags, boxes of food and ammunition, the tents and tent furniture, and finally Abdul and Mohammed's cooking boxes of pots and pans and kitchen equipment. By the time all of this had been sorted out and felt for weight, hefted by the Subedar or the Munshi or the Havildar, who now appeared, a tall, efficient-looking young soldier, it was divided into sixty-three loads. We would have sixty-three coolies, all at five rupees each per day. I groaned inwardly at the thought, wondering how long the stock in my money belt would last.

By nine-thirty we were off. On the way up the ugly street toward the hills, I turned off where the entrance to the General's camp was among the bushes. He was waiting for me in the reception tent, his aides standing under the guy ropes, peering in between the flaps.

"I know you will enjoy yourself in the hill," he said, using the singular. "It is very invigorating and chilly, like your home, yes?"

"We are looking forward to it."

"You may also find some 'beers' there." The General seemed to feel that we had come especially to shoot bear. He went on, rattling off the names of the different camping sites where he wished us to stay on the ridge beyond Dhankuta, the capital of his District. We should reach the town in two days.

"You will see some trees above Dhankuta," he continued. "I have planted them myself. His Highness has requested that all should plant trees in the country. I have planted these myself and I have forbidden anyone to touch them. It is" — he hesitated — "forest-ation."

The members of the Rana family seemed to have a characteristic style of speech with a certain hesitation in it, sometimes a kind of lisp also. In the General it became more exaggerated with unfamiliar words.

I stood up to go, and the General wished us "bon voyage," and his son behind him waggled his head in the sideways gesture which meant assent in India or in Nepal. I ran on out to the trail and caught up with the midstream of our coolies. It was already nearly ten o'clock.

The first day of the march with coolies was always trying. The men had signed up in little groups, members of the same clan, from the same village perhaps, in the hills. We had groups from seven tribes, Magars, Gurungs, Rais, Limbus, Khetris, Tamungs, and one Sherpa. The men were all listed in this way by the Munshi, their tribe designation like a surname at the end, and in fact the men thought of themselves as members of a tribe, not of a country. Nepal had no validity to them except as the name of the central valley, the omphalos, where Katmandu lay and the Great Ones resided. They did not think of themselves as Nepalis, but rather as Tamungs or Rais. If you asked a man his name, he would say Aka Bahadur Tamung — just like that. There was no exact equivalent to it in the West, for the tribal distinctions had long since ceased to carry any geographical designation. The Tamung people were scattered all over eastern Nepal and into the Bengal Duars and Sikkim.

Each one of these little groups would walk together with their loads, halt together, and cook their food in common. Usually each group of eight or nine men would have a boy or another man with them who was not entered on my pay roll. He carried a lot of his friends' gear and also acted as cook. The meal of the day for the coolies was in the evening when the rice was boiled. In the early morning they would have tea and cold stuff left over from the night before, mostly rice and a green vegetable. At midday they would often boil water and make tea, or if there was a roadside stall where sugar cane or tea or peanuts were sold, they would stop for a gossip with the usual merry woman proprietor.

This trail over the hills in back of Dharan Bazaar was a great route for the "paharis," the hill people, in the winter. The trail went right on up into Tibet over a pass, the Rakha La, beside Mount Everest. We passed a number of Tibetans coming down as we started up the long, steep dusty slope beyond the town. In addition, there were Lepchas, rather odoriferous little people, extremely dirty, and dressed in a sort of mixed Tibetan-Nepali style. Both men and women had very long, limp, straggly hair, but the women could be distinguished by the silver charm boxes which they wore. These were very decorative, flat, oblong, about two by four inches, with filigree designs on the cover and set with turquoises. They were worn suspended from a necklace of coral and turquoise beads. Usually there were some charms or prayers written on paper in the box, sometimes perhaps a relic. One woman had a cylindrical-style charm box, gold or gold-washed, hung from a necklace composed of a rope of many strands of fine red glass beads. I remembered seeing the style in Darjeeling among the Tibetans there.

Some of the men had charms consisting of small "potted lamas" in the amulet boxes worn on their necklaces. The potted lama has been much in vogue among the Tibetans for generations. When a great lama died, he would be cremated rather than simply exposed on the heights for the wolves and vultures as usually happened in a land without wood. After the cremation the bone ash would be mixed with clay and then molded into little statuettes or figures, often by means of a carved wooden block stamp. These would then be distributed. Some would be put into the "chortens" or memorial stupas near the monasteries, others given or sold to pilgrims. For a time there was a brisk trade in fake potted lamas roundabout Darjeeling where the hotels and the rest camps during the war provided an ever-present horde of tourists and GI's. The faked potted lamas were cleverly carved and painted of wood and looked exactly like the originals. Apparently tourists were not the only gullible people, for a Tibetan along the Dhankuta Trail sold us a potted lama which turned out to be one of the fake wooden ones, and yet his only possible customers in this area could have been devout hill Nepalis or perhaps one of the occasional Indian traders down at Dharan Bazaar. It was just luck that he ran into a group of unsuspicious Americans.

The climb up seemed interminable. By now the sun was

well out and it became very hot. Starting at Dharan Bazaar, which had an altitude of about nine hundred feet above sea level, we climbed straight up to the pass at the top of this first low Mahabharat ridge, which turned out to be forty-seven hundred feet. There were no trees to shade us, just scrubby bushes along the trail with every so often the gaunt hacked skeleton of a tree which was disappearing daily under the blows of the passers-by. Even on these steep slopes there were constant reminders of the search for arable land, little fields set at a thirty-degree angle, poorly braced with miniature retaining walls at their lower ends. Two seasons of the fierce monsoon rains and every scrap of topsoil would have disappeared, leaving stones and sand, interspersed with spreading, growing gullies. All these slopes above the town had been abandoned finally, left to wash down, and their remnants to grow over, not with grass or good trees, but only weeds and scrub.

In this desolation there was little to interest us. Occasional hunting parties of sun birds and flower-peckers, tiny hummingbird-like forms, would dart through the bushes looking for flowers or ripening fruit. From time to time a few scarlet-and-yellow minivets or a large gray cuckoo-shrike would fly out from one skeletal tree to another, the cuckoo-shrike making its loud tremolo whistle. Sometimes we would catch sight of a bird looking completely out of place, a thrush, perhaps, a bird of the forest, flying through this desolation erratically, almost desperately, like a cat caught out in the open in the middle of a thunderstorm. I wondered what would happen when the country for hundreds of miles became like this. Presumably many species of animals, insects, and birds would become extinct over vast areas which would serve like oceans to insulate or perhaps extinguish the remnants.

At the crest there was a fringe of forest, rather thin and ominous-looking, like a receding hair line. There were a few rhododendrons, some oaks, and a very few timber trees, and any quantity of stinging nettles and thorny bushes. By now we had long passed the coolies, and so we stopped here for a bit of lunch and waited. The Munshi came up, looking very excited and important on a small lathered pony.

"Hey, Munshi, where are the coolies?" I asked.

"Just now taking food, sir. They will be just now coming."

It all had a familiar ring.

"I think you had better go back," I said gently, "and tend to the coolies. See that they all get down the other side to our camping place. We want to have tents up and dinner going before dark."

The Munshi's open face became clouded with trouble, an expression that I was to see many times. He didn't enjoy dealing with coolies. He was too young, and they tended to make fun of him. He went back along the trail, leading his pony, looking hunched and sulky.

We went on down the other side of the hill. The climb down was just as steep as the one up and almost as far. By the time we had reached the bank of the Tamur River, one of the main branches of the Kosi, we were back at an altitude of barely a thousand feet. We walked for another two miles along the bank until we came to a surprise, a steel cable suspension footbridge crossing the stream. It was a good forty feet above the water, but we had been told by the General that it was very sad, that it would be submerged when the

Kosi Dam was built and the lower stretches of the Tamur became a lake. A new bridge would have to be built higher up the cliff and a new trail, too, for that matter, higher up the steep rock face where now a pair of small falcons, russet-colored kestrels, swooped and dove. We were in good time at our camping spot. The first coolies would not come for an hour or more. I decided to try a little hunting. Howie had unlimbered his fishing rod and the others were taking photographs.

Beyond the bridge there was a wide slope where the valley was less steep. Near the track along which we had come there were a few small fields and huts of a village of sorts, a collection of food shops mostly to serve the wandering hill people. I walked up to the head of the flat land where it narrowed into a gully reaching back into the hillside. Finally the place became a sort of canyon, narrow and steep with a dry stream bed choked with tall bushes and a few stunted trees clinging to the sides. Here I would hunt.

I sat down on a boulder. The little canyon was already in shade, although the afternoon sun was still bright in the Tamur Valley. It was beginning to cool off after the heat of the day. A faint wind wafted down from above, soft lambent fingers of breeze playing over my face as I sat looking upward. Far up the slope above me I heard a few scratchings, then a crow, the distinct surprising crow of a cock jungle fowl, so much like our own bantam roosters. I decided to try a trick I had learned in South India. I took out my handkerchief and holding it stretched tight between my hands, relaxed and then jerked it in a quick, diminishing rhythm. Held this way, the cloth made a noise just like the flapping of a cock after he has stretched his wings, the flapping that usually precedes the call. I made the noise two or

The great day of our formal audience with the Maharajah. From left: Francis Leeson, Edward Migdalski, Commanding General Shanker Shamsher, author, His Highness the Maharajah Mohan Shamsher, Major General Bijaya Shamsher, Howard Weaver, Major General Shri Dar Shamsher.

The view from Rekcha included the Saipal massif, the highest peak being 23,079 feet, unknown and unclimbed.

three times. There was what I took to be a surprised pause up the hill, and then the cock bird made his crow again, a little bit nearer this time, rather loud and defiant. He must have heard my handkerchief imitation. I did it again. Again came the crow, a bit nearer. Four more times and I stopped for fear of giving myself away. The bird seemed to be on top of me by now. Junglefowl are very territory-minded. The cock bird resents the intrusion of a rival male, even one who only flaps his wings without crowing. I waited patiently. I could hear the bird now clucking to himself and making-believe that he was interested in something up the way. He was scratching and pretending to be diverted, but in reality he was listening. His curiosity would eventually be too much for him. It worked. He suddenly came darting around from behind a bush twenty yards away, hackles raised, ready to face the intruder. We would dine well tonight.

Back at our camp site by the river there were problems to be faced. Some of the coolies were arriving, and their packs had to be sorted out, and the baskets stacked where they could be easily repacked in the morning. Francis was working hard. I felt almost guilty as I came in. I had been playing truant up the little canyon, away from the cares of the camp. We started to get the tents raised as more men arrived. It was well after dark before the Munshi appeared, tired and upset, three coolies still missing. One of the laggards had my bedding. I arranged a place on the floor of a tent, using a borrowed blanket. It hardly seemed to matter. After all, we were off. We had gotten well along the first leg up the Tamur, and we would eat well, roast junglefowl and roast pork for lunch tomorrow. It had been good hunting.

XIII

Dhankuta

ASIDE from the well-known Katmandu Valley, East Nepal gave us our first experience of an isolated Nepali hill town. We reached Dhankuta after a hard morning's climb of more than three thousand feet above the river where we had been camped the night before. Access to it was straight up from below. The town was on a ridge which ascended steeply from south to north. Above Dhankuta we could see the ridge met another east-west ridge, much higher, at right angles. Presumably that was where we would go on toward the hills.

There was something special, a particular quality about these hill towns. We were to see two of them, Dhankuta and Chainpur, and both impressed us with their distinctive atmosphere. Dhankuta consisted of perhaps four hundred houses fronting on narrow, winding, beautifully paved streets following the contours of the ridge. In a small flat depression caught between two shoulders of the hill was a neat parade ground. The houses were mostly of two stories, built of whitewashed stucco with carved wooden shutter windows. One or two were somewhat larger and withdrawn from the street, surrounded by walled gardens. Over the tops of their brick walls stretched orange trees, hung just now with the rich golden fruit for which the town was famous.

There was a sort of town hall in the center of the main street, built around a larger interior court containing sheds filled with old ordnance, mountain guns of a variety fit only for a museum. None looked as if they would work, except for one small weapon which seemed to be used for salutes. The pièce de résistance was an ancient Tibetan gun made of leather, in size and shape rather like a French bombard of the sixteenth century. The leather was put on in overlapping layers several inches deep, around a thin sheath of iron which actually formed the barrel. Presumably the charge for such a gun was a miscellaneous one of old nails and bits of glass rather than a round iron ball.

Across from the town hall were two high square brick walls, topped with an array of spikes. One enclosure was larger than the other. These were the District jails, one for men, the smaller one for women. Each had a huge wooden door with an impressive iron padlock of a type unknown to the Yale and Towne Company. Near the door was a round hole in the brick wall about six inches in diameter. I went over with the Munshi and looked in. I was met by a face at the other end.

"Baksheesh [a tip]," said the face after the first shock of surprise.

I rolled a four-anna piece down the hole and followed it with two more for the other faces which quickly crowded into view.

"How many people are there here, Munshi?" I asked.

"Thirty-eight men, sir, and six women in the other jail, or maybe six and a half."

"Six and a half?"

"One of the women is pregnant, sir," the Munshi giggled.

"Good Lord, what's she in for, and for how long?"

"Murder. The sentence is two years." The Munshi was well informed.

As we moved away, the men inside sang out to the Munshi asking for news, and I could understand some of his replies, telling about the party of strangers he was with. It was all very informal and rather jolly with much laughing and cat-calling back and forth. Even the jails seemed to be rather fun in the hills.

Farther along the street there was a procession, a number of young men carrying an image in a sort of sedan chair from one house to another. They were all singing and garlanded with flowers in the Hindu style. The image was of Krishna, and incense and little oil lamps were burning in front of it. The statue was well decorated and smeared with ghee, and rice and flower offerings. At each shop where the group stopped, the family of the proprietor would come out and make offerings to the image and there would be a fresh burst of singing and chanting. Something of the atmosphere of a mardi gras pervaded the scene. I asked the Munshi what it was all about.

"This is one of the days of Krishna," he replied. "We have holidays here all the time, maybe every three days or so. Now we are coming into the month of Marg. That is when all the weddings are held. It is an especial good-luck time."

The Munshi was very merry and carefree today. Dhankuta was his home and he loved to be here. Up the street he introduced me to his family, his brother who kept a store, his uncle across the way, and lastly his father. This was a big moment for the Munshi, and he and all his family saw him as a very dashing personage indeed, going up into the hills with all these foreigners. The brother put out some curious rather stiff locally made wooden folding chairs for us in the street, and we sat down in the shadow of a small temple and its bells which projected out on a sort of carved wooden rack. We sat about and ate some of the delicious oranges of Dhankuta, oranges that have made the town's name famous, we were assured.

We sat in the center of the street near the bells on their rack, but of course it did not matter. We were not interfering with traffic. There was no traffic. There were no wheeled vehicles, anyway, and never would be. If anyone was going anywhere up or down the street, they soon changed their minds when they saw all of us sitting there in the sun. It was far more fun to join the crowd and watch. Even the young men carrying the god Krishna seemed to lose interest in their procession after a time: the god in his palanquin was left unceremoniously, and they came to look on.

Just across from where we sat, in the second-floor balcony outside a window, there was a very large wooden cage suspended from the railing. In it was a beautiful cock Satyr Tragopan, one of the loveliest of the pheasants, a big bird the size of a half-grown hen turkey, all over scarlet with droplets of black and silver, and black ear tufts. The bird seemed very tame, looking down and watching the life of the street. I asked the Munshi where the pheasant came from. He questioned the owner who was in the crowd. I don't believe the Munshi had ever noticed the bird in his life until I pointed it out to him. Our guide was a townsman.

"He says the pheasant came from up in the hills where we are going," the Munshi replied excitedly.

I asked him to ask the man whether we might be able to

buy the bird on our return if we had not found any others. The Munshi said he would try to arrange it, but he looked dubious.

"It is a pet," he said, trying to explain the matter to me.

I saw another pet which I wanted very much to secure, an entrancing small café-au-lait-colored Nepali terrier. The people call these terriers "Bhutia" dogs, after the general name used for any of the hill tribes of the higher hills. They are smaller, about the size of a Cairn terrier, but of much the same sort of sheep-dog shagginess as the "apso" or Lhasa terrier. This little dog was still a puppy and was frolicking and gamboling merrily about the street with his master, a schoolboy. I had not seen any really attractive Bhutia dogs before, either in the Terai or in Katmandu. Among the wealthy people in Nepal there was no interest in the breed as there always has been in Tibet among the nobles and the chief lamas. The Ranas and the royal family were fascinated by foreign breeds, German shepherds, Labrador retrievers, and other exotic types which were considered far more fashionable than the indigenous kinds unknown to the Kennel Clubs. I asked the Munshi if there would be any chance of buying such a dog, even possibly this particular dog.

"Oh, no"—he seemed shocked. "It is a pet. The boy would cry to lose it."

When it came to people and things in Dhankuta, the Munshi was a man of sensibility.

We went on up the street finally, marveling at the order, the neatness, the charm of this town. Everything was clean and scrubbed-looking. Each housewife had charge of the segment of street in front of her house. It was scrubbed meticulously as well as her front doorstep. Every morning the women would be out with a fresh mixture of water and cow dung, that abrasive and cleansing agent, washing the street, seeing that the sacred "tulsi" plant, in its stucco pot on a pedestal, was watered. Then they would bathe themselves and sit for a time in the sun in the street gossiping, watching their fat contented babies. The paint was clean and fresh on the house walls. The goats even were clean, the chickens, the dogs. There were no obvious cur dogs about. Everything was as clean as a Dutch town. Furthermore, there was a strong religious flavor to it all. The temple was the center of the town's activities, the holy days observed with the full ritual. We passed a little group of girls going to the temple, dressed in their prettiest saris, their hair beautifully oiled and braided with flowers, carrying trays of offerings for a "Lakshmi puja" ritual. Their faces were bright, and the street echoed with their laughter.

So the whole town seemed, laughing, bright, and gay. We were struck by it, by the way everything fitted in. As we walked about Dhankuta we noticed the small local industries, the turners of brass, the weavers, the spinners, the traders — all seemed to have a place, to fit into a total town life. And the temple was over all, not a brooding, remote, implacable temple full of horrendous gods as in India, but a simple small temple with a few small images and a gentle, smiling priest. So the villages in India must have been four hundred years ago, before the coming of the Westerners. There must have been a rounded, integrated, total Hindu culture then before it all began to fragment under the impact of the West. Or perhaps it had begun to break down earlier under the impress of the Muslim invaders from the North. But this pleasant, clean village, with its appearance of wellbeing and detachment, hung in a state of suspension beyond the worries of the outside world. Nothing could touch it or shatter the shell which seemed to surround this entity, this perfect microcosm.

Beyond the town limits was a high old pine wood, a little farther up the ridge. This was a sacred grove which explained why the trees were not being constantly cut down for kindling by the townsfolk. We put up our tents on a little earthen platform leveled in front of the temple of the place. The townspeople were not disturbed by this alien incursion. Men and women passed by continually with trays of offerings for the temple, or simply to worship. The Munshi explained to me that of course firearms were forbidden here and that we could not collect any birds we might see or put out any small mammal traps. To all of this the Subedar nodded assent.

Meanwhile we had been busily putting up our own tents. The Munshi explained that the coolies were resting in their camp farther up the hill. I began to be slightly impatient with his voluble talk and lack of action. Getting off that morning had been delayed for almost two hours while the Munshi and the Subedar had made their own leisurely breakfast at the camp below Dhankuta. I was tired of listening to the man. The coolies should be helping us and he was doing nothing about it.

"Now, Munshi, the General, the Governor, sent you along with us to be helpful, did he not?"

"Yes, sir."

"Very well, as you apparently cannot control the coolies, you can come and assist us to put up the tents, right now," and I walked over and conducted the Munshi and the Subedar by the arm to one of the tents which we had spread out on the ground.

"I will show you exactly how to put it up and you can help us," I said firmly.

The tent went up in sulky silence.

"Furthermore," I added, "I wish to speak to the General on the telephone."

Dhankuta boasted telephone connections with Biratnagar, Dharan Bazaar, and even with Katmandu. I knew the Governor was in the habit of holding converse with his minions in Dhankuta every morning after his early prayers. I decided to try talking to him. I was particularly upset that the Munshi had been a notable failure with our coolies so far in getting them under way on time in the mornings or in persuading them to help us about camp. I foresaw difficulties when once we got into the hills and were really dependent on them for carrying firewood, water, and generally helping with tent-setting and other chores around the camp.

I was distressed with the Subedar, too. Here he was, especially detailed to assist us with hunting in the hills, and yet, when I had asked him if he was going to be able to get any men to help us trap mammals or birds, he had flatly replied in the negative. Presumably this did not sound like hunting to him as he knew it and was outside of his instructions. I determined to persuade the General to spell everything out over the telephone.

Next morning early, as the coolies were finishing their tea and warmed-over rice from the night before, and the final packing was getting under way, the Munshi came scampering along the path from his family's house in remarkably quick time. I told him that I wished to be shown the telephone. He turned and led me along the path back to the town, sparkling in the early sun, and onto a rise where there were two small brick Government buildings. One was a post office, for Nepal has its own internal mail delivery and stamps, even though it is not recognized by the International Postal Union. The other was the telephone headquarters. In the little brick shed there was a wooden table and several chairs and a box tacked to the wall. The door of this box was open. Spilling out onto the table below were the guts of the telephone system — dry cell batteries connected to wires, some old headphones, a miscellany of coils of wire and apparatus which looked as if the animal had just been disemboweled. A Nepali, all in white, was sitting at the table, bending over a receiver and telephone and shouting into it. At intervals he would vary his monologue with blowing into the mouthpiece, apparently a way of attracting attention. He also had a handle on the side of the box which he would ring vigorously. Evidently this was the only way he could dominate the other people on this one-party line, prevent them from ringing in and breaking up his soliloquy. The telephone was a one-line wonder, and the apparatus looked the sort which no self-respecting telephone company would have dared to inflict on its clients after the turn of the present century. I wondered what success we were going to have.

The operator seemed to know in advance about our visit, for he motioned me to a chair and shouted into the telephone that the visiting "Sahib" wished to talk to the General. Apparently he was already connected with Dharan Bazaar. There was a considerable delay. Perhaps the General was finishing his prayers. During this time our operator had to fight to keep his place on the line, blowing ferociously at all comers.

"No, no, Bhojpur," he would shout. "I am on the line. Keep off, Biratnagar. We are waiting for His Excellency."

After a time His Excellency got on the line. I could tell this because the operator suddenly lowered his tone, assumed a deferential look, and waited and listened, for a change, to what was being said to him. To each phrase he would reply, "Sircar, Sircar," inclining his head. Presumably Bhojpur, Biratnagar, and even Katmandu, were all now eagerly listening in. This was a party wire indeed. The receiver was handed to me.

"Good morning, Doctor. What can I do for you?" The General's voice sounded high and shrill, but clear amidst the static.

After a few politenesses I launched into my discussion of the trip so far, detailing each of the small incidents in which the Munshi or the Subedar had shown unwillingness to cooperate. I described what should have been obvious in the way of the help we should need from the coolies in camp and in raising and lowering the tents. I retailed again the sort of hunting we wished to do, including trapping small birds and animals. I said that we should like permission to buy such birds or animals as we might see, including small "Bhutia" dogs. I spelt it all out from A to Z.

"Yes, yes" — the General sounded impatient. "I have told them all that."

"I would appreciate it if Your Excellency would have the kindness to tell this again to the Munshi."

"Put him on," came the high voice, a tone higher.

I motioned to the Munshi, who picked up the instrument

hurriedly. A veritable torrent of shrieks and apparent imprecations — perhaps it was merely static — now came over the telephone. The Munshi almost bent double, whispering, "Sircar, Sircar," at intervals, his blank young face looking pained. He was getting what he deserved. I only hoped that he would remember all of it for more than a few hours.

Finally the session was over and the General rang off. The operator returned to his ministrations and the Munshi and I swept out. The town was bathed in the hazy sunlight of early morning. From the rise where the telephone office stood, we could look out over the tile roofs and the winding streets below. Curls of smoke rose from the eaves of some houses. Voices tinkled up toward us. The gray-green leaves of the giant fig trees near the temples twinkled in the sun as they waved. Cocks crowed, a goat blatted, and children laughed. I saw a whole troop of school children running along the street below, the little café-au-lait puppy with them. The scene glistened and sparkled. Something about the neat white stucco red-roofed houses seemed familiar, and I realized with a start that the view might easily be of a hill town in northern Italy.

Then the Munshi spoke at my elbow.

"Pardon, sir, I will go to my house now and take my food."

No wonder the man had turned up early. Now who would get the coolies to help us with the tents? I wondered when we would finally get off.

"All right, but hurry, hurry, hurry," I said after him, as he sped down the stone steps toward the street below.

Back at camp the situation was encouraging. The coolies seemed to have finished their breakfast and were beginning to assemble with their carrying baskets. They stood around mostly while all of us took down the tents and Mohammed and Abdul washed and packed up our breakfast dishes and pots. Rao rolled in along the path from town, his face beaming.

"Very good ghee here, sir." He held up for my inspection a large bundle of the stuff wrapped in green leaves. After him came John and Toni loaded with potatoes.

"All right, but hurry. We must get off soon."

Gradually the loads for the men were apportioned out. One or two of the coolies actually helped us of their own accord. One was a sturdy, dependable soul, a Sherpa named Pemba with a particularly flat, dish-shaped, Mongolian face. He was not only a help, but also colorful. He wore constantly a very gay coat made of a bright-patterned cloth, covered with prancing animals. I asked him once where he had gotten the coat.

"In Burma," he replied. He of all people had been there during the war in some sort of labor corps. The hills were full of surprises.

After nearly an hour we seemed to be ready to get off, but where was the Munshi? The Subedar was sent away to get him.

"Hurry, hurry," I called after him, but the Subedar had no more than sauntered around the corner when he returned. The Munshi had arrived, his face all smiles. With him was a boy carrying a metal tray on which was a pile of Dhankuta oranges under a cloth.

"This is a present" — the Munshi beamed. "It is from the family of the boy who owns the dog. They are so happy you did not ask to buy it."

We stared at one another in bewilderment. Anyway, the

oranges were delicious. As we ate them I lost sight of the Munshi for a time. When I saw him again I could not believe my eyes. He had taken all the coolies some distance away, leaving their packs behind, and was going painstakingly over the list of their names, checking them all off. This would take an hour at least. I hurried over to him.

"Munshi, what is it? Are the men all here?"

"Oh, yes, sir, but I must read them off. The General says so."

"Are these the same men who were in camp yesterday morning?"

"Yes, sir."

"And you read off their names then?"

"Yes, sir."

"Very well. Then that is done. Please have them come over and take their loads. We must get away. We have twelve miles to go. Hurry up!"

The Munshi looked sulky. I realized that a small audience of his friends and relatives from Dhankuta were standing near looking at the great man and marveling at his authority. Of course he wanted to show off.

"Must I call up the General?" I said, in a low tone. I hated to spoil his fun in a way, but there was no point in delaying. I hated, too, having to threaten this boy. It was all so much like "telling teacher."

The Munshi's face cleared and he stood up. He began ordering the men about briskly. They grumbled a bit, but soon were lifting their packs onto each other's shoulders. It was after nine, certainly time to be off. The others had gone on ahead. I waited until the last coolie had trudged out into the trail, waited until one of the aimlessly wheeling kites overhead above the pine trees flew down onto a branch, perched looking over the situation, and then with an eye on me swung down to the ground in an easy swoop and picked up a bit of refuse. The coast was clear and the last coolie gone. I could be off in my turn.

Beyond the pines the trail came out onto the open ridge. It was already hot in the sun. Crowds of hill people were coming down the trail from the heights, their huge carrying baskets full of oranges, or bales of wool or paper, or the strange fagot-like bundles of "infusion." They would stop outside one of the little boutiques, the roadside stalls where oranges or peppers or onions or potatoes could be bought. They would halt and reach behind putting their stick under the bottom of the basket, then lean back with a smile, pulling the tumpline down from their foreheads and wiping off the sweat with a greasy sleeve. They would laugh and begin to chatter among themselves, as if the weight of the load was nothing.

Into this pleasant welter along the path there came suddenly the clangor of horns and clarinets and the boom of a musket. It was a wedding party coming down the hill into Dhankuta. First came the band, eight or ten men with clarinet-like reed instruments, two drummers who capered a bit as they played, a solemn fellow with a pair of small cymbals, and finally two men with huge curving copper horns. The horns were far nicer-looking than the noise they made, a sort of wild bray. They looked like pictures of medieval horns called "serpents," except that these had one long curve for their full length of about six feet. The open trumpet-shaped end was carved to represent a dragon's or a serpent's mouth. Behind this group came the bride carried in a rude sort of hammock slung from a long pole, a local Nepali version of what was once known as a Wellington cot. Two Tibetans with wild flaring shocks of hair were carrying the litter. They had been hired for the occasion and seemed to be enjoying themselves hugely. Farther behind was a little knot of horsemen and a group of hangers-on, some carrying muskets and swords. Every so often along the trail one of these men would let off a musket as a sort of accompaniment to the music.

As we came up to this procession, they stopped to see the strangers go by. In the center of the horsemen was the young bridegroom dressed all in white, his face powdered with rice powder and a huge mark on his forehead, a "kumkum" with grains of rice stuck in it, to show that he had been to the temple that day. The boy looked about twelve. Round his neck was a small gold chain with a gold badge hanging in front, decorated with emerald drops. Our whole party lined up in front of the wedding party and in no time cameras were clicking.

Meanwhile we were just as much of a subject of curiosity to the wedding party as they were to us. I sometimes wondered what we should do if the Nepalis had cameras as well as ourselves. How would we all be able to manage and to pose each other if both sides were taking pictures at the same time? Perhaps in the next generation when tourists go out to remote places, the local natives will be just as camera-conscious as the visitors.

After a time we noticed that the cloth over the pole of the hammock was drawn to one side and the bride was peeking out. Kurt, with photographer's aplomb, asked one of the older men if we could photograph her, and permission was readily granted. The pole was lowered to the ground and the girl appeared, a pretty thing of about the same age as the boy, beautifully dressed in a hill girl's full skirt and jacket of scarlet brocade. Round her neck were ropes of red glass beads and a long necklace of gold coins. Closer around her neck was a wide jointed collar of beaten gold from the lower edge of which were suspended emerald drops. On her forehead was a gold marriage ornament hung from a cord which went over the head. On the lower edge of this were more emerald drops. She stared at us for a long time, and then smiled shyly for the cameras.

By now the press of coolies was enormous. All the people moving either up or down had stopped to see the goings-on. Below us the horns sounded and a musket boomed. The leading part of the wedding party was anxious to get away down to the delights of Dhankuta. We should be off ourselves. We packed up our cameras, and smiling and waving at the little couple and their escort, started off again.

The climb up to the ridge running perpendicular to Dhankuta took us two hours. As we rose we could look out to each side and behind over a huge panorama of Nepali countryside. All about Dhankuta and on the slopes of opposite ridges there was cultivation. The whole surface of these hillsides was terraced for farming or grazed by animals. The color of the landscape was an umber brown, rather hazy in the light. The little houses dotted on the fields were shades of brown too mostly, ranging from apricot to brownish-cream. The only green was the rare clump of trees near a house. There were spots of white, occasional houses, or plum trees in flower, but the general tone of the view was brown, a somber color. The only large stretch of green was the big stand of pines above the happy town of Dhankuta, now stretched below us on its ridge. Looking down farther into the valley bottoms, four and five thousand feet below us, the scene was still a monotonous brown. A small gray ribbon in each case marked the stream which sprawled over the flat in a number of channels. But the flat itself was a desolation. No cultivation existed there, so great was the mass of rock and boulders eroded from the hillsides by the reckless farming on the slopes. Widening gullies swept down in all directions from the heights, and in places there were the fresh open pale scars of avalanches. The slope of these hills and the heavy monsoon rains had not changed. This was a country meant for forests. I did not see how this wasting away of the land could go on much longer. The bones were showing clearly through already.

Right at the crest, where the Dhankuta ridge came up to join the higher ridge above, there was a stone-walled enclosure with a patch of thin spindly trees. These were the first trees we had passed in two hour's walking. It was the grove planted by the Governor about which he had told us so proudly. There were painted signs along the wall, evidently warning the people that this was the General's property and not to trespass. It was a more effective measure of protection than the mild proclamations which issued from time to time from the Durbar at Katmandu, telling people of the merit to be derived from planting trees each time a large tree was felled. Here was a living example to the people of the virtue of planting trees, but still in our travels it was the only time we observed the Maharajah's dictum being taken seriously. After all, people have to be able to read in the first place, and then have a certain measure of imagination, with land and funds to spare, before such gratuitous advice could be taken in and understood.

From the ridge at sixty-five hundred feet we could look straight away to the north. I had hoped that we might see a snow peak over there, perhaps Everest, but there was a chilling wind from the northeast, a keening wind which whistled over the ridge and drove through us. Clouds were massed to the north, and there was only one rift high up through which we could glimpse an impossible-looking bit of rock face interspersed with snow. The northern slope of the ridge showed us a similar vast panorama of lower slopes stretching down to the north into the complex of valleys which fed streams toward the main channel of the Arun Kosi River. Everywhere below us there was cultivation, everywhere the marks of a dwindling supply of arable land. I began to wonder where we were going to find any birds. There had been one small frightened flock of minivets in the General's trees. They had taken wing as we approached and flown off, looking as if they didn't know where their next perching spot was going to be.

There was a crossroads here where a trail coming up from the steep valley on the north side met the trail on which we were bound northeastward along the ridge. There were several long stone walls erected by the Buddhist people of the higher hills. These were prayer walls put up by the people as religious objects. By carving prayers on the stones, people gained merit. By walking round them on the right side, one automatically said a prayer. Some of the inset stones were thin slabs, beautifully carved in relief with images of Boddhisatvas, and colored, but the paint and the carving were much worn by weathering. With the current decline of Buddhism in the hills, the walls would go untended.

A flourishing little market was going on in the shelter of the walls out of the wind. A number of cheery market women must have walked up from Dhankuta or the huts above it at dawn with their packs of vegetables, peanuts, oranges, "biddies" or hand-rolled local cigarettes, matches, and odds and ends like nails or candles or bits of cloth or tiny mirrors. They were gossiping and chatting with the coolies, their conversational give-and-take being part of their stock in trade. It was a merry scene. We sat and waited awhile, out of the wind, for the coolies to catch up. It was time for lunch.

After an hour we moved on. Our course lay ahead on up the ridge to where we were told, after three days' march, we would get high enough to be beyond cultivation, in the forest, or what remained of it, above nine thousand feet. We started toiling along the ridge, into the teeth of the searching wind, feeling as we went that we were leaving behind the towns, the happy life of the hills. Ahead, it would be cold and dark in the dripping trees and the clouds. As we looked back and down, we could still see Dhankuta basking in the bright afternoon light, but already a vagrant cloud attracted by our ridge had spread a mantle between us and the sun's rays. We were entering another, a grander but a more somber world. Above the ridge ahead, sweeping on widespread pinions, came a pair of bearded vultures, lammergeiers, the largest of the birds of prey of Europe and Asia. They were the first we had seen in Nepal. They swept along above us, seemingly coldly disdainful of the puny mortals below. I hazarded a shot with number twos from my sixteen bore. I could hear the pellets after a perceptible time rattle off the wing quills of one of the birds. It never faltered, but swept on about its own business over the ridge with a swish, and was gone. We turned and struggled on up the trail, up and up toward the clouds.

XIV

Mangalbaré

IN THE EARLY MORNING, if we were lucky, the clouds would be off the tops of the ridges. When the light first filtered through our translucent tent walls, it was the coldest time of the whole day. I noticed that often the water in the cup by my camp bed would stay unfrozen during the night. Somewhere between five and six in the morning, it would freeze. Even though it was cold, there was an impelling fascination in Mangalbaré which forced us out of our warm sleeping bags, out of the tents and onto the rime-covered grass each morning. Untying the tent flaps with stiff fingers, we would impatiently burst through and out onto the strip of greensward, framed by giant sixty-foot rhododendrons, where we had made our camp.

If we were lucky, the whole vast panorama would lie before us, an enormous range of mountains, the highest in the world, all ice and snow, rearing up from a labyrinth of ridges and chasms like an implausible relief map. At the very bottom were the rivers, their wandering feeder channels spreading up and out like veins. Then the snow began on the dark purplish-brown lower hills, at first patchily, then farther up huge solid masses proclaiming glaciers, and finally the majestic individual peaks. On the right stood Makalu, enthroned, its twin supporting shoulders giving the effect of a statue, a man sitting in a great armchair. Then a sweep of snowy ridge, a graceful dip to a sharp peak, Peak Number Six, then Everest itself, looking as usual somewhat less impressive than the others because farther away. To the west of Everest and almost shielding it was the next formation, an enormous razorback ridge running east and west, sheer and sharp. Far to the left again was Gauri Sankar, eighty miles from where we stood, and marking the limit of our vision of these highest peaks.

Thin lines of cloud made horizontal breaks in the lower part of the view, obscuring some of the dark hills. A characteristic phenomenon on Everest itself was very apparent to us. This was Everest's noted ability as a cloud-maker. In the very earliest light the peak would be clear and unobscured, but after a few minutes, as it seemed, a small puff of white would appear off the leeward edge of the crest, like smoke from a chimney. This was snow blowing off the top, Everest's characteristic snow plume which many mountaineers have described. It has been estimated that on some days of great wind this plume may reach a length of thirty or forty miles. But in no time after the snow plume began to blow, a cloud would start just over the crest of the peak and soon the mountain would be shrouded from view.

We could not get tired of this panorama. A second view out over Kanchenjunga, sixty miles to the northeast, lay just over the ridge, in the lee of which we were camped. It, too, was a superlative sight, of vastness and majesty, but farther away and less awesome than the main Everest massif directly in front of us. Every day it was different. New clouds would obscure part of the mountains, playing across their faces in their idle course. Every day new ridges would stand out unobscured. Francis busied himself with a wash drawing he was making of the entire stretch from end to end. The rest of us hurried out with our cameras, both still and movie, to try to catch the whole magnificent sweep of it. With numbing fingers we would try to arrange our lenses and check our light meters. It was excessively difficult to make a panorama shot with the movie cameras owing to stiffened oil and grease of the camera parts, the stiffness of our fingers, and the consequent jerky progression of the camera on its tripod. We would try and try again. By the time the first shafts of sun penetrated down to us, streaking across the grass between the trees, it was already too late to photograph any more. The clouds would be making up from the lower valleys. The thin horizontal streaks of cloud, stretched lifeless across the hill masses, would have suddenly mushroomed into billowy, living, moving creations, sweeping across the peaks and blotting the whole from view. By eight o'clock the mountains would be largely gone and the tents beginning to smoke as the frost ran off them, and we would adjourn to breakfast.

Our time in Mangalbaré was not wasted. There was no village here, only a single Government hut beside the trail, which ran on up the ridge to the inner approaches of Everest itself. It was the first place that we had managed to find in our wanderings in Nepal where there was real jungle. Beyond the stretch of meadow land where our camp was pitched, there was a long expanse of rhododendron forest stretching up to the ridge in back of us, the crest of which wore a thin fringe of silver firs (*Abies*), interspersed with clusters of tall thin-stemmed bamboo and occasional spreading yew. It was a somber, dark, shadowy expanse. The season was too early for flowers or blossoms, and the most notable characteristic of this forest, it seemed to me, was the silence. The only noise was the soughing of the wind in the trees, the occasional tinkle of some streamlet falling away over the moss and rocks underfoot, or the single "click" of a Blue-fronted Redstart, a beautiful miniature blue thrush-like bird about the size of an English robin which would perch on the edge of the forest on a branch or stump and slowly flirt its chestnut tail up and down. This silence was very noticeable and all-pervasive. If there was a noise at all, it seemed to press into the vastness of the surroundings to no effect. No noise could last for more than a fraction of time in this great space.

The first morning when I fumbled my way out through the tent flaps, Mohammed was standing outside the cook tent with his mouth open staring at the wood. As he saw me he came over, obviously much excited, for Mohammed.

"Sahib, there was a bear here just now," and he pointed up the slope.

I ran over in the direction he indicated and sure enough there was a fresh bear track in the heavy frost which lay on the grass, leading up from below, going within a few yards of our tents, and on across an old snow bank into the trees. I went over to the stone hut which lay a few hundred yards beyond our camp and routed out the Subedar.

"Now, Subedar, here is your chance to show your skill. There was a bear just now by the camp. Let's go and hunt it up."

The Subedar was "just now taking food." There would be no question of securing his co-operation for an hour at least. However, after assuring me that there was no use following, as the animal was obviously on the move, he told me that he had sent notes to the local hunters and that they would soon be coming to assist us. I returned to camp to breakfast and the inquiring gaze of my companions.

"The Subedar says that it's no use hunting up a moving bear like that," I reported. "And, anyway, he has summoned the local boys to hunt for us. We must wait for them."

Fortunately we did not have to depend on the Subedar for our own hunting. After breakfast we were all out, Dick and Howie to set out their trap lines, Ed and I to look for birds, Kurt, Francis, and Gertrude Legendre to take photographs. I spent most of the morning putting up my silk bird nets and wandering slowly through the forest, moving very little, standing or sitting most of the time, listening and looking, trying to measure the value of the place and what it held for us. It often has seemed to me that much of bird or animal collecting or study was sheer luck compounded with the ability of the hunter to assess the locality. Some places just were birdy or gamey, others not. At first sight it was not easy to tell. I finally decided that we never had come across a really good collecting place in all our wanderings in Nepal. There just didn't seem to be any. Of them all, though, Mangalbaré was one of the best. At least it had a big stretch of forest.

That first morning I saw a number of birds that we had not previously met with at lower altitudes. The most striking was the Yellow-billed Blue Magpie, first cousin of the Red-billed species found at the five-thousand-foot level. This bird was the same shape and size, but a paler gray-blue color on the back, wings, and tail, with a yellow bill and a delicate transitory yellow wash on the breast and flanks. They were shy and skillful at concealing themselves behind branches and tree trunks. Only their curious call, rather like the rusty note of a serpent eagle, gave them away.

Another distinctive new species was the Nutcracker, a bird as big as a small crow and closely related to that family, which was common here. We saw them often, usually perched on the very tip of a tree, a bulky brown bird with a blackish crown and wings and white spangles on the brown body plumage. What was very noticeable was their tails. The whole under surface of the tail was white, and at times they would lift it carefully, high enough so that the white surface was exposed. It stood out like a beacon, evidently a display signal of some sort. They would fly sometimes over the camp in a deliberate way, uttering a crow-like call, "kraa, kraa."

Below the camp in a clearing in the heavy growth of rhododendrons, here as tall as maples at home, there was a small patch of the Daphne bushes in bloom, their delicate purplish waxy flowers exhaling a faint gardenia-like aroma. Here as I stood quietly I heard a single bell-like syllable, faint but clear and musical. Then in the clearing ahead I saw three or four birds on the grass, quite still, looking at me. One flew up to a small tree finally, and I realized they were bullfinches, a soft gray bird with orange-red tints about the head, a white rump, and shiny black wings. They were very quiet and shy, and only the single note betrayed them, that and the momentary flash of the white rump. This one glimpse of the birds was our only one in Nepal. It happened so often: a species would be seen once, a flock sometimes flying by, and then never again. It seemed to be entirely a matter of chance whether or not we met them. A collector would have to spend many months in a locality to see anywhere near a complete cross-section of the birds which might sometime or other fly through. And by that I do not mean purely migratory birds, but rather the numerous species that apparently wander erratically through the hills, sometimes through a vertical progression of many thousands of feet.

Back in camp there was something doing. It was nearly lunch time and warm in the sun. The Subedar was in his element explaining to Abdul and Mohammed about the men who had arrived. In the forefront was an extraordinary-looking hill man, dressed in ragged homespun woolen garments with a small woolen turban on his head. He wore enormous waxed mustaches which stretched out on either side of his cheeks for a good four inches. Across his knees as he sat idly on the grass was a long percussion-cap single-barrel rifle. It looked at least a hundred years old. The Subedar was so excited that as I came toward them he drew himself up and saluted. The hunter rose to his feet.

"This is Don Pal," the Subedar introduced him. "He has come to guide us to the bears."

Don Pal must have been fairly well along in years for a Nepali, although age is difficult to tell. He looked at least sixty, which meant, I suppose, that he was in his forties. After some conversation it appeared that Don Pal had one or two bears up his sleeve that he was itching to show us, the real thing in fact. I talked the matter over with Gertrude Legendre and we decided to join forces for an afternoon with the mighty hunter. Mohammed obliged with some cold meat and chappatties and a bottle of cold tea, and without waiting for lunch we started off, the two of us, the Subedar,

Don Pal, and three lesser fry, who seemed to me to have sprung up out of the ground. A moment before they had not been there. Now they were with us to clutter up our party and make obtrusive noises. So it always seemed to be in Nepal. It was impossible ever to have few enough people for hunting. It simply wasn't done.

We trotted back along the rough track through the forest over which we had climbed coming to Mangalbaré. After a mile or so, we struck off and started up through heavy bushes, many of them of the spiked variety. They looked like wild blackberries. In addition, they were covered with water, either from rain the night before or distilled from the clouds. In a short time we were soaking wet and scratched. I had a rent in my sweater. We were also breathing hard, as we had been going uphill fast. Don Pal, who was now in the lead, suddenly stopped and turned toward us with a theatrical gesture indicating caution and suspense. The Subedar whispered to me hoarsely that there might be a bear near. We crept forward as silently as we could. At least, the wetness of everything served to muffle sounds. We came out at last on top of a huge boulder which stood out on the hillside commanding a fine view above the surrounding trees. Don Pal motioned to us to look down to one side where, in a dark tangle of brush, we could just discern a darker spot.

"It is where the bear sleeps," the Subedar said in a melodramatic stage whisper.

"Balu," said Don Pal portentously, looking wise and comical at the same time. He picked up a small rock and heaved it into the brush. It crashed down noisily, and was followed by another and another. Silence followed.

"Gone," said the Subedar, shrugging his shoulders.

We went on through the brush, threading our way ever upward toward the ridge which ran steadily for several miles here at about ninety-five hundred feet. In a few more minutes of fast work we reached it and came out on another small alpine meadow where we sank down panting. Don Pal was neither tired in the least nor depressed. As we came to the crest, he broke into a joyous sort of gamboling lope, prancing easily up the last few hundred yards. The exercise had, however, brought out a new characteristic of the man. He had an unparalleled personal reek about him, of a degree seldom met with. It had an absolute "animal house in the Zoo" quality. Gertrude and I carefully sat down to windward. We rested, breathing heavily, and then called for a future plan of operations. The Subedar consulted with Don Pal while we ate our hastily constructed lunch. Then we stood up and looked over the ridge down the other side. Beyond, the ground fell off very steeply for two thousand feet, then more gradually for another four thousand. Far down, we could see the windings of the Tamur River and the cultivated lower slopes of the valleys a mile or more down and a good six or seven miles away. The lower slopes were bathed in warm afternoon sun, a faint blue haze intervening. At our altitude clouds had already made up over our heads and it was chill in the light wind.

From far below we heard the wild blare of horns. There must be a wedding party somewhere down below. The noise carried thinly but clearly. In the utter silence of these hills it had a remote, almost magical quality. Perhaps they were ghost horns of a wedding many years ago. Perhaps the noise had simply been suspended all this time in this eerie sound vacuum, I thought to myself. It was strange hearing the horns in the hills coming from some distant lower place and never seeing the people.

Don Pal explained what we were to do, and the Subedar translated. First, we would go straight down a couple of thousand feet to a cave or two that he knew of, then up again farther to the west along the ridge, and if we found no bear, we might look for either of the two species of goat-antelopes said to occur here, the Serow or the Goral. All of this sounded encouraging, and we started off, plunging down the hillside with abandon in the wake of the gayly cavorting Don Pal. Half an hour of stiff descent, through alternate bands of bushes and open meadow and thicker trees, brought us down into a belt of heavy forest, mostly tall rhododendrons mixed with oaks and patches of bamboo.

Here our pace slowed, and here again Don Pal, not even breathing hard, assumed once more his theatrical stance. The mighty hunter was at work. We crept forward, up and down over minor side ridges through the dripping undergrowth, sloshing through streams, bamboos whipping back in our faces and splashing us with accumulated water. Finally, by inches we crept around a last bend to see another cavity in the side of a steep hill, surrounded by bushes. Again there was the throwing of rocks while we waited tensely. The rocks rattled down and stopped finally in the underbrush. No bear.

Don Pal gestured us forward, and this time we swung up the slope, climbing steadily westward. On the way up, in several open stretches, we had again the throwing of stones into clumps of bamboos under the shelter of groups of out-cropping rock. Always the stones clattered down into silence.

"He is looking for Goral," whispered the Subedar.

Another hour of this, and Gertrude, an experienced hunter, and I were winded and disillusioned. The Subedar, on being questioned, admitted that Don Pal had seen a bear in one of the lairs that we had tried just now, about two years before. He had not seen any bears in this area recently. This was the sort of information that always came out afterward, never before a hunt.

"But what about the bear that went by camp this morning?" I persisted.

"Oh, that. Don Pal does not know that bear," the Subedar replied.

My Hindustani was never adequate at these moments for the rejoinder which I should have liked to make to the Subedar. He was an exasperating man.

Meanwhile Don Pal had decided to go off on his own a few hundred yards to investigate a possible "Goral yard" where they might be resting up during the daylight hours. We sat awhile in the open, drooping a bit after the events of the last hours. An errant cloud swept over us, blotting out sight and sound and covering us with a fine rain.

Suddenly there was a tremendous "boom" and a great series of shouts and calls. We recognized the voice of Don Pal. That "boom" must have been from his old muzzle-loader. The Subedar jumped to his feet and started hailing the mighty hunter in the long-carrying wailing tone that mountain people use. The first word that shot back to us clearly from Don Pal was "balu."

"He has seen a bear," said the Subedar, looking genuinely startled.

There was great chatter from our companions as we dashed forward over hill and dale toward the spot from

Our view from our tents at Mangalbaré, the vast panorama framed in 60-foot rhododendrons, Mount Everest showing clear nearly in the center of the picture with a smaller sharp peak (possibly Peak 22,110 feet, called Number Six) to the right, and farther still to the right, the superb outline of Makalu, nearly blocked by a tree. This picture represents the Everest massif at a new angle, unknown to mountaineers, for the approaches on this southern side have never been mapped.

A bride in east Nepal, dressed in scarlet brocade, and necklaces, one of beaten gold with emerald drops.

whence came the bellowings of Don Pal. Everyone was surprised, not least of all Don Pal himself, we surmised, from his shouts. The clouds cleared and we came out on a long stretch of open meadow land interspersed with rocks and clumps of bushes. The great man was standing at the head of the meadow. He wasted a few valuable moments showing us how he had cast a rock into a clump of bamboos to see if he could start up a Goral, and instead a big bear had careened down the hillside. Finally we set off down the obvious trail, the Subedar and Don Pal in the lead, muttering to themselves as they noted the broken grass stems and small branches, bits of scuffled turf and upturned stones, marking the bear's rapid descent. At the bottom of the long meadow, a quarter of a mile down the hillside, the forest started again.

We plunged into it after the two men, who had by now outdistanced us. Suddenly we heard loud peals of laughter just ahead. There they were, the Subedar and Don Pal, literally holding their sides as they teetered back and forth on the slope under the trees. As we came up to them holding on to branches and trunks to support ourselves on the hillside, they pointed speechless at the ground. The bear had been traveling so fast that it had never stopped, but had simply let go with a bad case of diarrhea for a long way down the slope.

"He was so scared," gasped the Subedar, trying to explain to us why it was all so funny.

After a time we went on, but a few more hundred yards and we had lost the trail.

"It doesn't matter," explained the Subedar. "We could not catch up anyway."

We turned and started the long climb back up the hillside.

On the way we came to a spot between two rocks in an open space where a fox had dined royally on a Satyr Tragopan Pheasant. It was the only sign of these noble birds that we were to see during our stay in the hills. We managed to shoot two Nepal Wood pigeons during that climb, so that I felt our afternoon had not been entirely wasted. On the return walk I made Don Pal go behind us, as the breeze was in our faces. The man was quiet but not in the least crestfallen, although the ends of his mustaches were definitely drooping. He admitted that he had not shot a bear in two years. It never occured to him to be sorry that he had fired off his gun at the bear, scaring the daylights out of it, or that his whole method of stalking the elusive "balu" was hardly calculated to succeed. This was apparently the way he always hunted bear.

When we tottered into camp just at dusk, I realized that we had climbed over six thousand feet up and down since we had left shortly before noon. We sent Don Pal off with a five-rupee note. He scampered away down the trail like one of his wholly mythical Goral, or even somewhat like a thoroughly startled bear. The Subedar, too, went off at a slightly slower pace, vowing that he would produce some extra fine hunting for us the next day.

The Munshi had been resting all this time. Now he came to me, looking rather pinched by the cold, his head wrapped in a scarf. It appeared that he would like to go to Theratum, our nearest village, a day's march away and considerably lower down one of the spurs of the ridge we were on. He would take a few coolies and bring back rice. I agreed instantly and sent him off with the necessary rupees.

"Take a couple of days down there, Munshi, it will do you good."

The Munshi's face brightened for the first time since we had come to Mangalbaré. All this cold and the talk of bears was not his style really.

After that, I left Don Pal and the bear hunting to those who might care to try. Gertrude went out again on two different days with one or other of the boys, but they were not successful. Don Pal maintained his poise and his agility over the rocks and up and down hill, but nary a bit of game did he produce. Meanwhile three other lesser hunters had appeared in answer to the Subedar's summons, and I sent these men out each day, giving one of our extra shotguns to two of them who had no muzzle-loaders of their own. One of these men finally procured a barking deer for us, a very welcome addition to the failing meat supply, but Goral, Serow, and Tahr were never seen. There were apparently enough Don Pals around with muzzle-loaders to keep the available supply down to the vanishing point.

Another animal that we were interested in was the Musk Deer, an exceedingly shy little creature about the size of a setter, with thin legs and no horns, the males having instead long protruding canine teeth in the upper jaw which stick down below the lower lip rather like those of a miniature Saber-tooth Tiger. The males have a curious surface gland near the navel which becomes distended and full of a clotted oily secretion during the rutting season. The animals are shot by local hunters at this time for the gland, which is the origin of the traditional musk of commerce. Musk Deer had apparently become extinct at this altitude according to Don Pal and his cohorts, and could now only be found much higher, up toward the Tibetan border. Several of the local people brought us in the musk pods as they are called, the dried gland in its ball of Musk Deer fur, stamped with a black sealing wax seal. They wanted to sell them to us, but I imagined their prices in the hills were probably higher than the pods would be worth in Calcutta. I had been told that, like everything else, the musk trade has dropped off.

The other hunters were quite successful in getting us birds. Although they never found any pheasants, they did manage to get us some very rare things, a Brown Parrotbill, a mouse-brown finch-sized creature with a long tail, and a curious thick yellow bill, the exact shape of the bill of a cockatoo. Parrotbills were always rare and hard to secure. They were secretive birds, traveling in small flocks, the lowland species in the very tall grass of swamps in the Terai, or the hill kinds in thick bamboos and pines at the high mountain levels. I saw one flock one day above our camp on the edge of a precipice in a grove of thin tall bamboos. This was the small parrotbill called Hume's Suthora, a tiny creature, much smaller than a chickadee, but of the same build and coloring, though again with the strange thick cockatoo-like bill. The flock of fifty or more birds simply flowed like a continuous streamlet through the bamboos, never stopping for an instant, chittering and chattering softly to each other, moving, always moving. I managed to collect myself sufficiently to shoot two birds, one of which I lost in the thick underbrush, but by then the whole flock had vanished, moving almost as a unit with a kind of total undulating rhythm. These occasions were always unnerving. The chittering of the birds, the constant movement, made me nervous and unsure of my aim. That, and the certain knowledge, too, that I would not see the species again. I had never tried to collect birds before in such a place. I had never seen so many species, which, seen once, were not encountered again.

One of the worst experiences of that sort came one of the early mornings when we were trying to photograph Everest. Just as I had the camera set, a whole flock of grosbeaks came toward us, flying gently and calling their loud unmistakable tinkling note. Of course, my collecting gun was down at the tent. Of course, too, that was the only time we saw the species.

Some of these finches were very shy. I saw a flock one day on a rocky exposed ridge flying toward me. They apparently caught sight of me when still a good hundred yards off, for the whole flock wheeled in the air and dashed away. One of our hunters, however, was luckier. On two days he brought in two species that we had not secured, both rose-finches, one a male the color of my childhood's favorite ice-cream mold, chocolate, with a center of raspberry ice. Round the head, the bird was all raspberry ice, the back and wings streaked dark chocolate, a delectable combination.

Another species that we saw only once was the White-headed Thrush, a whole flock of which flew in near dusk one afternoon, and perched in the very tops of the rhododendron trees all about us. Try as I would I could not see the birds after they had alighted. I could see them easily as they flew from tree to tree, but once in the tops of these huge thick rhododendrons, they froze, or, if they did move, were too obscured by the tangle of branches sixty feet above me. In the end the whole flock simply packed up and flew off, leaving behind a severely frustrated ornithologist.

After supper Ed and I went out with our headlight flash-lights to try for the Wood Owl which had been calling the previous night around the camp. There was one bird which apparently ranged through this territory and probably had a nest on the cliff which rose behind us. He would call, a double-note, very resonant, "who-who," and another owl a half-mile away would answer, and finally a third, perhaps three-quarters of a mile off. We waited and watched, but when the owl moved, he was farther away instead of nearer, and we could not get out on the cliff face in the dark.

The breeze had come up from the northeast again and it was very cold standing under the trees with the wind sweeping down on us from the icy slopes of Kanchenjunga. The moon was obscured by clouds which were sweeping over us, and as we turned back toward camp we switched on our headlights. For a moment I was startled when my light caught two flashing green-gold eyes. Then I saw it was only a jackal. One, two, three, ran away over the open slope ahead of us. As we reached camp, it was to the accompaniment of a great outburst of their unearthly laughter.

The Subedar was still in camp, waiting near the kitchen fire. He looked solemn. After a time he bade us good night and went off toward the stone hut. Abdul spoke up, half grinning, half serious.

"Subedar says those jackals are not jackals"—Abdul looked a bit sheepish. "He says that is the goddess Budini, who lives in this place, laughing at us. She has this place protected. That is why you cannot get any bear or other things."

"The Subedar is concerned with bears," I replied. "We are concerned with birds and small things, rats and mice and shrews. We have done well enough altogether."

Whether or not the goddess Budini had anything to do with it, our luck changed that night. In the first light before dawn, I turned, feeling something pressing down on me. It was the tent side, sagging under snow. It had snowed most of the night, we found, as we struggled out half awake to prop up the canvas and sweep off the tent sides. It had stopped snowing now, but it was bad enough already. There was a good six or more inches.

That was a hectic day. We had to decide what the probabilities were with the weather. The Munshi and the Subedar struggled over from the stone hut about eleven, very sour and depressed. None of the coolies had appeared out of their leaf shelter huts. Fortunately the Munshi had returned the day before with his coolies and rice from Theratum, so that we had food for the time being, but what of the future? The clouds were heavy and menacing. Small flurries of snow descended at intervals all morning. The pass back over the ridge behind us would definitely be blocked to coolies at this rate. Our task was to decide whether we could outwait the snow, stay on and have it melt in a few days of good weather, or leave, get out while the going was good, if this marked a definite cycle of bad weather ahead. Certainly the prospects of staying were gloomy. The coolies and our own men would not stir outside in this snow. Even in our own party, I turned out to be the only one who had waterproof boots with me.

At this point the Subedar provided a bit of comic relief, a high point in his efficiency as a great hunter. He had been surveying the slopes about us and suddenly interrupted to ask if he could borrow a gun. I handed him a shotgun, and he rushed off while we still clustered about the damp smoking fire, under the lee of the leaf-hut kitchen, discussing the weather. In a little while there was a loud bang and a triumphant shout from the Subedar on the hillside above us just at the jungle edge. A few minutes later, a very crestfallen

Subedar appeared around the corner of our shelter, a badly lacerated Yellow-throated Marten in his hand, still attached by one leg to one of Dick's mammal traps, one of the sets which he had not yet visited that morning. The Subedar with characteristic zeal had been keen enough of sight to see the marten in the snow at that distance, but just not clever enough to visualize why a marten in its senses had refused to run away as he approached it. He shook his head, downcast, and muttered to himself, probably something about the goddess Budini.

Our conclave finally ended in a decision to get out the next day while the going was good. We could have no guarantee that we could outstay the snow, and that our food would hold out as well. The rest of the day was spent packing, getting our specimens all wrapped and arranged in their carrying crates, and preparing the camp for an early start the next morning. It was tiring, wet work, especially the mushing out through the snow to pick up the bird nets and the traps, the latter often very hard to locate. There were two birds in the nets, one a great surprise, a woodcock, one of a pair which lived just uphill from us in a wooded gully. I learned one thing that day, that it is impossible to remove a bird from a wet net. The tangle was inextricable, until the whole affair had dried in the sun.

Looking round the camp in the late afternoon, I hated the thought that tomorrow we should be leaving this strange place. The snow covered the rhododendrons with a soft canopy of cake frosting. The silence was even greater today. The goddess Budini's minions had fled before the snow. No bird sang, no horns sounded from the lower valleys. We were shut off, blanketed, wrapped in cotton wool. And then the snow began again.

XV

Farewell to Nepal

OUR LAST NIGHT in Mangalbaré was a sleepless one. From time to time we all had to get up and rebrace our tents, shake off the weight of heavy wet snow, rearrange the guy ropes and the inner tent posts, and occasionally help clear the large eating tent. The thin tent walls were no match for this moisture and soon streams ran down the inside, depositing small pools of water on our bedding. Fortunately it was less cold, just above freezing, I estimated, my thermometer having been broken earlier, so that the mush and the snow did not freeze hard. In the stillness, shut in by the driving snow, I wondered if we would ever be able to get off by morning.

At dawn, however, we were favored. The snow stopped just before light came, leaving us fourteen inches of its bounty. The day dawned clear and crisp, but the clouds had miraculously vanished. For the last time we were to see that full unexcelled panorama of the Everest massif, which we had been privileged to photograph for the first time from the south side. This morning, as if to reward us, Everest itself was clear, and my panorama with the movie camera flowed smoothly without jerks. Now, provided my light exposure was right, we had a picture of the whole range as clearly as it could ever be seen.

The mountains rose up in front of us, burnished almost, immaculate in the first light. The rays of the sun sparkled off the tops of our surrounding trees, as if they were hung with crystal chandeliers. The light was blinding, so vast was the expanse of gleaming white off which it was reflected. In the freshly washed air, the range looked so close that we could almost have touched it, serene, calm, and majestic, but not awesome as it was at other times. It had a kind of familiarity now like an old friend, gleaming in the sun. With the nearness of it we could see the ridge clearly on which Leigh-Mallory and Irvine had last been glimpsed on that fateful expedition of 1924, toiling upward until they were blotted out by a snow flurry, never to be seen again. I realized this was a beautiful mountain with its outliers, but not one to be taken lightly. Everest was implacable. As the clouds began to make, to swirl upward, I felt again that sense of majesty, of grandeur underlain by brooding violence, which the panorama imparted.

However, now we had to get going. Everyone was grumpy this morning. All except myself had wet feet. I could hardly blame anyone for feeling badly. The prospect ahead was not pleasant. After breakfast, the Havildar, usually so quietly efficient, appeared from the group of leaf huts, where he was staying with twenty-two of the coolies, to report that they all wished to stay abed and in their huts today.

"No," I said, full of firmness. "We are leaving this morning. I want everyone up here in camp in half an hour."

The Havildar went off downhill through the drifts, and I mushed over to the stone hut. The Munshi and the Subedar and an assortment of coolies were herded into the place which reeked with smoke and unwashed bodies. The Munshi smiled politely in answer to my greeting, but averred that he would like to stay in today. I reached out my hand as if to shake hands with him, and when he had stretched out his, I clasped it and held on to it.

"Now, Munshi, we are leaving right now, at once, and you are going to help us and direct the coolies." Still holding his hand, I walked out of the hut. The Munshi was panic-stricken.

"But my clothes, my luggage," he panted.

"Tell the coolies to bring it over to the camp at once, and come themselves with their baskets," I commanded.

The Munshi shouted at them, and turning I saw the Subedar hopping through the snow after us, come to see the fun, smiling at the discomfiture of the Munshi.

"Come on, Subedar. You must help us too!"

Back in camp there was a certain amount of preparation, but not enough. Abdul was sitting rocking on his heels, off in some daydream of his own. At the miserable fire Rao was lazily talking with John and Toni. I roused everyone with black looks and harsh words, I am afraid. I asked the Munshi before the others whether he was a man or a boy, much to his embarrassment. I was resolved to get going in time today even if everyone hated me for it.

The Havildar's men had not appeared, so I sloshed through the soft white drifts to their camp half a mile downhill. The little leaf huts were dry enough inside, although exposed, being really an old buffalo grazier's camp used only in the summer time. The men were all inside, smoking and chatting, their fires going, rice bubbling in pots. There seemed to be no intention of getting underway. They were perfectly willing to sit here, unmindful of the fact that in a few days they would be starving. I decided on direct action. Rushing into the first hut, I shouted out that we were all leaving, getting out.

"Come on! Come on, hurry!" I yelled, grabbing first one man and then another. As I did so, I tipped over the cooking pots. The boiling water ran out, but not the rice. Picking up big armfuls of snow, I dashed the stuff on the fire. Smoke and steam welled up, blinding the occupants. They must have thought I had gone mad, for one and all rushed out of the huts as if a swarm of bees were after them. Then what a turmoil there was of shouts and yells! Soon they were all chortling with laughter about the comical behavior of the Burra Sahib, but at least they were out, and gradually one by one they picked up their baskets and food pots. Still calling back and forth the latest anecdote about the white man's strange way of doing things, they trudged on up to camp, lifting their bare legs high to try to keep their poor thin trousers or skirts from getting wet.

Another hour and the rest had straggled in from outlying huts where the Subedar and the Havildar, aping my methods, had gone to rout them out. Still another hour and we were pretty well ready. Everyone had finally stopped grumbling long enough to finish up the work of packing and loading. Sixty-seven coolies altogether appeared and took on loads. By about twelve-thirty we finally got them all off. It was a sight to see them trudging away from the camp in single file, the skin around their eyes coated with saffron or ochre as a partial protection against the glare. Not a man in the group was shod. All were walking in bare feet. I felt sorry for them, but this was no time for pity.

The day kept fair, and although clouds welled up all about us, shutting off the mountains, it was still sunny most of the time and fairly warm. We started north toward a long ridge which gradually descended into the valley of the Arun Kosi River, three days' march away. We slipped and slid along over rocks and up and down through patches of forest and clear meadows trying to stay on the trail which went down from Mangalbaré. It was rough work. The snow had covered whatever track there was, covered, too, the boulders and rounded stones. Everyone fell sooner or later, but at least there were no broken bones, nor was any of the equipment lost. The coolies found it especially hard going. We realized that it would have been impossible to climb back over the ridge. Only downhill was possible, and even that was very tricky. The Munshi made the worst going of anyone. He was sulky because I had made him lose face before the others, although he had only vestiges of face left in any case. The coolies had laughed at him, as it was. Also, as he told me later, he was afraid some of us were going to be killed falling down the hill, and then it would all be on his head.

Indeed, the Munshi was not the gay, careless blade he had been when we started up into the hills. The weight of his experience bowed his shoulders now, and gave him a careworn look. In fact, for the first time in his life he showed some indication of growing up. As for the Subedar, his emotions seemed to be so mixed, half pleasure over the discomfiture of the whipper-snapper of a Munshi, half pain over his own lack of success as a mighty hunter, that I never knew where we really stood. I only hoped that he would last out the trip and not go sour on us before we got back. At least he was of some use with the coolies, for the men were a rugged, independent lot. I had been lucky to get away with what I had done that morning. If they had become angry instead of taking it all as an insane but persuasive whim of a mad foreigner, I am not sure how things would have turned out. But suffice it to say that they did turn out well.

By dusk we had gotten down below six thousand feet, where the snow magically ceased. It was gone, and the air felt hot and stuffy, although it was actually not too far above freezing and there was frost in our camp that night. We stopped by the bank of a small stream inhabited by a family of dippers who flew up and down uttering sharp alarm whistles all night. A party of Tibetans camped near us and some of the coolies and some of our men bought heavy homespun woolen blankets from them, now that the need was largely over, and we had passed below the region of the snows. Looking up in the gloaming I could hardly believe that we had come down from those gloomy, forbidding ridges high above, so dark and dank-looking were they with the heavy jungle, the clouds wreathed about them, and the snow.

The next days were solid pleasure. We had gotten down safely from our ridge with over four hundred specimens, hundreds of feet of film, and no broken bones. The weather at the lower levels seemed an endless joy and a reprieve. The third day we came to our second hill town, Chainpur, an immaculately clean village placed along the top of a forty-five-hundred-foot ridge. Over the houses towered banyan and fig trees of noble height, giving shade to the streets and the little squares below. The red tile roofs were grouped at odd angles, making a flowing, undulating pattern along the ridge.

Like Dhankuta the effect was of a mediaeval hill town in northern Italy or the Dolomites. All about valleys fell away to lower levels with the glint of water at the bottom. The lower slopes were hazy greenish-gray spotted with the white or delicate pink of fruit trees in flower. Above towered the higher slopes, darker, patched with woodland, and at the top, covered with snow. High up through the clouds which seemed to swirl endlessly over the heights, we could get glimpses of the snow peaks, half-revealed, lost in a raging cosmos of their own.

Here we camped for a day and observed the life of the town, a remote, self-contained, peaceful life of its own. Here again we were in the time of weddings. The center of the village was filled with two processions at one time, two weddings, each with its train of relatives, musicians, and hangers-on. The boom of the muskets was incessant, the blare of the strange antique instruments all-pervading. From nearby hillsides we could hear other horns echoing across the valleys. Everyone seemed to be getting married. Even Rao told us that he had had an offer. When one of the dignitaries of the village had found that he was a Hindu of the proper "jhat," the right caste to marry, he had shyly suggested that Rao might be interested in one of his daughters. Rao asked me what I thought, but I argued against it. He was already married, he would have to give a dowry of at least fifty rupees to the family, and what on earth would his wife say if he produced a little Nepali kitten from the hills? Rao said they were pretty, these hill girls, and besides she would help his wife around the house. His mind was not really firmly made up, however, and the novel idea gradually wore off. It was just that the fever was catching.

Most of the town seemed to be dressed in their best bib and tucker. The streets were immaculate, the two small temples shining with cleanliness, everyone was smiling, open-mouthed at all the goings-on. Everyone, that is, except a small group of Tibetans who shyly approached us. Would we buy some potted lamas? Of course we would, and trading commenced. Two of the Tibetans had been hired by one of the wedding parties to carry the bride in her Wellington cot. The others stood about looking rather mournful except when they smiled encouragingly at us in order to consummate a sale. We bought a couple of the painted clay and bone images finally, each in its little amulet box. As the Tibetans stood there, I thought to ask them what they were doing in Chainpur. Why had they come to this town? The Subedar translated for me and asked the question. The men stood first on one foot and then the other. Finally they came out with it. They were brothers, five of them. They had come down over the Rakha La Pass looking for a sixth brother who had not returned the previous spring from his winter's trip down into the lowlands as a porter. They had traced him as far as here, and now they had heard that he had been killed in a quarrel with a Tamung tribesman, a porter also who came from near Chainpur. The brothers were seeking the man. I asked what they would do if they found him.

"They will make him pay indemnity," said the Subedar, "and that will depend on how much he can pay."

"How much, then, is life worth here, Subedar?" I asked.

"For such a man, perhaps he will have to pay a hundred rupees," was the answer.

In American money that would be somewhere between twenty and thirty dollars, more than Rao would have had to pay for a wife.

The next morning we left Chainpur and its village of lotus-eaters, and struck down toward the Kosi River. By evening we had come to the river valley itself. From the time we left Chainpur until we reached the lowlands of the Terai again at Dharan Bazaar, we were constantly in open country. In fact even before reaching Chainpur, we had already lost the jungle. Our path took us through the whole middle zone, the range from six thousand feet above sea level down to Terai level less than one thousand feet. In all that area there was no real stretch of forest for the forest-haunting birds that might inhabit this zone. On the way down, we had lunch beside a small patch of perhaps an acre of rhododendrons which had not yet been cut. They were in flower, their rich scarlet blossoms lighting the tops of the trees like beacons. During the hour and a half that we sat near the small wood, I saw a number of birds come in from nowhere, visit the trees, explore them, and pass on out the other side. First there was a small flock of Fire-tailed Sunbirds, the males with bright orange-red rumps and tails. Then came a single Scimitar-babbler, looking worried and nervous. While I walked through the shrubbery, trying to get a sight of the babbler, I flushed a small quail, which flew away on down the hillside. Then finally we saw a dark green long-tailed Malkoha, a strange skulking species of cuckoo with a high-arched chartreuse-green bill. He came into the trees from some bushes lower down, scuttled about a bit, half on the ground, half in the lowest branches, looking for cover, then scuttled on and away. In addition, a flock of Crested Buntings, black-crested, sparrow-like birds, flew in and then out again, and a solitary brown and black chat, a miniature member of the thrush family. I wondered how far these birds traveled during an average day, searching for the remnants of wooded places, going through them with their own brand of fine-toothed comb.

At the river's edge, when we reached it later, we found a small settlement, a ferryman and his assistants, some dugout canoes, and a wayside shop. Seeing my shotgun, the ferryman came out and said hopefully that there were a number of duck on the river. After some conversation, it was fixed that I would try going after the birds in one of his canoes. Then ensued the wildest little bit of duck shooting I have ever attempted. I climbed into the canoe along with my guide and four of his paddlers. We shot out into midstream from the boulder-strewn bank in no time. The current here was fast. There was nearly a mile of smooth stream between rapids. On either side the bank was rather steep, especially across the river where a tall cliff rose directly out of the water. It was nearing sunset, a lovely time of day, everything pink verging toward purple below, while the tops of the hills hemming us in were still in the bright sunlight. A small flock of black cormorants flew over, directly in midstream. My self-appointed friend and guide and all his assistants immediately dropped whatever they were doing, and pointing at the cormorants, shouted at me, "Shoot! Shoot!"

This and the merry-go-round attitude of the boat when left to its own devices were well calculated to rattle me. In any case I did not want to shoot a cormorant, so waved my hand at the birds and shook my head. Directly in front of us, as we half paddled, half drifted with the stream, was a sand spit. In the lee of it, in shoal water, was a small spring of teal. As we drew near, they rose, facing upstream, and flew high into the air far ahead of us, then turned and came downstream toward us, peeling off against the face of the cliff, coming down at tremendous speed. Using number fours, I stood up in the teetering craft and fired once as far ahead of the little flight as I dared, not taking aim, just feeling the movement of the birds. There was a mighty boom which echoed back and forth across the river, and two birds, hit with the one shot, fell into the water, the rest sweeping on down low over the rapids below. I almost fell out of the boat as all the men in it shouted and screamed at once, beat their paddles against the gunwales, and left us quite at the mercy of the current. For the second time in Nepal, I was dubbed a wizard, this time rather inclining to believe it myself.

For the next twenty minutes we ran a ragged zigzag course back and forth across the swiftest part of the current, banging headlong into rocks along the way, trying to retrieve the birds. One was dead, but floated away at a great rate from us, the other, wounded, swam over to the opposite bank and proceeded to dodge about among the rocks near the shore. Why the canoe was not stove in a dozen times was beyond me. The men sang and yelled and laughed about the amazing sight of two ducks falling at one shot, quite overlooking the fact that the proof is in the eating, and if we did not secure the birds no one would believe us. Besides, we needed meat as usual and two teal would make a more bountiful curry for us all than one. Much to my relief, we finally secured both birds, but failed to get in another shot, as the Gadwall, Pintail, and occasional Ruddy Shelducks which flew by all kept their distance. The teal, Green-wings, were much appreciated.

The next day we marched on down the bank of the Kosi through a mile-wide valley which enclosed the river at this point. It was dry and dusty and the river looked low, with large sand bars along its course. At one or two points we saw small crocodiles sunning themselves well out on the banks, but they were alert and launched hurriedly into the water if we approached too close.

The days were warmer than two months before when we were marching along a similar valley in West Nepal. At midday we were definitely tired and hot. There was no jungle here, no shade trees even along the trail. Nothing but bare rock screes and talus met our glance, aside from the occasional small patches of cultivation on raised terraces, well above flood level. Very few birds were visible, a scattering of duck along the river, one small green heron, and a flock of Ibis-bills on a sand bar. The Ibis-bill is a very large plover, the size of a large curlew, with soft gray plumage and a decorative dull-reddish curved, sickle-shaped bill. These were Tibetan birds, come to winter at lower altitudes like the Ruddy Shelducks and their human compatriots, the Tibetans themselves.

We passed many Tibetans here, all going up now instead of down. It was the end of February, time to start up again into the hills, time to seek again the high windswept pastures and stony plains of Tibet. Some of the people were porters, bent under the weight of a load of aluminum and brass cooking-pots, rolls of cloth, felt hats, always in extraordinary demand in Tibet, and miscellaneous tools and gadgets. Others were lamas, back again on their way home after a winter's visit at the shrine of Gaya, or in Calcutta.

As I went a bit up a small ravine away from the main valley of the Kosi, I came to the camp of a lama. Here were shade, a few trees, and a pool where a small hill stream must have recently dried, leaving water in part of its channel.

The old lama was seated by a rock, in the lee of which a small fire was burning, his face solemn, his expression turned inward, telling his beads. A servant was tending the fire, boiling something in a pot. Another man lay asleep against his pack. I was about to turn away when the lama's eyes opened, he spied me and smiled, and reached out a welcoming hand. He stood up then, alertly for one of his age, and gave me a courtly greeting, in broken English and Hindustani.

"Salaam, Baba, how do you do," he smiled pleasantly, but not in the rather ingratiating, subservient manner so many employed.

This man was not about to beg. He was greeting me as a man of standing. The cleanliness and good condition of his ample red robes bespoke the man of quality. This was no ordinary Tibetan monk.

"Salaam, Lama," I replied. "Where do you come from and where do you go?"

We exchanged news of the road and of our travels on it. As far as I could make out, the lama was going to Drowa, a big monastery sixteen marches away. He had business there.

"How is everything in Calcutta?" I asked.

We could as well ask news of a lama as anyone else. My radio picked up lots of Indian jazz music, but very little news.

"In Calcutta it is quiet now," he said, half in Hindustani, half in English. "No trouble," by which I took it he meant no Hindu-Muslim rioting.

"But in Indonesia there is much trouble," he added as an afterthought.

I was surprised to be talking about Indonesia with a lama on the banks of the Kosi River.

"Yes, there is much trouble there, and India is very worried concerning it, and she is against the Dutch."

All of this came out in an offhand way, as if we were sitting in a club somewhere discussing the headlines in a newspaper.

"What news of China?" I asked.

"Oh, China is very bad." He made a grimace. The network of strong lines in his brown face crinkled and twisted and writhed like a devil dancer's mask. "Mao Tse-tung take everything. Kuomintang finish, 'hogia.' " The last is an expressive word.

"And Tibet?"

"Tibet not so good." Again his face crinkled and this time he looked very sad. "Maharani of Sikkim run away to Tibet just now with Tibet lama. She had a child by him. Very bad. Our religion will suffer. Dalai Lama should punish, but Maharajah of Sikkim is under Indian protection." He looked grave and shook his head.

This gossip was more than I had bargained for. An Asian Court scandal involving high personages, a celibate monk, and international repercussions!

"What should be done?" I asked.

"Dali Lama is young now. The Gyalpo should act. The lama and the woman are in Lhasa. They should be killed as an example to the people and the lamas." The old priest's face was stern.

After a few moments more I took my leave. The lama rose gracefully again, and his two servants bowed and stuck out their tongues at me respectfully in proper Tibetan style. I went on down the ravine to the main valley again, refreshed after my talk, having forgotten, for a time, the trials of sixty-seven coolies, a dwindling food supply, grumbling servants, and the hundred and one problems of the trip which was nearing its end. I could not have felt better if I had just reread the whole of *Kim.*

That night we camped along the river bank again, tired out after the greater heat of this day's march at a lower altitude. In the evening light we could look up above the surrounding lower hills and see, just under a heavy blanket of clouds, burnished scarlet-orange in the sun, the purple-shadowed higher hills blanketed in snow. The cloud must have been resting on top of the ridge, but the lower slopes of what the Subedar said was Mangalbaré were plain to our view.

"I'm sure glad we're not up there right now," said Ed, voicing what was in all our thoughts. The snow had still held on Mangalbaré.

The next day, our sixth since leaving the hills, was a long, tedious, tiresome climb up from the Kosi, up and up a side ridge, on the other side of which somewhere was Dhankuta. By nightfall, we had ascended a good five thousand feet in the hot sun and were high on the ridge itself, in a cold wind which blew through us, and with clouds pressing all about. Tents were a long time getting up and we took refuge in a small hut, one of four or five which comprised a village in this bitterly uninviting spot. The hut next us was occupied by the body of a man, a traveler who had died that morning of some disease or other. The simple village people were quite uneasy and undecided as to what to do with the body. The householder, who was entertaining us with a bottle of "rakshi," a stimulating local beverage distilled from rice, and dishes of peanuts and cracked corn, asked our advice. At that the Munshi, who had been standing near, interjected himself. With an exclamation of impatience he drew the man aside and explained to him that we were not Hindus and knew nothing about such things.

Meanwhile Kurt, who had been off by himself, returned grinning with triumph. He had succeeded in buying a dozen eggs at a neighboring hut for an unannounced sum. We asked him how he had managed — Kurt's Hindustani was not a strong point.

"Oh, I just clucked like a hen and made the motion of dropping an egg, then I picked it up, broke it, cooked it over a fire, and ate it." Kurt smiled knowingly.

"When we get back to the States, let's have Kurt order dinner for us at a restaurant that way sometime," said Howie.

Later the resulting omelet was a great success.

The following day's walk was a short one back along the ridge to Dhankuta. As we were taking down our tents that morning, I had one of those frustrating experiences that occasionally happen to all collectors. I had just turned from talking to the Subedar and was walking toward my shotgun which was leaning against a bedding roll, when up from the farther side of the ridge, riding easily on the wind, came a flock of big swifts, White-throated Spinetails. They came deceptively slowly, hardly moving their wings, just a few feet overhead. I broke into a run, raced for my collecting gun, feeling through my pockets feverishly the while for ammunition, picked up the gun, loaded, turned, and fired all at once — and missed. The swifts continued lazily and easily on over the ridge and were never seen again. That proved to be our one and only chance to collect these mysterious ten-inch creatures, whose vast powers of flight and erratic movements make them one of the more fascinating and desirable species to observe and study.

During the day we saw another bird for the first and last time, not half so rare but curious none the less, the beautiful Wall-creeper, a gray square-tailed bird like a nuthatch, with a slender black bill and bright crimson on the wings. This bird is a creeper, like our Brown Creeper at home, but climbs about on walls or cliff faces as energetically as the Brown Creeper skitters up the trunk of a tree, searching through the crevices for insect larvae, caterpillars, and bugs.

Dhankuta was as pleasant as ever, shining in the afternoon sun. The place had a familiar look like an old friend. We treasured its warmth, its familiarity. Very soon we would not see it again. Very soon we would reach the Terai, turning our backs on the sixteenth century and facing once more jeeps, trucks, trains, with all the mental assumptions that go with them. No more would we walk down a main street which had never known a wheel or the harsh glare of an electric light. Soon we would be faced with telephones which actually worked well enough for people to want to use them and to call us on them. I thought of calling the General in Dharan Bazaar, but the telephone house when I came to it was deserted. The remaining entrails of the machine were scattered on the little table and wires and batteries were dripping down onto the earthen floor. The telephone was temporarily out of order, I heard later. From the look of it, I would have said permanently out of order, but there are always time and hope in the hills.

Two days later, we were in Dharan Bazaar and I paid off our coolies. A whole afternoon was spent arranging the accounts of the men and writing chits of recommendation for the Subedar and the Havildar. The Munshi had disappeared. He did not come round for a tip or a letter as the others had. In my farewell interview with His Excellency, the Burra Hakim, resplendent in his frock coat, he asked me what I thought of the men he had sent with me, beginning with the Munshi. I was tired and bored with the Munshi, but I decided that nothing would be served by saying so. I merely commented instead that he was young.

"He is a silly boy," said the General, with the suspicion of a giggle. "Let us say no more about him."

That evening the General's servants came to our camp with bountiful leaf platters filled with curried stuffs, rice, "chura," hard-boiled eggs, and spices. It was our farewell present from his wife, the Rani Sahiba, whom we had never seen.

The next morning the jeep and truck arrived from Biratnagar, from our kind friend Mr. Bahadur, and we loaded our precious cargo aboard, over five hundred birds by now and about fifty mammals, besides all our films and equipment. Now we closed the door on the sixteenth century, on the silences of the high cliffs, the villages with their quality of being suspended in time, the tinkling bells of the temples, the haunting bray of the curling serpent horns. Now we were going home, climbing into the unfamiliar vehicles, rattling and bumping over the roads.

Biratnagar was as dusty as ever, but at least we could get a good hot bath with the aid of pails of water, our first such in over three weeks. We had a day there packing and crating our material, putting the last touches to our boxes before they started off by train for Calcutta and the long voyage home. Our bird collections now amounted to some sixteen hundred specimens from Nepal, the mammals to about two hundred. The birds belonged to a total of three hundred and thirty-one species and subspecies, and in addition we had identified another fifty in the field, mostly the larger sorts, herons, ducks, egrets, hawks. Thus, we had observed three hundred and eighty-one forms of birds in Nepal. This was better than Surgeon Scully's list of three hundred published in 1879, but still well below Hodgson's grand total of five hundred and sixty-three, but probably it would now be imposible to match Hodgson's list: he was in the country over twenty years. In addition, the forests have been so drastically reduced since his time that some species known to him may now have vanished from Nepal. Collecting and observing birds in Nepal today is so different from what it must have been like in Hodgson's time that it is as if a bird student in Kentucky nowadays had only Audubon's journals to use as a reference list of Kentucky birds.

Even if we had not found the Mountain Quail, the Pink-headed Duck, and the Pygmy Hog, we had at least rediscovered the Spiny Babbler. And besides, we had collected a number of Himalayan birds, some ten species altogether, which had not previously been recorded from Nepal. In addition, a few months later I described eight new subspecies of birds from Nepal, distinct geographical populations which differed from their neighbors in some obvious character of color or size.

Moreover, what of the break for which I was looking? That, too, became apparent months later in the Museum, studying our bird collections. Tabulating all the forms of resident birds which we had collected along the Himalayan foothills from west to east, I found that a total of twenty-one species had two distinct populations or subspecies within the territory of Nepal. Of these, fourteen, or sixty-seven per cent, showed that the distinct break in the fauna occurred in the eastern part of Nepal, about the region of the valley of the Arun Kosi River.

Trying to assess the factors which could be operating here to serve as an outward barrier preventing the continous exchange of populations, keeping the birds separate and distinct, I could find only one important phenomenon. No geographical or geological factors seemed to enter in, but right down this valley from north to south there is an isohyet, a band west of which the annual rainfall is fifty inches, east of which the total annual rainfall is seventy-five inches. Correlated with this was a distinct change in year-round climate, greater humidity, and a more even spread of rainfall in the east, drier conditions and more contrast between winter and summer in the west. Characteristically the bird populations had responded to this environmental change. Those species which had two subspecies in the two areas showed a uniform adaptive response to the increase in humidity, following a theory known as Gloger's Theory. According to this theory, bird populations tend to be darker, to have more dark pigment in their plumage, in regions of greater humidity; and so it proved to be in this case.

All of this came to me much later, of course, after months of research at home. At the time of our leaving the mountain kingdom I had only the list of specimens and species, the notes in my journals, the records, and the specimens themselves. I had been able to note also one other interesting phenomenon. This was the startling disappearance of bird and animal life from the middle zones of the hills, the area between one thousand and seven thousand feet in altitude, where farming and deforestation had worked such havoc. Certain species of birds were confined to this zone entirely and may well have become extinct in Nepal.

Not only this, but the destruction of the forests will tend to perpetuate itself. Forest-tree species cannot usually grow without shade and without humus soil. Thus, new barriers are being created with great climate and habitat differences compared to previous times. In the long run all sorts of changes will take place. Species will drop out. In future aeons they will be replaced by other species. Evolution will go forward taking advantage of each changing situation. Even in remote Nepal there will be no biological *status quo*.

Finally the packing was done, the Oudh Tirhut Railway informed that we should be needing one of their tourist cars again, and a plan evolved for loading our precious trunks of specimens, our tents and the remainder of our luggage, on bullock carts for transport the mile to the Jogbani Station, and we made our final farewells in Biratnagar. Mr. Bahadur was genuinely touched at our leaving and we were sorry to say good-bye to him. He had been a real friend in need. The last afternoon a telephone call came all the way from Katmandu from General Bijaya wishing us, on behalf of the Durbar, farewell and a good voyage home.

The last morning in Biratnagar I woke up early with the dawn and walked out of the factory guest house onto the little stretch of grass. The air was very clear, the dust had settled, and it was cool. Far to the north in the dawn light were the clear tips of the snow peaks rising in space like the dragon teeth of Cadmus, magical and evanescent. It seemed only a moment before the sharp shapes were blotted out by puffy clouds and the hills were gone, snuffed out like a mirage, but as I turned back to the house, I knew that I had that vision with me always — the great peaks, the purple hills below, the mountain villages with their laughter, their horns echoing faintly along the valleys. Then, too, the birds, flocks of them, calling to each other, flying free from ridge to ridge. I had seen all of this and it was distilled, preserved clearly for an instant of time, a microcosm in the high hills of Nepal.

THE END

BIBLIOGRAPHY
INDEX
INDEX OF BIRDS

Bibliography

A list of books published on Nepal in recent years.

HODGSON, B., *Essays on the Languages, Literature and Religion of Nepal and Tibet.* London, 1874.

AITCHISON, U. (compiler), *A Collection of Treaties, Engagements and Sanads Relating to India and Neighboring Countries.* Vol. II. Calcutta, 1892.

BROWN, PERCY, *Picturesque Nepal.* London, 1912.

NORTHEY, MAJOR W. B., *The Gurkhas: Their Manners, Customs and Country.* London, 1928.

NORTHEY, MAJOR W. B., *The Land of the Gurkhas.* Cambridge, 1937.

LANDON, P., *Nepal.* 2 vols. London, 1928.

POWELL, E. A., *The Last Home of Mystery: Adventures in Nepal.* London, 1932.

MORRIS, C. J., *Gurkhas.* (Handbooks for the Indian Army.) Delhi, 1933.

WRIGHT, D. (translator), *History of Nepal.* Cambridge, 1937.

ALI SHAH, (the Sirdar Ikbul), *Nepal: The Home of the Gods.* London, 1938.

A list of publications on the birds of Nepal.

1846. *Catalogue of Mammals and Birds of Nepal* by J. E. Gray. Natural History Museum, London.

1879. "A Contribution to the Ornithology of Nepal by Surgeon J. Scully, in *Stray Feathers*, vol. 8.

1928. "A List of Birds of Nepal" by S. H. Prater, in volume I of *Nepal* by Percival Landon, Constable and Co., London.

1948. "Some birds of the Gandak-Kosi Watershed including the Pilgrim Trail to the Sacred Lake of Gosainkund" by B. E. Smythies, in the *Journal of the Bombay Natural History Society* vol. 47, pt. 3.

1949. "Some Notes on the Birds of the Nepal Valley by Mrs. D. Proud in the *Journal of the Bombay Natural History Society*, vol. 48, pt. 4.

1950. "Birds from Nepal, 1947–1949" by S. Dillon Ripley in the *Journal of the Bombay Natural History Society*, vol. 49, pt. 3.

1950. "More Notes on the Birds of the Nepal Valley" by B. E. Smythies in the *Journal of the Bombay Natural History Society*, vol. 49, pt. 3.

Index

Index of Birds